W9-AWA-044

Future Prospects of The World According to The Bible Code

Joseph Noah

New Paradigm Books Boca Raton 2002

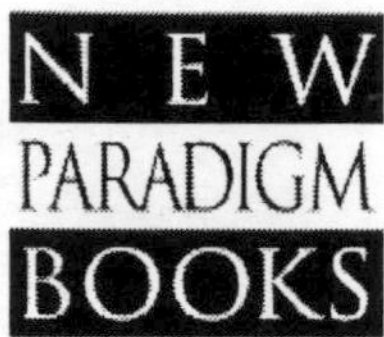

NEW PARADIGM BOOKS
22783 South State Road 7
Suite 97
Boca Raton, FL 33428
Tel.: (561) 482-5971, Toll-Free: (800) 808-5179
FAX: (561) 852-8322
E-mail: <jdc@flinet.com>
<http://www.newpara.com>

FUTURE PROSPECTS OF THE WORLD ACCORDING TO THE BIBLE CODE
By Joseph Noah

Cover design by Peri Poloni, Knockout Design
<http://www.knockoutbooks.com>
3784 Archwood Road
Cameron Park, CA 95682
E-mail: <peri@knockoutbooks.com>

First New Paradigm Books Quality Paperback Edition, February 1, 2002
New Paradigm Books ISBN Number: 1-892138-07-7

10 9 8 7 6 5 4 3 2 1

Dedicated to My Grandchildren

Clayton, a loving little boy
and
Jessica, his older sister, wise beyond her years
Both of whose questions about life
Inspired this book
More than they will ever know

TABLE OF CONTENTS

FOREWORD

The book that you are about to read concerns the history and future prospects of the world. Its revelations were found encrypted in the Holy Torah, the first five books of the Old Testament. There is a prediction that the same code will be discovered in the holy testaments of the *Vedas* and the Koran. It is not the intent of this book to discredit your religion in any way or lure you away from it. If you love God above all things and mankind as yourself, it is your religious faith that enlightened your soul and your character, and you must cling to it.

The Bible Code confirms that only God knows the future. This book does not, therefore, contain prophecy; rather, it clarifies prophecy given to us long ago. Much of it was given in the form of metaphor because we were not ready for the facts at that time. Bible Code matrix slides give us descriptions of actual events and prospective dates when they may occur, based upon the current state of the world. Sixty-one of the more than 200 matrix slides used in the development of this book were selected to be included with the text. When I write about those I have not included, I write as if the reader could see the entire sequence.

On the morning of the 11th of September, 2001, the world changed with the destruction of the World Trade Center in New York. President Bush described it as the beginning of a long struggle between good and evil. He was right. According to the Bible Code, it was the start of a ten-and-a-half-year countdown, the time and half time as prophesied in Daniel 12 of the Old Testament and in the last book of the New Testament, the Revelation to St. John.

The Bible Code brings a final warning to mankind. We have caused the current sickness of the earth and it must repair itself to accommodate the coming Golden Age. Two-thirds of us professing to believe in God have not yet developed the godly character necessary to survive the coming cleansing process that is described herein and by most religions of the world. The coming earth changes can be gradual, or abrupt and catastrophic, in nature. If we don't change the way we deal with each other, it will probably be the latter. The Bible Code tells us what we must do to survive.

1

The Bible Code

One day in 1997, while searching for a good cup of coffee, I wandered into the coffee shop of a Barnes & Noble bookstore in Billings, Montana. On my way out, I scanned the best seller shelves, where a book entitled *The Bible Code*, by Michael Drosnin, caught my eye. I bought the book and took it home to my mountain hideaway. I began to read it immediately, and I didn't stop until I was finished. From that day on, my life was totally changed. Could it be true that a secret code was encoded in the first five books of the Old Testament known as the Torah?

I was someone who had always read the Bible with a great deal of skepticism regarding the literal meaning of what is written. I had tried to learn as much as I could by treating much of it as metaphor, just as some of the parables taught by Jesus are metaphor. With my engineering background, I had a hard time believing that all our troubles started with Eve's eating a forbidden fruit, that two each of all the animals in the world got into Noah's Ark, or that our bodies will rise from their graves during the "Rapture" that, so it is said, will precede the Apocalypse. It all took more faith than I could muster. But, as I read *The Bible Code,* an idea suddenly occurred to me: The Bible could be a book of answers for all ages. Certainly God, who created the entire universe, would have no problem creating such a document.

The testaments of the world's great religions were written many centuries ago. As our knowledge has increased, a greater and greater divergence has come about between science and religion. We must rely more and more on faith to hold on to our religion. In the face of Darwin's theories on evolution, for example, we must look for a deeper meaning in the statement in Genesis that God created the world in seven days.

The Torah was given to Moses thousands of years ago. What was the level of knowledge at that time? The average person couldn't read or write. Life was all about getting the sheep to pasture and growing enough food to survive. The educated, i.e. the priests and scribes, read the Torah to the people, teaching them what it meant to the best of their comprehension. Society was very primitive, and the Torah was written to its level.

What do we tell a small child when he asks us where babies come from? We would probably say that babies are a gift from God. This answer can be seen as correct, though purposely lacking in detail. When the child gets a little older and notices mommy's tummy getting bigger, we may say that God is growing a baby brother or sister in there and that, as soon as it is big enough, the doctor will take it out in the hospital and mommy will bring it home. That can also be viewed as a correct answer that is geared to the child's level of understanding. The first Bible I bought for my preschool granddaughter was a durable hardcover book, but it had comic-book style pictures and story text. She loved it, and learned it by heart because she could understand it. As she gets older, she will get others that suit her level of development.

The idea that the Torah contains hidden information goes back to Daniel 12:4 and the words, "But you, Daniel, keep the words secret and the book sealed until the time of the end." The Book of Daniel also states that (12:10) "none of the wicked shall understand [the book after it is unsealed] but the wise shall understand." I now believe that God has done for the world as a wise father would do for his child. The Bible may be a book within a book within a book. Which book we can read depends upon our knowledge, our capabilities, and the need we have to understand the information.

I believe these books are decipherable through the Bible Code, and that the modern computer makes this possible. Is the information available to us today because we are ready for it, or have we been guided to it because we are entering into a very important period and the information is now vital? Maybe both!

In Michael Drosnin's *The Bible Code*, the author discusses the work of Professor Eliyahu Rips of the Mathematics Department at Jerusalem's Hebrew University, an orthodox Jew and one of the world's leading experts on group theory. He credits Dr. Rips with the discovery of the equidistant letter sequence ELS (the Bible Code) in the Torah, and with the creation of a computer program that can decipher that Code. Writes Drosnin, "His work on the Bible Code has been reviewed and confirmed by famous mathematicians at Harvard, Yale and Hebrew University. It has been replicated by a senior code-breaker at the U.S. Department of Defense and has passed three levels of secular peer review at a leading U.S. math journal." I learned from a different source that two other prominent scientists, Doron Witztum and Yoav Rosenberg, worked with Dr. Rips on the project (I found verification for this in the Bible Code itself, as you will later see).

I decided that, given these scientists' credentials, I was hardly qualified to question the Bible Code's validity. What I desperately wanted was to get my hands on the computer program and discover answers to philosophical questions that I've pondered for as long as I can remember—questions that we've all asked, such as Who are we really? Why are we here? and Where are we going when this life is over? I wanted answers to questions regarding the beginnings of life, the right of a woman to end a pregnancy, the death penalty, the Hollywood effect, the causes of AIDS, the direction the Internet is headed in, and much more.

I finally managed to obtain a Bible Code decoding program, and some of the things I've learned will astound you. But in order for you to understand the results, you will have to bear with me while I explain more about the mechanics of my code searches.

The Bible Code decoding program searches the Torah for words that have an equidistant letter sequence (ELS) throughout the Torah or in a designated book such as Genesis. The great Jewish sage R. Moses ben Nahman (Ramban or Nahmanides, 1195-c.-1270 A.D.) asserted in his *Commentary on the Torah* that Moses received the Torah from God in a single string of 304,805 uninterrupted letters. The Bible Code decoding proGram lOads a *D*atabase of the Torah into a computer in a way analogous to this. I think of it as though the Torah were wrapped around a cylinder. Imagine a large cylinder in front of you, with a long string of letters wrapped around it in a tight spiral from top to bottom. Now, draw a square on that portion of the cylinder that faces you, enclosing approximately 30 by 40 letters as though it were a page. This is called a slide. You can picture it as a crossword puzzle with Hebrew letters filling all the squares. Imagine that some of these letters are highlighted and spelling out words. When you enter a word such as "God" in an ELS search, the program will search for the same sort of letter combination as I have highlighted several sentences above. The above sequence happens to be a five-letter equidistant letter sequence; I refer to it as a five-letter skip.

The object of an ELS search is to find two or more words in close proximity to each other, with the skip distance as short as possible. As in a crossword puzzle, the letters may be read forwards or backwards, vertically, horizontally or diagonally. The position of the first or last letters, depending upon whether you are reading the word forwards or backwards, is very important; however, any of the letters can be important.

When you make a search on the first two words that are the subject of your slide, you box in the section of the cylinder that looks like a page. After that, you search for words in close ELS proximity that are related and pertinent to your subject and can be developed into a sentence. You have to analyze the sentence to determine if it makes biblical sense in relation to the knowledge we already have. It should be noted, however, that the Bible Code does not only confirm Bible teaching, but also provides new knowledge that can't be found literally stated in the Bible. Moreover, it identifies which areas are parable, metaphor, and in a number of cases religious doctrine that is myth.

I was given a document that a friend of mine had downloaded from the Internet. I don't use the Internet myself, for reasons which I'll disclose later. The author of the document stated that he was no longer researching the Bible Code because he had found the words "God" and "Satan" in close proximity, which he considered blasphemy. I did the same search myself, and, sure enough, the two words were there; the word "God" was directly above the word "Satan" and the search was very compact. I investigated further, and found the story that God had created Satan and that He would defeat him during the end time. Now, someone could take that sentence out of context and say that it might read that Satan created God and that God would be defeated in the end time. That wouldn't make biblical sense, however. Another author stated that in one slide Jesus had appeared as a false prophet. Further investigation of that resulted in the prediction that Jesus would return to defeat the false prophet.

I have read several articles in which the validity of the Bible Code is discounted because, it is asserted, any large text will show a relationship of words when incorporating an ELS code search. This is true. It was reported that the author of *The Bible Code,* Michael Drosnin, had challenged anyone to find a prediction for the assassination of Yitzhak Rabin in an ordinary book such as *Moby Dick.* A mathematician at the Australian National University did find in Melville's classic novel the word "assassination" associated with 13 public figures who were assassinated, including Yitzhak Rabin, according to Mark Hitchcock in his *Bible Prophecy.* It should be noted, however, that the average searches in my book were found not in a large text like *Moby Dick,* but on average in a text the equivalent of a single page of approximately 300 words! Take the slide regarding the U.S. presidential race of 2000, in Chapter Two, for example. This compact slide (**Subject: FLA/Vote**), found in Genesis 2:22 to 3:7—"Nothing shall subdue the FLA 1,000-miracle votes given to Bush by God"—came to light prior to the final 2000 election results, in a Genesis text of 288 words. Out of nine primary words in the sentence, four had an ELS of 115 ("miracle" is hidden under "FLA").

The prediction was displayed in the slide as a concise sentence relative to the subject of the search. I'm sure all will agree that the searches in this book are not random associated words that could be found anywhere.

I am aware that some people will take issue with many of the searches in this book. That is because the messages they contain often conflict with current mainstream religious theology (they must, in order to provide new knowledge), or that those people just don't like the messages. These messages cut across political correctness, getting to the root causes of our problems, advising us that we shall be held accountable for our actions.

Many of my searches failed to come together no matter how hard I tried. I changed subject words, used various synonyms, searched the entire Torah and then separate books of the Torah, to no avail. I have had to assume that my ideas regarding those subjects were incorrect. The following slide (**Subject: Bible/Code**), found in Numbers 32:6 to 32:14—"The Bible Code is the word of God"[1]—allayed my concern whether the Bible Code is truly the word of God. The close proximity of positions and skips left me in no doubt that it is. Note that one of the letters of "God" shares a letter of code. Moreover, a letter of "God" touches a letter of "word," and a letter of "word" touches a letter of "Bible." The compactness of this slide indicates a high degree of accuracy in deciphering the code. The legend contains information about the search. It gives the book of the Torah in which the search was carried out, the skip sequences, the position of the first letter of the word taken from the Torah text, the Hebrew word, its English translation, and a highlighting symbol so that it can be recognized on the slide. Below that, the words are put into sentence form. If necessary, words are added in parentheses to grammatically shape the sentence. It's possible that the syntax could be different from the one presented, but what is shown is what makes the most sense to me. The message should make biblical as well as moral sense, and support historical and current scientific knowledge. When a new concept is involved, I try to determine if it is reasonable, probable, or even possible. Quite often, someone else has explored it. I

Letters	Position
ר צ י ע ז ר ו א ת א ר צ ג ל ע ד ו ה נ ה ה מ ק ו מ מ ק ו מ מ ק נ ה ו י ב א ו ב נ	242025
ב ו ו ב ע נ ה א ר צ א ש ר ה כ ה י ה ו ה ל פ נ י ע ד ת י ש ר א ל א ר צ מ ק נ ה ה	242154
ב נ י ר א ו ב נ ה א ח י כ מ י ב א ו ל מ ל ח מ ה ו א ת מ ת ש ב ו פ ה ו ל מ ה ת נ	242283
כ ו ק ו י ר א ו א ת ה א ר צ ו י נ י א ו א ת ל ב ב נ י י ש ר א ל ל ב ל ת י ב א א	242412
מ ה א ש ר נ ש ב ע ת י ל א ב ר ה מ ל י צ ח ק ו ל י ע ק ב כ י ל א מ ל א ו א ח ר י	242541
ע ש ה ה ר ע ב ע י נ י י ה ו ה ו ה נ ה ק מ ת מ ת ח ת א ב ת י כ מ ת ר ב ו ת א נ ש	242670
י א מ ר ו ג ד ר ת צ א נ נ ב נ ה ל מ ק נ נ ו פ ה ו ע ר י מ ל ט פ נ ו ו א נ ח נ ו	242799
ב נ י י ש ר א ל א י ש נ ח ל ת ו כ י ל א נ נ ח ל א ת מ מ ע ב ר ל י ר ד נ ו ה ל א	242928
ל ח ל ו צ א ת ה י ר ד נ ל פ נ י י ה ו ה ע ד ה ו ר י ש ו א ת א י ב י ו מ פ נ י ו	243057
ה נ ה ח ט א ת מ ל י ה ו ה ו ד ע ו ח ט א ת כ מ א ש ר ת מ צ א א ת כ מ ב נ ו ל כ מ	243186
י נ ו מ ק נ נ ו ו כ ל ב ה מ ת נ ו י ה י ו ש מ ב ע ר י ה ג ל ע ד ו ע ב ד י כ י ע	243315
נ י י ש ר א ל ו י א מ ר מ ש ה א ל ה מ א מ י ע ב ר ו ב נ י ג ד ו ב נ י ר א ו ב נ	243444

Shape	Word	Translation	Verse	Position	Skip
א	אלוה	God	Numbers 32:6	242308	256
ק	קוד	code	Numbers 32:11	242562	258
מ	מלה	word	Numbers 32:13	242684	-262
ת	תנך	bible	Numbers 32:14	242691	258

1. Bible/Code: (The) Bible Code (is the) Word (of) God.

look to the writings of philosophers, scientists and theologians for guidance before I make up my mind.

The searches have been done in Hebrew and translated as well as possible into English. Many English words have no Hebrew equivalent, and vice versa. English names, for instance, require letters to be translated phonetically into Hebrew sounds. The reference for most translated words in this book is *Webster's New World Hebrew Dictionary*. In some cases, the words were phonetically translated into Hebrew letter sounds on a Hebrew/English virtual keyboard and used as transliterated words.

Whether I use the past, present or future tense of a word makes little difference, because the Bible Code transcends time. Hebrew root words are used as much as possible without prefixes, suffixes, or reference to tense, gender or number. In most cases, two-letter words are not used unless they integrate perfectly into the slide. This is because, in every search, small words often show up at random. References to the words "is" or "not" can seldom be used. Often they appear to incorrectly verify or negate the Code search—even those searches that are known to be historical fact. Compactness, word location, and minimal ELS of the primary root words, indicate accuracy.

I discovered something while researching the Bible Code that makes it truly miraculous. Although I searched it in Hebrew, it appears that it can be searched in any language. I worked with an international group when I started experimenting with the Code. People of different nationalities asked me to research things about their country. As I was trying to change foreign names, such as the name of a volcano, for example, into Hebrew sounds, the Bible Code seemed to recognize exactly what I was referring to, and I got credible historic data as well as future prospects. Then I decided to try a simple search in various languages. I picked something that I consider to be a given and that almost everyone knows. The search focused on the phrase **(Subject: Name/God)** "I am who I am" (Exodus 3), as translated in the *New Revised Standard Version*. I found it in English in Genesis 24:25 to 24:30, in German in Exodus 32:29 to 32:31[2], in Hebrew in Numbers 23:26 to 23:30, in Tagalog (the prin-

Letters	Position
ל פ י א י ש ו י א מ ר מ ש ה מ ל א ו י ד כ מ ה י ו מ ל י ה ו ה כ י א י ש ב ב נ ו	127358
ו ה כ י א י ש ב ב נ ו ו ב א ח י ו ו ל ת ע ל י כ מ ה י ו מ ב ר כ ה ו י ה י מ מ	127387
מ ב ר כ ה ו י ה י מ מ ח ר ת ו י א מ ר מ ש ה א ל ה ע מ א ת מ ח ט א ת מ ח ט א ה ג	127416
מ ח ט א ת מ ח ט א ה ג ד ל ה ו ע ת ה א ע ל ה א ל י ה ו ה א ו ל י א כ פ ר ה ב ע ד	127445
ו ל י א כ פ ר ה ב ע ד ח ט א ת כ מ ו י ש ב מ ש ה א ל י ה ו ה ו י א מ ר א נ א ח ט	127474
ה ו י א מ ר א נ א ח ט א ה ע מ ה ז ה ח ט א ה ג ד ל ה ו י ע ש ו ל ה מ א ל ה י ז ה	127503
ש ו ל ה מ א ל ה י ז ה ב ו ע ת ה א מ ת ש א ח ט א ת מ ו א מ א י נ מ ח נ י נ א מ ס	127532
א י נ מ ח נ י נ א מ ס פ ר כ א ש ר כ ת ב ת ו י א מ ר י ה ו ה א ל מ ש ה מ י א ש ר	127561
ה א ל מ ש ה מ י א ש ר ח ט א ל י א מ ח נ ו מ ס פ ר י ו ע ת ה ל כ נ ח ה א ת ה ע מ	127590
ה ל כ נ ח ה א ת ה ע מ א ל א ש ר ד ב ר ת י ל כ ה נ ה מ ל א כ י י ל כ ל פ נ י כ ו	127619
כ י י ל כ ל פ נ י כ ו ב י ו מ פ ק ד י ו פ ק ד ת י ע ל ה מ ח ט א ת מ ו י ג פ י ה	127648

Shape	Word	Translation	Verse	Position	Skip
ג (circle)	גת	Gott/God	Exodus 32:29	127406	-119
י (diamond)	יש	Ich/I	Exodus 32:30	127436	-147
נ (shaded)	נאמא	name	Exodus 32:30	127438	-57
ב (hourglass)	בנ	bin/am	Exodus 32:31	127494	115
ו (box)	ויר	wer/who	Exodus 32:31	127529	54

2. Name/Gott: Ich bin wer ich bin. (German)

cipal language of the Philippines), in Numbers 7:79 to 9:7, in Arabic in Genesis 42:9 to 42:14, and in Hindi in Genesis 31:7 to 31:13. All of these searches were very compact, with the skip lengths low and close together. Apparently, if you can learn the sounds of the Hebrew alphabet, it is likely that you can search the Bible Code in your native language. More experimentation needs to be done in this area.

After discovering that the Bible Code appears to be phonetic, requiring only that words be formatted in Hebrew sounds, I did a search to verify if this theory were correct. The results of this search, included next, indicate that indeed it was. **(Subject: Torah/Code**), found in Genesis 29:32 to 30:14, confirms that the Torah Code is readable by phonetics in all languages.[3]

In transliteration, such as names and places into Hebrew, correct phonetics is extremely important. If the primary words of the subject and the associated words are in close proximity, that in itself indicates confirmation. This was obvious from searching documented historical events, but in historical searches I knew exactly which words to search on. I believe that everything that is, was, or ever will be, is in the Bible Code. Today is tomorrow's past, so if anything is there it must all be there—past, present, future and more. How could there be more? We'll discuss the concept of prospects in a later chapter.

There seems to be a veil that covers the future, however, especially regarding relationships between humans and human-caused events. I think this is because we don't have the necessary data on a future event to do an accurate search. Every such forecast and date is suspect because it is only a prospect. We all have free will, the option to change our minds, our plans, decisions, beliefs, goals, etc. If we could see the future in advance, life would be like a play with our roles prescribed. Life is a learning process based upon decisions that we make on a daily basis. Some are good and some bad, but we learn something from every decision we make. It seems that access to knowledge of the future would interfere with that process. There is probably a safeguard in the Code to prevent this from happening.

Position	Letters
41287	כ י ר א ה י ח ו ה ב ע נ י י כ י ע ת ה י א ה ב .נ י א י ש י ו ת ה ד ע ו ד ו ת ל ד ב נ ו ת א מ
41414	י כ י י ל ד ת י ל ו ש ל ש ה ב נ י מ ע ל כ נ ק ר א ש מ ו ל ו י ו ת ה ד ע ו ד ו ת ל ד ב נ ו ת
41541	ל י ע ק ב ה ב ה ל י ב נ י מ ו א מ א י נ מ ת ה א נ כ י ו י ח ר א פ י ע ק ב ב ר ח ל ו י א מ ר
41668	א ת ב ל ה ה ש פ ח ת ה ל א ש ה ו י ב א א ל י ה י ע ק ב ו ת ה ר ב ל ה ה ו ת ל ד ל י ע ק ב ב נ
41795	ת א מ ר ר ח ל נ פ ת ו ל י א ל ה י מ נ פ ת ל ת י ע מ א ח ת י ג מ י כ ל ת י ו ת ק ר א ש מ ו נ
41922	ה ב ג ד ו ת ק ר א א ת ש מ ו ג ד ו ת ל ד ז ל פ ה ש פ ח ת ל א ה ב נ ש נ י ל י ע ק ב ו ת א מ ר
42049	א מ ו ו ת א מ ר ר ח ל א ל ל א ה ת נ י נ א ל י מ ד ו ד א י ב נ ו כ ו ת א מ ר ל ה מ ע ט ק ח ת
42176	א ה ל ק ר א ת ו ו ת א מ ר א ל י ת ב ו א כ י ש כ ר ש כ ר ת י כ ב ד ו ד א י ב נ י ו י ש כ ב ע
42303	י ו ת ק ר א ש מ ו י ש כ ר ו ת ה ר ע ו ד ל א ה ו ת ל ד ב נ ש ש י ל י ע ק ב ו ת א מ ר ל א ה
42430	ש מ ה ד י נ ה ו י ז כ ר א ל ה י מ א ת ר ח ל ו י ש מ ע א ל י ה א ל ה י מ ו י פ ת ח א ת ר ח מ
42557	ו ס פ ו י א מ ר י ע ק ב א ל ל ב : ש ל ח נ י ו א ל כ ה א ל מ ק ו מ י ו ל א ר צ י ת נ ה א ת נ
42684	כ נ ח ש ת י ו י ב ר כ נ י י ה ו ה ב ג ל ל כ ו י א מ ר נ ק ב ה ש כ ר כ ע ל י ו א ת נ ה ו י א
42811	י ו ע ת ה מ ת י א ע ש ה ג מ א נ כ י ל ב י ת י ו י א מ ר מ ה א ת נ ל כ ו י א מ ר י ע ק ב ל א

Shape	Word	Translation	Verse	Position	Skip
ש	שפה	language	Genesis 29:32	41293	-510
ה	הכל	all	Genesis 29:34	41427	139
ת	תורה	Torah	Genesis 30:4	41672	-127
ק	קוד	code	Genesis 30:11	41925	-127
ק	קריא	readable	Genesis 30:11	41931	-136
ק	קולי	phonetics	Genesis 30:14	42067	-262

3. Torah/Code: (The)Torah Code (is) readable (by) phonetics (in) all language(s).

Suppose an assassination attempt is planned against a state leader, such as the one described in Drosnin's *The Bible Code*. Two leaders were shown by Bible Code searches to be targets of assassination, Yitzhak Rabin and Benjamin Netanyahu. It's well known that the predicted Rabin assassination occurred while Netanyahu survived his term in office. Both events were prospects; one occurred, the other didn't. The prediction that Netanyahu would succeed Rabin as president did prove to be accurate, however. This occurred against all odds. Why? Because human will prevailed.

You will find in later chapters of this book that the Bible Code predicts the prospect of many calamities to beset the earth and mankind over the next ten years. We are in what the Bible calls the end times. Must these calamities take place, in which two-thirds of mankind may perish? The answer is, absolutely not! We have a choice. I believe it is not too late to change our prospects, but at the same time I am a realist. Too few people will change their lives to the extent necessary, or soon enough, to avert all of these future prospects—but there may be enough change to avert some of them. The collective will of mankind can move mountains or prevent them from moving. The choice of paradise on earth or the destruction of mankind is fully our decision to make.

It is ironic that Michael Drosnin, a self-professed atheist, should be the author to bring acclaim to the Bible Code. The following three Code searches were done on information provided in Michael Drosnin's book. The first slide (**Subject: Drosnin/Author**), found in Numbers 32:25 to 33:36, is a Code record of Michael Drosnin, 1996, author of the (book entitled) *The Bible Code*. The second slide (**Subject: Bible/Code**), found in Numbers 31:51 to 32:27, confirms that the Bible Code computer programming creators were Eliyahu Rips, Doron Witztum and Yoav Rosenberg. The third slide (**Subject: Computer/Decoded**), found in Numbers 16:3 to 17:10, confirms that in 1990 the computer decoded the Torah message sealed by God in the Book of Daniel. As you can see, the searches support what Michael Drosnin reported in his book.

Some members of the scientific community have alluded to the pitfalls of a lay person's doing searches in the Bible Code. I agree that certain ethical and procedural criteria must be observed, but I don't agree that you must be a physicist or a mathematician to achieve accurate results. As far as I can tell, the Bible Code is not very well understood by anyone at this point. A number of distinguished scientists agree that a code does exist in the Torah. That's good enough for me. To borrow a phrase from Anthony Robbins, "You don't have to understand electrical theory to flip the switch and see the light." Since the Torah is a holy book, I believe that all Code searches must be treated as though they were sacred. Again, this means that valid Code search results must make biblical sense and exhibit the highest moral and ethical values. Building a Bible Code search is like compiling a computer program. The old cliché, garbage-in, garbage-out, is applicable here. If you love God and you do unto others as you would have them do unto you, you're probably on firm ground.

Searches must be conducted on a computer program that uses an approved version of the Torah and has the capability of finding the closest possible ELS word relationships. There are several available on the market at this writing. I've had the best results using the following criteria. First, obtain a good Hebrew dictionary. I used *Webster's New World Hebrew-English Dictionary* and *The New Bantam-Megiddo Hebrew-English Dictionary*. Then you must learn the Hebrew alphabet letter sounds and some basics about the language. Before conducting a search, you should formulate an idea and then write a short statement that accurately expresses it. Make it read like a newspaper headline, e.g. "Russian Coal Mine Explosion, Many Miners Dead." For this search, I would make my subject: "Russian/Mine." Then I would search on "coal," "explosion," "miners," "dead" and "many." You're looking for an association of primary nouns, adjectives, verbs and adverbs, but not articles, conjunctions and prepositions. Underline the primary words of the statement leaving out words such as "is," "will," "not," "did," etc., and search the words in the order of the statement. Also, leave out words that are less than three Hebrew letters; if possible, use a four-letter word if it can accurately replace a three-letter word. If the original syntax is changed, the search may change, because the program keeps track of the sum total of ELS compactness. Each word searched changes the value. In one search, I removed a word, searched on the next word, then searched again on the word that I had previously removed. It came up again, but in a different location. As the search turned out, the new location supported my hypothesis better. If a compact search doesn't develop, start over and try changing the words without changing the meaning of your original hypothesis. If compactness still doesn't develop, chances are your idea is incorrect. I used the Bible Code itself to determine what constitutes an accurate search. The following slide (**Subject: Code/Accuracy**), found in Genesis 4:24 to 6:9, advises that Bible Code accuracy contains a Bible subject, correct word sound (transliteration phonetics), a compact matrix, and close short skip distances. The slide also gives examples showing the letters of pertinent words touching each other, letters superimposed, and pertinent words crossing each other.[4]

Let's take another look at Daniel 12:4: "But you, Daniel, keep the words secret and the book sealed until the time of the end." The passage also states that "*none of the wicked shall understand* (the book after it is unsealed) *but the wise shall understand*" [italics mine]. I was intrigued by this passage because of the difficulties I was having with some of my searches. I decided to do the following search (**Subject: Computer/Matrix**), which was found in Exodus 28:33 to 31:10. The search verified that a Torah Code computer matrix is presented in truth when the matrix structure is inspired by God through prayer. This means that if we are one with God, the words and sentence syntax will simply come to mind. But we must first yield our will to His. Anyone can accurately search for truth in the Code, but how many are prepared to surrender his or her will to God's? Unfortunately, very few, I believe. This is what is meant by "none of the wicked shall understand." The wise, of course, align themselves with the will of God. Doing so ensures that the Bible Code cannot be used for evil purposes.

Michael Drosnin remarked that he had no idea who encoded the Torah but that the source could not have come from this world. I decided to search for the source itself, and, since Gabriel appears

Letters	Row
כ י ש ב ע ת י מ י ק מ ק י נ ו ל מ כ ש ב ע י מ ו ש ב ע ה ו י ד ע א ד מ ע ו ד א ת א	5284
ד מ ב י ו מ ב ר א א ל ה י מ א ד מ ב ד מ ו ת א ל ה י מ ע ש ה א ת ו ז כ ר ו נ ק ב ה	5434
ה מ א ת ש נ ה ו י ו ל ד ב נ י מ ו ב נ ו ת ו י ה י ו כ ל י מ י א ד מ א ש ר ח י ת ש	5584
ה י ו כ ל י מ י ש ת ש ת י מ ע ש ר ה ש נ ה ו ת ש ע מ א ו ת ש נ ה ו י מ ת ו י ח י א	5734
ו ת ש נ ה ו י מ ת ו י ח י ק י נ נ ש ב ע י מ ש נ ה ו י ו ל ד א ת מ ה ל ל א ל ו י ח	5884
י מ ו ש ש י מ ש נ ה ו י ו ל ד א ת י ר ד ו י ח י מ ה ל ל א ל א ח ר י ה ו ל י ד ו א	6034
י ו ל ד א ת ח נ ו כ ו י ח י י ר ד א ח ר י ה ו ל י ד ו א ת ח נ ו כ ש מ נ ה מ א ו ת	6184
ר י ה ו ל י ד ו א ת מ ת ו ש ל ח ש ל ש מ א ו ת ש נ ה ו י ו ל ד ב נ י מ ו ב נ ו ת ו	6334
כ ו י ח י מ ת ו ש ל ח א ח ר י ה ו ל י ד ו א ת ל מ כ ש ת י מ ו ש מ ו נ י מ ש נ ה ו	6484
ו נ ח ל א מ ר ז ה י נ ח מ נ ו מ מ ע ש נ ו ו מ ע צ ב ו נ י ד י נ ו מ נ ה א ד מ ה א	6634
י נ ח ב נ ח מ ש מ א ו ת ש נ ה ו י ו ל ד נ ח א ת ש מ א ת ח מ ו א ת י פ ת ו י ה י כ	6784
מ ל ע ל מ ב ש ג מ ה ו א ב ש ר ו ה י ו י מ י ו מ א ה ו ע ש ר י מ ש נ ה ה נ פ ל י מ	6934
י צ ר מ ח ש ב ת ל ב ו ר ק ר ע כ ל ה י ו מ ו י נ ח מ י ה ו ה כ י ע ש ה א ת ה א ד מ	7084
ה א ל ה ת ו ל ד ת נ ח נ ח א י ש צ ד י ק ת מ י מ ה י ה ב ד ר ת י ו א ת ה א ל ה י מ	7234
ע ל ה א ר צ ו י א מ ר א ל ה י מ ל נ ח ק צ כ ל ב ש ר ב א ל פ נ י כ י מ ל א ה ה א ר	7384
י מ א מ ה ר ח ב ה ו ש ל ש י מ א מ ה ק ו מ ת ה צ ה ר ת ע ש ה ל ת ב ה ו א ל א מ ה ת	7534
א ר צ י ג ו ע ו ה ק מ ת י א ת ב ר י ת י א ת כ ו ב א ת א ל ה ת ב ה א ת ה ו ב נ י כ	7684
י מ מ כ ל י ב א ו ל א י כ ל ה ח י ו ת ו א ת ה ק ח ל כ מ כ ל מ א כ ל א ש ר י א כ ל	7834
ל ה ב ה מ ה ה ט ה ו ר ה ת ק ח ל כ ש ב ע ה ש ב ע ה א י ש ו א ש ת ו ו מ נ ה ב ה מ ה	7984
א ו ב ע י מ ל י ל ה ו מ ח י ת י א ת כ ל ה י ק ו מ א ש ר ע ש י ת י מ ע ל פ נ י ה א	8134
ו ר ה ו מ נ ה ב ה מ ה א ש ר א י נ נ ה ט ה ר ה ו מ נ ה ע ו פ ו כ ל א ש ר ר מ ש ע ל	8284
ש ב ע ה ע ש ר י ו מ ל ח ד ש ב י ו מ ה ז ה נ ב ק ע ו כ ל מ ע י נ ו ת ת ה ו מ ר ב ה	8434
ו כ ל ה ח י ה ל מ י נ ה ו כ ל ה ב ה מ ה ל מ י נ ה ו כ ל ה ר מ ש ה ר מ ש ע ל ה א ר	8584
י מ ו י ס ג ר י ה ו ה ב ע ד ו ו י ה י ה מ ב ו ל א ר ב ע י מ י ו מ ע ל ה א ר צ ו י	8734

Shape	Word	Translation	Verse	Position	Skip
ק	קול	sound	Genesis 4:24	5293	600
מ	מלה	word	Genesis 5:5	5607	-453
מ	מרחק	distance	Genesis 5:12	5897	-599
א	אמה	matrix	Genesis 5:22	6342	600
א	אות	letter	Genesis 5:26	6505	600
ת	תנך	bible	Genesis 5:26	6509	-598
נ	נכון	correct	Genesis 5:26	6518	-594
ד	דיוק	accuracy	Genesis 5:32	6803	150
ק	קוד	code	Genesis 5:32	6803	-300
ד	דהום	compact	Genesis 5:32	6809	-151
ק	קצר	short	Genesis 6:3	6948	-302
ל	לוג	skip	Genesis 6:5	7092	298
ק	קרוב	close	Genesis 6:5	7093	-1
נ	נושא	subject	Genesis 6:6	7107	5
מ	מכיל	contains	Genesis 6:9	7257	449

Code/Accuracy: Bible Code accuracy contains Bible subject, correct word sound, compact matrix, close, short skip distance.

in the Bible as the messenger of God, I started with him. The following search **(Subject: Gabriel/Author)** was found in Exodus 10:14 to 10:16, and verifies that the Archangel Gabriel is indeed the author of the Torah Code.

It appears that the seal discussed in Daniel was a technological clock. We had to reach a certain level of technological development before we could access the coded information. As we develop faster and bigger computers, we may even be able to search the Bible Code in three dimensions. That would provide a source of information that we can't even imagine now. The technological clock concept makes sense when you realize that, with the advent of the computer age, our knowledge is accelerating at a frightening pace. But history tells us that socialization is always far behind technology. That makes our current world a very dangerous place indeed!

2

History: The Proof

The proof that the Bible Code really works lies in its accuracy in providing data on past events. I'm a natural skeptic, so I devoted a lot of time to doing searches on past world catastrophes in order to determine if I could find them encoded in the Bible. I found that if I knew enough of the details of an event, I had no problem finding it in the Code. This is probably because the cause-and-effect relationship has already played itself out. Being history, all human choices have already been made. Of course, future dates are prospects with many possibilities.

I performed a search on the disastrous earthquake that occurred in Tangshan, China, on July 28, 1976. Over 650,000 people lost their lives and 780,000 were injured. I found the exact date on which it occurred. I then searched for future earthquakes in China and found two possible years, 2006 and 2010. Whether a quake occurs or not in these years may reflect on choices yet to be made by the people and government of China, during the period in question. The following slide (**Subject: Earth/Quake**), found in Exodus 13:3 to 14:14, revealed that, in China, a great and disastrous earthquake surely took place on July 28, 1976.[5]

In April, 1902, Mont Pelée volcano on the Caribbean island of Martinique slowly came to life. At first, the population of the port town of St. Pierre was unconcerned. People went about their daily

Letters	Position
ד ב ר מ ש ה ו י ש א ל ו מ מ צ ר י מ כ ל י כ ס פ ו כ ל י ז ה ב ו ש מ ל	96019
ר ה ו צ י א ו מ מ צ ר י מ ע ג ת מ צ ו ת כ י ל א ח מ צ כ י ג ר ש ו מ מ	96194
צ ר י מ ל י ל ש מ ר י מ ה ו א ל י ה ו ה ל ה ו צ י א מ מ א ר צ מ צ ר י	96369
כ ל א ת ו צ י א מ נ ה ב י ת מ נ ה ב ש ר ח ו צ ה ו ע צ מ ל א ת ש ב ר	96544
ש ר צ ו ה י ה ו ה א ת מ ש ה ו א ת א ה ר נ כ נ ע ש ו ו י ה י ב ע צ מ ה	96719
י מ מ ב י ת ע ב ד י מ כ י ב ח ז ק י ד ה ו צ י א י ה ו ה א ת כ מ מ ז ה	96894
י מ ת א כ ל מ צ ת ו ב י ו מ ה ש ב י ע י ח ג ל י ה ו ה מ צ ו ת י א כ ל	97069
כ י ב י ד ח ז ק ה ה ו צ א כ י ה ו ה מ מ צ ר י מ ו ש מ ר ת א ת ה ח ק ה	97244
ל א ת פ ד ה ו ע ר פ ת ו ו כ ל ב כ ו ר א ד מ ב ב נ י כ ת פ ד ה ו ה י ה	97419
כ ל פ ט ר ר ח מ ה ז כ ר י מ ו כ ל ב כ ו ר ב נ י א פ ד ה ו ה י ה ל א ו	97594
ל ה י מ א ת ה ע מ ד ר כ ה מ ד ב ר י מ ס ו פ ו ח מ ש י מ ע ל ו ב נ י י	97769
מ ב ע מ ו ד ע נ נ ל נ ח ת מ ה ד ר כ ו ל י ל ה ב ע מ ו ד א ש ל ה א י ר	97944
י מ ו א מ ר פ ר ע ה ל ב נ י ש ר א ל נ ב כ י מ ה מ ב א ר צ ס ג ר ע ל	98119
ל ח נ ו א ת י ש ר א ל מ ע ב ד נ ו ו י א ס ר א ת ר כ ב ו ו א ת ע מ ו ל	98294
מ כ ל ס ו ס ר כ ב פ ר ע ה ו פ ר ש י ו ו ח י ל ו ע ל פ י ה ח י ר ת ל פ	98469
ל נ ו ל ה ו צ י א נ ו מ צ ר י מ ה ל א ז ה ה ד ב ר א ש ר ד ב ר נ ו א	98644
ס פ ו ל ר א ת מ ע ד ו ע ד ע ו ל מ י ה ו ה י ל ח מ ל כ מ ו א ת מ ת ח ר	98819
פ ר ע ה ו ב כ ל ח י ל ו ב ר כ ב ו ו ב פ ר ש י ו ו י ד ע ו מ צ ר י מ כ	98994
ו ה ח ש כ ו י א ר א ת ה ל י ל ה ו ל א ק ר ב ז ה א ל ז ה כ ל ה ל י ל ה	99169
ר י ה מ כ ל ס ו ס פ ר ע ה ר כ ב ו ו פ ר ש י ו א ל ת ו כ ה י מ ו י ה י	99344
ה נ ט ה א ת י ד ע כ ל ה י מ ו י ש ב ו ה מ י מ ע ל מ צ ר י מ ע ל ר כ ב	99519
נ ש א ר ב ה מ ע ד א ח ד ו ב נ י י ש ר א ל ה ל כ ו ב י ב ש ה ב ת ו כ ה	99694
ו ב י ה ו ה ו ב מ ש ה ע ב ד ו א ז י ש י ר מ ש ה ו ב נ י י ש ר א ל א ת	99869
ב י מ ו מ ב ח ר ש ל ש י ו ט ב ע ו ב י מ ס ו פ ת ה מ ת י כ ס י מ ו י ר	100044
ג א ח ל ק ש ל ל ת מ ל א מ ו נ פ ש י א ר י ק ח ר ב י ת ו ר י ש מ ו י ד	100219

Shape	Word	Translation	Verse	Position	Skip
נ	נורא	disastrous	Exodus 13:3	96922	-343
ב	בטח	surely	Exodus 13:9	97249	-348
ר	רעידת	quake	Exodus 13:13	97446	-525
א	אדמה	earth	Exodus 13:15	97621	-175
ס	סין	China	Exodus 13:21	97952	-181
א	א אב	7/28	Exodus 14:3	98136	527
ת	תשלו	1976	Exodus 14:6	98311	-180
ח	חזק	great	Exodus 14:14	98852	168

5. Earth/Quake: China, great disastrous earthquake, surely 7/28/1976.

business in this quaint European-style village assuming the volcano was just blowing off steam. After all, the last violent eruption of Mont Pelée had been in 1767. Towards the end of April, ash started falling on the town in ever-increasing amounts, and the populace began to grow nervous. A local election was scheduled for the tenth of May. The French governor, concerned that too many citizens would leave before the election was held, downplayed the danger and dispatched troops to prevent people from leaving the island. On the seventh of May, the La Soufrière volcano erupted on the island of St. Vincent, some 90 miles away. This had a calming effect on the people of St. Pierre, because it was believed that event would take the pressure off Mont Pelée. Then, on the calm, sunny morning of the eighth of May, at 7:50 a.m., without warning, four gigantic explosions blew Mont Pelée to bits. Over 30,000 people in St. Pierre were incinerated or suffocated in a matter of minutes. Only four residents survived to tell the story of the holocaust that took place that day.

The following slide (**Subject: Volcano/1902**), found in Deuteronomy 28:30-28:65, told of many thousands of dead in St. Pierre after an explosion of Mont Pelée on 5/8/1902.[6]

It was two days after Christmas of 1996 that America awoke to the recounting of a horror story on the news. A six-year-old girl had been found dead in her home in Colorado the day after Christmas. The gruesome murder had all the markings of being perpetrated by a sexual predator. Her father had found her body in a basement room of their stylish brick mansion. The child had been wrapped in a blanket with her hands tied and had duct tape over her mouth. JonBenet Ramsey was a beautiful little girl who lived in an upscale neighborhood of Boulder. She was the daughter of John and Patsy Ramsey, a wealthy Boulder couple, and had a nine-year-old brother, Burke. JonBenet was a talented child with everything to look forward to. Her mother had taken her to child talent shows and beauty pageants where the little girl had always amazed the crowds. The story of her death captured the hearts of millions of people across America and all around the world. The incredible thing about this case is that, for over four years, to the date of this

Shape	Word	Translation	Verse	Position	Skip
ה	האר	Mont	Deuteronomy 28:30	293021	-334
ה	הדף	explosion	Deuteronomy 28:44	293689	362
א	אלפים	thousands	Deuteronomy 28:56	294403	351
ה	הר געש	volcano	Deuteronomy 28:56	294404	-349
ח	חלל	dead	Deuteronomy 28:56	294416	-345
ה	הרבה	many	Deuteronomy 28:56	294418	357
ת	תרסב	1902	Deuteronomy 28:61	294738	-2
פ	פיר	Pierre	Deuteronomy 28:61	294741	355
א	א אייר	5/8	Deuteronomy 28:62	294790	-334
פ	פילא	Pelee	Deuteronomy 28:65	295083	13

6. Volcano/1902: Many thousands dead (in) (St.) Pierre (after an) explosion (of) Mont Pelee Volcano (on) 5/8/1902.

writing, no one has been charged with JonBenet Ramsey's murder. There were no credible signs of an intruder. A ransom note demanding $118,000 was found and reported to have come from a writing pad in the house. The Ramseys have since moved to Atlanta, Georgia. They have written a book, *The Death of Innocence*, that tells their side of the story.

The brutal end of JonBenet's short life was recorded in the Bible Code. A slide emerged (**Subject: Ramsey/1996**), found in Deuteronomy 1:19 to 1:44, recording that JonBenet was killed in December, 1996, in the cellar of her home.

In the spring of 1912, the British luxury liner *Titanic* left port in Southampton, England, on its maiden voyage to New York. The ship was equal to its name. It weighed 46,000 tons and was considered unsinkable due to its unique construction of 16 watertight compartments. First-class passengers included socicty notables such as John Astor, Benjamin Guggenheim and Isidor Strauss. There were 2,200 passengers listed on the manifest, but only 707 passengers would make it to New York. It was just before midnight on April 14 that disaster struck. The ship hit an iceberg some 95 miles south of Grand Banks, Newfoundland, sinking in about three hours. The *Titanic* disaster was found in the Book of Numbers. The slide (**Subject: Titanic/Ship**), found in Numbers 22:29 to 32:14, revealed that the ship *Titanic* struck ice on 4/14/1912, with over a thousand souls lost in the accident.

On June 16, 1999, CNN broadcast a worldwide breaking news flash that John F. Kennedy Jr. was missing off the coast of Massachusetts while piloting his private aircraft. His wife, Carolyn, and her sister, had accompanied him on the flight. They had left New York to attend a family wedding the following day.

When I first heard the news, I could hardly believe that yet another tragedy had beset this family. I was experimenting with the Bible Code at the time, and I decided to do a search on the accident. I used Kennedy/Plane as my subject, unsure that I could keep the search separated from John F. Kennedy Jr.'s famous father. As it turned out, I obtained much of the information about the accident while the search was still going on. I had to develop several scenarios as to what could have happened. The worst-case scenario unfortunately appeared. I got a very compact slide indicating that the plane had submerged on July 16, 1999, and that all three people on board were dead. This information was coded in Genesis. I did another search that indicated that the plane would be found and that the bodies would be recovered within a few days. I was able to do all this within an hour of the news bulletin. As the story developed, exactly as my searches had indicated, I became convinced that the Bible Code was in fact a gift from God that, if properly used, could be a great source of guidance to mankind. The following slide (**Subject: Kennedy/Plane**), found in Genesis 41:45 to 42:31, revealed that John Kennedy Jr.'s plane was lost on 7/16.1999, three dead.

One of the worst disasters in modern history occurred in the spring of 1887. Northern China's Yellow River overflowed its banks, causing utter catastrophe in the lower provinces. The river starts in the Kunlun Mountains of the northwest Tsinghai province and winds its way south, then east through agricultural areas, before emptying into the Yellow Sea. In 1887, unusual summer rains caused the river to swell to as much as 40 miles wide and 50 feet deep in some parts, devastating every region through which it passed. So many people died in the flood, and later of cholera, that it's not known how many perished. Estimates range between anywhere from two to seven million. The following slide (**Subject: China/Flood**), found in Leviticus 7:37 to 8:19, told of the disastrous Yellow River flood in China; millions lost in the summer of 1887.[7]

On May 26, 2000, a tragedy occurred at the Lake Worth Middle School in Lake Worth, Florida. On the last day of school, a teacher dismissed a 13-year-old student named Nathaniel Brazill from class early for misconduct. The student later returned to class with a pistol and shot the teacher in the face, killing him instantly. The teacher was Barry Grunow, married and the father of two. The following slide (**Subject: Brazill/Grunow**), found in Genesis 47:22 to 49:30, revealed that Nathaniel Brazill was the murderer of U.S.A. teacher, Barry Grunow, on May 26, 2000.[8]

Shape	Word	Translation	Verse	Position	Skip
מ	מליון	million	Leviticus 7:37	150730	-678
ק	קיץ	summer	Leviticus 8:4	150968	965
נ	נורא	disastrous	Leviticus 8:4	150980	-414
א	אבוד	lost	Leviticus 8:5	151004	-545
נ	נהר	River	Leviticus 8:5	151006	-528
צ	צהוב	Yellow	Leviticus 8:9	151236	687
ת	תרמז	1887	Leviticus 8:13	151417	539
	חרסינה	China	Leviticus 8:15	151514	137
מ	מבול	flood	Leviticus 8:19	151780	6

7. China/Flood: Disastrous Yellow River flood (in) China, million(s) lost (in the) summer (of)1887. (One letter of the words "yellow", "1887" and "million" is hidden beyond the slide border.)

Shape	Word	Translation	Verse	Position	Skip
ב	כא אייר	5/26	Genesis 47:22	73305	606
ת	תשס	2000	Genesis 49:15	75829	14
ב	ברזל	Brazill	Genesis 49:15	75850	-248
ג	גרנו	Grunow	Genesis 49:15	75851	-124
מ	מורה	teacher	Genesis 49:20	75982	-131
ב	ברי	Barry	Genesis 49:24	76086	-124
א	ארהב	USA	Genesis 49:24	76117	-6
נ	נתנל	Nathaniel	Genesis 49:30	76490	-112
ק	קטלן	murderer	Genesis 49:30	76495	124

8. Brazill/Grunow: Nathaniel Brazill (was the) murderer (of) USA teacher Barry Grunow (on) 5/26/2000. (Three letters of the word "5/26" are hidden beyond the slide border.)

Letters	Position
גדלהאישוילכהלוכוגדלעדכיגדלמאדויהילומקנהצאנומקנהבקרועבדה	35099
שמיצחקויחנבנחלגררוישבשמוישביצחקויחפראתבארתהמימאשרחפרובי	35271
ייצחקלאמרלנוהמימויקראשמהבארעשקכיהתעשקועמוויחפרובאראחרתו	35443
יויהוהבלילהההואויאמראנכיאלהיאברהמאביכאלתיראכיאתכאנכיובר	35615
אוויאמראלהמיצחקמדועבאתמאליואתמשנאתמאתיותשלחונימאתכמויאמ	35787
שלומאתהעתהברוכיהוהויעשלהממשתהויאכלווישתווישכימובבקרוישב	35959
העירבארשבעעדהיומהזהויהיעשובנארבעימשנהויקחאשהאתיהודיתבתב	36131
ויאמרהנהנאזקנתילאידעתייוממותיועתהשאנאכליכתליכוקשתכוצאהש	36303
ורבקהאמרהאליעקבבנהלאמרהנהשמעתיאתאביכמדבראלעשואחיכלאמרהב	36475
מטעמימלאביככאשראהבוהבאתלאביכואכלבעבראשריברככלפנימותוויא	36647
קליולכקחליויקחויבאלאמוותעשאמומטעמימכאשראהבאביוותקחר	36819
תהבידיעקבבנהויבאאלאביוויאמראביויאמרהננימיאתהבניויאמריעק	36991
פניויאמריצחקאליעקבגשהנאואמשכבניהאתהזהבניעשואמלאויגשיעקב	37163
ואכלהמצידבנילמענתברכנפשיויגשלוויאכלויבאלויינוישתויאמרא	37335
צורבדגנותירשיעבדוכעמימוישתחולכלאמימהוהגבירלאחיכוישתחוול	37507
אביוויאמרלאביויקמאביויאכלמצידבנובעבורתברכנינפשכויאמרלויצ	37679
תדבריאביוויצעקצעקהגדלהומרהעדמאדויאמרלאביוברכניגמאניאביו	37851
נגבירשמתיולכואתכלאחיונתתילולעבדימודגנותירשסמכתיוולכהאפו	38023

Shape	Word	Translation	Verse	Position	Skip
(hourglass) ת	תשנ	1990	Genesis 26:14	35136	-342
(shaded) ע	עירק	Iraq	Genesis 26:18	35301	-344
(circle) י	יא אב	8/2	Genesis 26:34	36161	-344
(square) פ	פרוץ	invaded	Genesis 27:20	37163	190
(diamond) כ	כווית	Kuwait	Genesis 27:25	37354	169

9. Iraq/8/2/90: Iraq invaded Kuwait (on) 8/2/1990.

In 1990, the U.S. led a great world alliance against Iraq's Saddam Hussein after his invasion of Kuwait on August 2 of that year. He was defeated the following year, on February 28, 1991. The following slide (**Subject: Iraq/8/2/90**), found in Genesis 26:14 to 27:25, verified that Iraq invaded Kuwait on 8/2/1990.[9]

The U.S. presidential election of 2000 almost stopped the writing of this book. When the primaries started, I did a Bible Code search that indicated an enormous probability that Governor George W. Bush would win. The slide was extremely compact and in every way exhibited a high degree of accuracy. Since I believed that G.W. Bush was exactly what the country needed at this point in our history, I was gratified, and didn't give the outcome of the election any further thought. However, when the seventh of November rolled around, I couldn't believe the results: the apparent victory of Al Gore. Could I have been so wrong in interpreting my Code search of this election? I was depressed and confused, not only because my candidate was losing, but also because my confidence in interpreting the Bible Code was shaken. I stopped writing and began to examine my entire theory of the Code.

Every place I searched, however, G. W. Bush appeared to be the winner. About a week after the election, I was watching the CBN News when I heard Pat Robertson mention that thousands of his listeners were fasting and praying for a Republican victory. I wondered if this could be a miracle in the making. I immediately went to my computer and started to search the election using different parameters. George Bush was only a few hundred votes ahead at this point, out of approximately 100 million votes. If he did win, it would truly be a miracle in every sense of the word. I remembered that Governor Bush had had a crisis early in his life and had turned to his religion for help. My first search (**Subject: Accepted Jesus**), found in Numbers 22:38 to 23:14, verified that Governor Bush had accepted Jesus and was therefore blessed by God. This was inspiring, but being blessed didn't mean he would win the presidency. I then decided to search for a miracle, and I found it. The following slide (**Subject: 2001/President**), found in Exodus 37:24 to 38:19, verified that the president chosen is Bush

ה ז ה ב ט ה ו ר כ כ ר ז ה ב ט ה ו ר ע ש ה א ת ה ו א ת כ ל כ ל י ה ו י ע ש א ת מ	135882
ו א מ ת י מ ק מ ת ו מ מ נ ו ה י ו ק ר נ ת י ו ו י צ פ א ת ו ז ה ב ט ה ו ר א ת ג	135956
ב ס ב י ב ו ש ת י ט ב ע ת ז ה ב ע ש ה ל ו מ ת ח ת ל ז ר ו ע ל ש ת י צ ל ע ת י ו	136030
ת ה ב ד י מ ע צ י ש ט י מ ו י צ פ א ת מ ז ה ב ו י ע ש א ת ש מ נ ה מ ש ח ה ק ד ש	136104
ע ל ה ע צ י ש ט י מ ח מ ש א מ ו ת א ר כ ו ו ח מ ש א מ ו ת ר ח ב ו ר ב ו ע ו ש ל	136178
ה י ו ק ר נ ת י ו ו י צ פ א ת ו נ ח ש ת ו י ע ש א ת כ ל כ ל י ה מ ז ב ח א ת ה ס	136252
ת ת כ ל כ ל י ו ע ש ה נ ח ש ת ו י ע ש ל מ ז ב ח מ כ ב ר מ ע ש ה ר ש ת נ ח ש ת	136326
ע ה ק צ ו ת ל מ כ ב ר ה נ ח ש ת ב ת י מ ל ב ד י מ ו י ע ש א ת ה ב ד י מ ע צ י ש	136400
ע ת ה מ ז ב ח ל ש א ת א ת ו ב ה מ נ ב ו ב ל ח ת ע ש ה א ת ו ו י ע ש א ת ה כ י ו	136474
ח א ה ל מ ו ע ד ו י ע ש א ת ה ח צ ר ל פ א ת נ ג ב ת י מ נ ה ק ל ע י ה ח צ ר ש ש	136548
מ נ ח ש ת ו ו י ה ע מ ו ד י מ ו ח ש ק י ה מ כ ס פ ו ל פ א ת צ פ ו נ מ א ה ב א מ	136622
מ ו ד י מ ו ח ש ק י ה מ כ ס פ ו ל פ א ת י מ ק ל ע י מ ח מ ש י מ ב א מ ה ע מ ו ד	136696
מ כ ס פ ו ל פ א ת ק ד מ ה מ ז ר ח ה ח מ ש י מ א מ ה ק ל ע י מ ח מ ש ע ש ר ה א מ	136770
ה ש נ י ת מ ז ה ו מ ז ה ל ש ע ר ה ח צ ר ק ל ע י מ ח מ ש ע ש ר ה א מ ה ע מ ד י ה	136844
ז ר ו ה א ד נ י מ ל ע מ ד י מ נ ח ש ת ו ו י ה ע מ ו ד י מ ו ח ש ו ק י ה מ כ ס פ	136918
צ ר ו מ ס כ ש ע ר ה ח צ ר מ ע ש ה ר ק מ ת כ ל ת ו א ר ג מ נ ו ת ו ל ע ת ש נ י ו	136992
ל ע מ ת ק ל ע י ה ח צ ר ו ע מ ד י ה מ א ר ב ע ה ו א ד נ י ה מ א ר ב ע ה נ ח ש ת	137066
ת ד ת ל מ ש כ נ ו ל ח צ ר ס ב י ב נ ח ש ת א ל ה פ ק ו ד י ה מ ש כ נ מ ש כ נ ה ע	137140
א ה ר נ ה כ ה נ ו ב צ ל א ל ב נ א ו ר י ב נ ח ו ר ל מ ט ה י ה ו ד ה ע ש ה א ת כ	137214
ל מ ט ה ד נ ח ר ש ו ח ש ב ו ר ק מ ב ת כ ל ת ו ב א ר ג מ נ ו ב ת ו ל ע ת ה ש נ י	137288
י ה י ז ה ב ה ת נ ו פ ה ת ש ע ו ע ש ר י מ כ כ ר ו ש ב ע מ א ו ת ו ש ל ש י מ ש ק	137362
ב ע מ א ו ת ו ח מ ש ה ו ש ב ע י מ ש ק ל ב ש ק ל ה ק ד ש ב ק ע ל ג ל ג ל ת מ ח צ	137436
ר י מ ש נ ה ו מ ע ל ה ל ש ש מ א ו ת א ל פ ו ש ל ש ת א ל פ. י מ ו ח מ ש מ א ו ת ו	137510
א ת א ד נ י ה פ ר כ ת מ א ת א ד נ י מ ל מ א ת ה כ כ ר כ כ ר ל א ד נ ו א ת ה א ל	137584

Shape	Word	Translation	Verse	Position	Skip
ח	תפלה	prayer	Exodus 37:24	135905	-374
ה	השיב	answer	Exodus 37:26	135987	143
ק	קול	vote	Exodus 37:27	136055	-448
פ	פלא	FLA/miracle	Exodus 38:1	136191	-229
א	אלף	thousand	Exodus 38:1	136191	229
ע	עדף	excess	Exodus 38:2	136264	-158
א	אלוה	God	Exodus 38:5	136401	-232
נ	נבחר	chosen	Exodus 38:11	136655	73
נ	נשיא	president	Exodus 38:11	136660	-222
ת	תשסא	2001	Exodus 38:14	136808	-148
ב	בוש	Bush	Exodus 38:17	136949	-75
א	ארהב	USA	Exodus 38:19	137099	-143

10. 2001/President: (The) president chosen (in) 2001 (is) Bush (with an) excess (of a) thousand vote(s) (in) Fla. God's miracle answer (to) USA prayer. (Note: "Miracle" is also the transliteration of "Fla." and phonetically spelled backwards is "thousand," two words meaning "Fla. miracle thousand." The word "thousand" is shown as a positive skip, therefore is hidden from view under "miracle.")

with an excess of 1,000 votes in Fla., God's miracle answer to U.S.A. prayer.[10] I was truly amazed! By now, the Florida Supreme Court had endorsed the vote-counting means used by the Democrats to eat away at Bush's lead. I decided to search for whether that slim lead would hold. The following slide (**Subject: FLA/Vote**), found in Genesis 2:20 to 3:7, verified that nothing shall suppress the FLA 1,000 miracle votes given to Bush by God.[11]

I understand that Vice-President Gore believes the election was stolen from him. Perhaps it was! I believe that when it was all over, G.W. Bush did indeed hold an over-1,000-vote lead when all of the overseas ballots were included. In any case, without those 1,000 miracle votes, Governor Bush could not have won the election. My searches were completed two weeks after Election Day, long before the U.S. Supreme Court was involved. It is interesting to note that the phonetic transliteration of the Hebrew word for *miracle* into English is FLA.

There is little to say about the World Trade Center tragedy of September 11, 2001 that hasn't already been said. President G. W. Bush has said that he believes that it is his calling to deal with this catastrophe. After reviewing the above Bible Code searches, I believe most people will agree. The following search (**Subject: 9/11/ bin Laden**), found in Exodus 16:4 to 19:1, verified that Osama bin Laden destroyed the U.S.A. World Trade Center on 9/11/2001.[12]

The purpose of this book is not to look into the past. We already know what happened yesterday. I have many slides that accurately identify historical events recorded in the Bible Code. I, also, had to be convinced. I've included some of them in this chapter to convince the reader that the Bible Code is a fact. As verified by historical slides, it's the close proximity or compactness of primary words and their relationship to each other describing the event that confirm the accuracy of the slide. Since the Bible was written thousands of years ago, the Code must include past, present, and all possibilities of future events. The problem with searching future events is that, until they occur, we can only view them as prospects for the future. Prospects can change for better or for worse, depending upon decisions we make along the way.

Letters	Position
ולעופהשמימולכלחיתהשדהולאדמלאמצאעזרכנגדוויפליהוהאלהימתרד	2631
שרלקחמנהאדמלאשהויבאהאלהאדמויאמרהאדמזאתהפעמעצממעצמיובשרמ	2746
והיולבשראחדויהיושניהמערומימהאדמואשתוולאיתבששווהנחשהיהער	2861
עצהגנותאמרהאשהאלהנחשמפריעצהגננאכלומפריהעצאשרבתוכהגנאמרא	2976
עאלהימכיביומאכלכממנוונפקחועיניכמוהייתמכאלהימידעיטובורע	3091
ותאכלותתנגמלאישהעמהויאכלותפקחנהעינישניהמוידעוכיעירממהמו	3206
ויתחבאהאדמואשתומפנייהוהאלהימבתוכעצהגנויקראיהוהאלהימאלהא	3321
ידלככיעירמאתהמנהעצאשרצויתיכלבלתיאכלממנואכלתויאמרהאדמהא	3436
אמרהאשההנחשהשיאניואכלויאמריהוהאלהימאלהנחשכיעשיתזאתארורא	3551
ובינהאשהובינזרעכובינזרעההואישופכראשואתהתשופנועקבאלהאשהא	3666
מאמרכישמעתלקולאשתכותאכלמנהעצאשרצויתיכלאמרלאתאכלממנוארור	3781
שדהבזעתאפיכתאכללחמעדשובכאלהאדמהכיממנהלקחתכיעפראתהואלעפר	3896
כתנותעורוילבשמויאמריהוהאלהימהנהאדמהיהכאחדממנולדעתטובורע	4011

Shape	Word	Translation	Verse	Position	Skip
ד	דכא	suppress	Genesis 2:20	2655	573
ה	האם	shall	Genesis 2:22	2768	121
ב	בוש	Bush	Genesis 3:2	2995	-235
נ	נתון	given	Genesis 3:2	3005	345
א	אלף	thousand	Genesis 3:5	3114	-115
פ	פלא	FLA/miracle	Genesis 3:5	3114	115
ק	קול	vote	Genesis 3:5	3115	115
א	אין	nothing	Genesis 3:5	3120	-227
א	אלוה	God	Genesis 3:7	3236	-115

11. FLA./Vote: Nothing shall suppress (the) FLA. thousand (miracle) vote(s) given (to) Bush (by) God. (Note: The transliteration of "FLA" and "miracle" are phonetically the same so "miracle" does not register in the search. "Thousand" is "FLA" and "miracle" phonetically spelled in reverse therefore covered by the symbols for FLA.)

Shape	Word	Translation	Verse	Position	Skip
ת	תשסא	2001	Exodus 16:4	101365	-644
מ	מרכז	Center	Exodus 16:26	102638	423
ב	בן לדן	Bin Laden	Exodus 17:9	103695	-223
ח	חרב	destroyed	Exodus 17:9	103731	-637
כ	כג אלול	9/11	Exodus 17:9	103740	-636
א	ארהב	USA	Exodus 18:6	104385	-213
ס	סחר	Trade	Exodus 18:9	104575	-646
ע	עולם	World	Exodus 18:13	104810	208
ו	וסמה	Osama	Exodus 19:1	105646	-4

12. 9-11/Bin Laden: Osama Bin Laden destroyed (the) USA World Trade Center (on) 9/11/2001. (One letter of the words "9/11" and two of "2001" are hidden beyond the slide border.)

3

The Source: The Akashic Records

The Akashic Records may be said to be the destiny of a soul in its entrance into materiality. They are the records that the individual entity itself writes patiently upon the skein of time and space. These records are opened when self is attuned to the infinite, and they may be read by those attuned to that consciousness. They are records in the Book of Life.

The above paragraph is a paraphrase of "Reading 2533-8," given early in the last century by the modern-age prophet Edgar Cayce (1877-1945). Author Jess Stearn introduced me to Edgar Cayce in the 1970's when I read his best-selling biography of Cayce, *The Sleeping Prophet*. Many books have been written about this amazing individual. *The Edgar Cayce Companion* (A.R.E. Press, 1995), by B. Ernest Frejer, contains the most comprehensive study of Cayce's 14,000-plus readings in the Akashic Records that I have seen to date. All of his readings are on file at the Association of Research and Enlightenment (A.R.E.), in Virginia Beach, VA.

Edgar Cayce is usually referred to as a psychic, seer or visionary. The Bible Code, however, identifies him as a Prophet of God. Some of his readings will be featured in the following chapters of this book.

The next slide (**Subject: Cayce/Prophet**), found in Exodus 22:22 to 30:10, reveals that Cayce, U.S., 1877 to 1945, was a Prophet of God.

When I first read about the Akashic Records, I tried to verify their existence through other sources, but the little I could find in English led me right back to Cayce. It has only been recently that I have found an independent source in English that described "Akasha," a book called *The Wisdom of the Vedas* (1992), by J. C. Chatterji. *Veda* means "wisdom" or "science." The book is a treatise on the ancient Sanskrit compositions of the sacred Hindu mantras, and on the commentaries about them called the Brahmanas. The writings date back to thousands of years B.C. It is believed by the faithful that these mantras were received from God. This belief is verified by the Bible Code, as you will see in a later chapter.

According to these writings, *Akasha* refers to an ethereal time/space continuum filling all creation. It has been referred to as sound (vibration), air, fire, water and earth. If we refer back to the Cayce reading above, it appears that each of us has a recording within the Akasha of all our thoughts and deeds, called an Akashic Record. The Bible refers to the Book of Life in a similar manner. The following slide (**Subject: Akasha/Continuum**), found in Genesis 22:4 to 23:17, verifies that the Akasha continuum of the *Vedas* equals sound (vibration), air, fire, water and earth.

There are many accounts today of near-death experiences during which people have had their entire lives flash before them in seconds and have reviewed those lives as if on a movie screen. It's possible that those people were tuned in to their Akashic Records, underwent a self-judgment, and determined it was too early to leave. They've reported that after they recovered they were no longer afraid to die and that their lives were changed for the better by the experience.

If everything has been recorded in the Akasha since the beginning of time, if time is relative and the time-space continuum is all-encompassing, then it would be reasonable to expect the Akasha to contain a record of everything, including past, present and future. That would be complex enough, but humanity's collective will includes an infinite number of choices to be made also. That means that the Akashic Records would not only include the past, present and future, but also all the prospects of that which could have occurred. It is a concept that staggers the imagination.

Since our lives are regulated from sunrise to sunrise, it appears to us that there is a beginning and an end to everything. It is difficult for us to imagine that time is only an illusion. But Albert Einstein is quoted as saying, in 1955, that "the distinction between past, present and future is an illusion, however persistent."

Somewhere, I read an explanation of the relativity of time that may be helpful here. Imagine a curving river with three fishermen on its banks. The fishermen are a mile apart and can't see each other, but you are on a mountaintop, able to observe the entire scene below. Now, imagine a boat passing the middle fisherman. The boat is in the middle fisherman's present, but it is in the first fisherman's past and the third fisherman's future. Since you are above it all, everything is in your present. As you can see from this example, time is relative to the vantage point. If you were outside of our three-dimensional, time-bound world and looking in, from your vantage point you would see past, present, and future prospects all at once.

There is something else to consider, however. From the mountaintop you saw the past, the present, and the prospect of the boat's passing the third fisherman. But the pilot of the boat has choices he can make. He can decide to stop and try the fishing by the second fisherman. If he does and the fishing is good, he may never go up the river any farther. When he catches his limit, he may return down the river again, passing the first fisherman. Up to this point, what we saw from the mountaintop was the past, the present, and the perception of two prospects of the future. Suppose the pilot of the boat decided to stop and camp for the night between the second and third fishermen. The fishermen have choices to make also. The third fisherman may call it a day, go home, and never see the boat at all.

As you can see from the above, there is no predestined future. There are only prospects of the future, which depend upon the collective choices of us all. Only the All-Seeing Eye of God can determine what all of those collective choices will be. God told the prophet Jonah that He would destroy the ancient city of Nineveh because of the wicked ways of its people, and told Jonah to announce to the populace His impending judgment. Upon hearing the prophecy, the people of Nineveh repented and the city was subsequently spared, but Jonah was embarrassed, because he had prophesied an event that didn't come to pass. Based upon this testament, God apparently knew that, with a warning, repentance would be the collective choice of the people of Nineveh. When the choice of repentance was made, God followed it up with mercy. He was apparently teaching a lesson to Jonah as well as to all those reading the story.

Only God knows the future, as you will see in a Bible Code search of a later chapter. I believe God guided the true prophets of the past through the web of prospects directly to the actual choices that were made.

The Akasha is remote from our three-dimensional world and therefore contains the whole. We can access it from the vantage point of an out-of-body experience. While in a self-induced trance, Edgar Cayce was able to accomplish this at will, apparently accessing thousands of records; those having near-death experiences had no control over the experience, and were able to access only their own record. I believe that in the current era we have been given the Bible Code as another source through which to access the Akashic Records. Regarding the future, however, we can only see prospects and probabilities.

In 1934, Edgar Cayce was asked the following, in Reading 443-005: "As given through this channel, we understand that the Akashic Records are recorded on the ether. Then cannot an instrument be invented to induct ether and thus tap in on the Akashic Records?" Cayce answered that the electronic instrument that they had in mind would not work—adding, however: "But would necessitate rather a varied or different form, but using much of the same theory as is used here in its activity. Yet this may be done—eventually, will!" I am convinced he was talking about the modern electronic computer, which was not yet invented at the time of his reading, but with which we can now access the Bible Code.

It's now apparent that the Akashic Records were provided to Moses thousands of years ago encoded in the Torah. According to tradition, he was told that not one letter should be changed. This would be necessary to maintain the integrity of the Code. The holy writings have been faithfully copied ever since under the strictest of quality control procedures. Any page that varied in the slightest from the original had to be destroyed. The quality of Old Testament text reproduction was verified in 1947 when a Bedouin shepherd boy discovered the 2,000-year-old Dead Sea Scrolls in the desert caves near Qumran.

The following slide verifies that the Akashic Records and the Bible Code are indeed the same, identical: **(Subject: Akashic/ Records)**, found in Leviticus 23:31 to 24:7.[13]

Letters	Position
ל מ ל א כ ה ל א ת ע ש ו ח ק ת ע ו ל מ ל ד ר ת י כ מ ב כ ל מ ש ב ת י כ מ ש ב ת ש ב ת ו נ ה ו	177741
י ע י ה ז ה ח ג ה ס כ ו ת ש ב ע ת י מ י מ ל י ה ו ה ב י ו מ ה ר א ש ו נ מ ק ר א ק ד ש כ ל מ	177891
ע ד י י ה ו ה א ש ר ת ק ר א ו א ת מ מ ק ר א י ק ד ש ל ה ק ר י ב א ש ה ל י ה ו ה ע ל ה ו מ נ	178041
ש ב י ע י ב א ס פ כ מ א ת ב ת א ו ב ת א ה א ר צ ת ח ג ו א ת ח ג י ה ו ה ש ב ע ת מ י מ ב י ו מ	178191
מ י מ ו ח ג ת מ א ת ו ח ג ל י ה ו ה ש ב ע ת י מ י מ ב ש נ ה ח ק ת ע ו ל מ ל ד ר ת י כ מ ב ח	178341
מ צ ר י מ א נ י י ה ו ה א ל ה י כ מ ו י ד ב ר מ ש ה א ת מ ע ד י י ה ו ה א ל ב נ י י ש ר א ל	178491
ד ב ק ר ל פ נ י י ה ו ה ת מ י ד ח ק ת ע ו ל מ ל ד ר ת י כ מ ע ל ה מ נ ר ה ה ט ה ר ה י ע ר כ	178641
ר ל פ נ י י ה ו ה ו נ ת ע ל ה מ ע ר כ ת ל ב נ ה ז כ ה ו ה י ת ה ל ל ח מ ל א ז כ ר ה א ש ה	178791
א ש י י ה ו ה ח ק ע ו מ ל ו י צ א ב נ א ש ה י ש ר א ל י ת ו ה ו א ב נ א י ש מ צ ר י ב ת ו כ	178941
ו י נ י ח ה ו ב מ ש מ ר ל פ ר ש ל ה מ ע ל פ י ה ו ה ו י ד ב ר י ה ו ה א ל מ ש ה ל א מ ר ה	179091
ו ו נ ק ב ש מ י ה ו ה מ ו ת י ו מ ת ר ג ו מ י ר ג מ ו ב ו כ ל ה ע ד ה כ ג ר כ א ז ר ח ב נ ק	179241
ח ת ע י נ ש נ ת ח ת ש נ כ א ש ר י ת נ מ ו מ ב א ד מ כ נ י ת נ ו ב ו מ כ ה ב ה מ ה י ש ל מ	179391
ת ו א ב נ ו ב נ י י ש ר א ל ע ש ו כ א ש ר צ ו ה י ה ו ה א ת מ ש ה ו י ד ב ר י ה ו ה א ל מ ש	179541

Shape	Word	Translation	Verse	Position	Skip
ק	קוד	code	Leviticus 23:31	177761	-154
א	אקשק	Akashic	Leviticus 23:37	178060	-299
א	אותו	same	Leviticus 23:39	178216	-451
ע	עדות	record	Leviticus 23:41	178361	150
ז	זהה	identical	Leviticus 24:7	178816	146
ת	תורה	Torah	Leviticus 24:7	178822	150

13. Akashic/Record: (The) Akashic Record (and the) Torah Code (are the) same, identical.

4

The Word: Testaments of God

So far, we have briefly discussed the Torah and the *Vedas* of the Hindu mantras as testaments of God. It should be noted that the Bible Code verifies that the Christian New Testament and the Holy Koran, as well as the teachings of Buddha and Confucius, are also the Word of God. There are probably more. Buddhism is a path to enlightenment and does not preclude its followers from believing in the one true God. There are variations of Buddhism and other religions that believe that self-enlightenment is possible to attain without God. According to the Bible Code, these teachings are not of God. It would be reasonable to infer that all religions that are from God believe in the one God, and contain the central theme that we must love Him above all things and love each other as we love ourselves.

Throughout the ages, messianic figures have emerged in different parts of the world to bring the same message over and over again. Such figures usually appear when a society is totally off course. Their testaments teach us how to organize a good and just society. Plato, the great philosopher of ancient Greece, advised us that all things of goodness, truth, and beauty are of God. It is reasonable to believe that a society based upon these principles is as God intended us to live.

If the above is true, then why are there differences between the testaments? It should be noted that when the testaments were received, societies were at different stages of development, with different languages, cultures and historical backgrounds. The messages, although basically the same, were presented in conformance with the needs of the society concerned. One element was common among all of them, however: These were primitive societies that needed simple answers to complex questions.

Even their views of God were different. In some testaments, God is viewed as a king, and He is praised and feared as a king would be. Prayer is regulated into strict rituals where deviation may be considered blasphemy. Other testaments view God as a father figure; He is revered as a loving father. Jesus encouraged this view, probably because a father is truly loved while a king is often merely respected. When asked by his disciples how they should pray, Jesus recommended a prayer whose first line addressed God as, "Our Father, Who is in Heaven." Do these different testaments mean one must be right and another wrong? Of course not; they mean only that there are differences in the way we can view God and His message. In all of the testaments, God is viewed with the utmost of reverence, although in different ways.

Unfortunately, the perceived differences between these holy testaments have been exploited throughout history, resulting in confusion and even so-called holy wars. We are all brothers and sisters in the eyes of God. I would imagine that the only blasphemy greater than killing our brothers and sisters in His name would be a total denial of God. In reality, these holy wars are carried out more in the name of greed and/or revenge than in the name of God. Those profiting from such wars convince the populace that they are fighting a holy war sanctioned by God. The people are often told they will go to heaven if they die fighting the so-called infidels. The profiteers are usually better educated than the solders, which is why they can easily manipulate them.

I found seven slides verifying that there is only one God and that Rama, Krishna, Moses, Buddha, Jesus, Confucius and Mohammed were His messengers. There are probably more. It is interesting to note that of those religions searched, only three, Judaism, Confucianism and Islam, did not fall into the trap of worshipping their messenger as God. It is probably because of this that, when Gabriel gave the last Testament of God to Mohammed, it was explicitly stated that "there is only one God and Mohammed is His Messenger."

The lesson that the Bible Code gives us on this subject means that at least 90 percent of the world's population believe in the same basic religious doctrines. When the common man or woman finally understands and accepts this, no government can ever lead him or her into a war based upon religious hatred, because it will have been accepted that we are more alike than we are different.

The following slide entitled (**Subject: Three/Message**), found in Genesis 45:13 to 46:17, identifies that three sacred messages, the *Vedas*, Torah, and Koran hold an embodied code from God.[14]

Regarding Islam, the following slide (**Subject: Gabriel/ Mohammed**), found in Numbers 14:10 to 15:38, verifies that Gabriel offered Mohammed the Holy Koran, the final message of God till the Tribulation.

Letters	Position
צ ר י ח ו א ת כ ל א ש ר ר א י ת מ ו מ ה ר ת מ ו ה ו ר ד ת מ א ת א	69453
ק ל נ ש מ ע ב י ת פ ר ע ה ל א מ ר ב א ו א ח י י ו ס פ ו י י ט ב ב	69572
מ ו א ת ב ת י כ מ ו ב א ו א ל י ו א ת נ ה ל כ מ א ת ט ו ב א ר צ מ	69691
נ כ מ א ל ת ח ס ע ל כ ל י כ מ כ י ט ו ב כ ל א ר צ מ צ ר י מ ל כ מ	69810
ש ל ש מ א ו ת כ ס פ ו ח מ ש ח ל פ ת ש מ ל ת ו ל א ב י ו ש ל ח כ ז	69929
ג ז ו ב ד ר כ ו י ע ל ו מ מ צ ר י מ ו י ב א ו א ר צ כ נ ע נ א ל י	70048
ו ס פ א ש ר ד ב ר א ל ה מ ו י ר א א ת ה ע ג ל ו ת א ש ר ש ל ח י ו	70167
ב א ב א ר ה ש ב ע ו י ז ב ח ז ב ח י מ ל א ל ה י א ב י ו י צ ח ק ו	70286
ג ו י ג ד ו ל א ש י מ כ ש מ א נ כ י א ר ד ע מ כ מ צ ר י מ ה ו א נ	70405
ל ו ת א ש ר ש ל ח פ ר ע ה ל ש א ת א ת ו ו י ק ח ו א ת מ ק נ י ה מ	70524
י א א ת ו מ צ ר י מ ה ו א ל ה ש מ ו ת ב נ י י ש ר א ל ה ב א י מ מ	70643
ו ש א ו ל ב נ ה כ נ ע נ י ת ו ב נ י ל ו י ג ר ש ו נ ק ה ת ו מ ר ר	70762
י ו ב ו ש מ ר נ ו ב נ י ז ב ל ו נ ס ר ד ו א ל ו נ ו י ח ל א ל א ל	70881
ר י ו א ר ו ד י ו א ר א ל י ו ב נ י א ש ר י מ נ ה ו י ש ו ה ו י ש	71000
י ר ח ל א ש ת י ע ק ב י ו ס פ ו ב נ י מ נ ו י ו ל ד ל י ו ס פ ב א	71119
י מ ו ח פ י מ ו א ר ד א ל ה ב נ י ר ח ל א ש ר י ל ד ל י ע ק ב כ ל	71238
ק ב כ ל נ פ ש ש ב ע ה כ ל ה נ פ ש ה ב א ה ל י ע ק ב מ צ ר י מ ה י	71357
ש ב ע י מ ו א ת י ה ו ד ה ש ל ח ל פ נ י ו א ל י ו ס פ ל ה ו ר ת ל	71476
ר י ו ע ו ד ו י א מ ר י ש ר א ל א ל י ו ס פ א מ ו ת ה ה פ ע מ א ח	71595
צ כ נ ע נ ב א ו א ל י ו ה א נ ש י מ ר ע י צ א נ כ י א נ ש י מ ק נ	71714

Shape	Word	Translation	Verse	Position	Skip
ג	גלום	embodied	Genesis 45:13	69456	-244
מ	מכיל	hold	Genesis 45:13	69469	356
ת	תורה	Torah	Genesis 45:18	69694	365
א	אלוה	God	Genesis 45:22	69933	478
ק	קדוש	sacred	Genesis 45:22	69942	-601
ש	שדר	message	Genesis 46:1	70290	-119
ש	שלוש	three	Genesis 46:5	70528	-119
ק	קוד	code	Genesis 46:6	70546	230
ק	קורן	Koran	Genesis 46:11	70788	116
ו	ודס	Vedas	Genesis 46:17	71025	238

14. Three/Message: Three sacred message(s), (the) Vedas,Torah (and) Koran, hold (an) embodied code (from) God.

5

The Law: Cause and Effect

Everyone knows that the universe was established in accordance with various natural laws that maintain universal order. The balance of inertia, gravity and centrifugal force on bodies in motion maintains equilibrium in the solar systems of the galaxies. The earth, functioning as a living organism, constantly renews itself. The sun acts as the spirit force of earth's being, which, if withdrawn, would cause the earth to die. Its energy recycles the earth's elements in measured balance to maintain life. We have only discovered a few of the countless laws that govern creation, but we know that it is their perfect harmony that enables us to survive.

If you push hard enough on a body at rest (cause) to overcome gravity, friction, inertia and other forces, the body will move (effect). This is a physical cause-and-effect relationship.

Most of us are also aware that there is a similar law of cause and effect governing social relationships. If I am kind to you, you will probably be kind to me. If I am hateful towards you, you will probably reciprocate in kind. One of the central themes that Jesus taught us is that we will reap what we sow. The Torah and the Holy Koran explain it as an eye for an eye and a tooth for a tooth: If you kill by the sword, you will be killed by the sword. Today's cliché is, "What goes around, comes around." It all means the same thing: Everything we do, think, or say is related to *cause* (the reason for), and the repercussions of those actions are *effect* (result of), good or bad. Experiencing this is how we learn. The Law of Cause and Effect rewards us when we do right and punishes us when we do wrong. It's as simple as that—a perfect system of justice. When this concept is understood, we realize that we are not being rewarded or punished directly by God, but by His established law, and, in effect, by our own triumphs and failures. Just as defying the law of gravity by jumping from an airplane without a parachute guarantees physical disaster, so does committing murder have an equally disastrous effect on our soul in that it disrupts its development. In human relations, however, the effect doesn't always immediately follow the cause. If you steal from someone, perhaps no one will ever find out. Does that mean that you have beaten the Law of Cause and Effect? No; the transgression is simply documented in your Akashic Record and awaits the proper circumstances to unfold for justice to occur. Someday, someone will steal something similar from you, and probably you will not relate it to your earlier theft. You may even set up the justice scenario yourself, by perhaps forgetting to lock your car door, or leaving something valuable lying around. But justice is nevertheless served. When we commit a wrong, we are always punished, not by God, but by the Law of Cause and Effect. There is no escape except by grace—by the mercy of the court, so to speak. It all depends upon whether we have learned our lesson and are resolved never to repeat the transgression. I will revisit the concept of grace later.

We never purposely do anything that we are sure will cause us pain and suffering. We would never intentionally put our hand on a hot stove, because the effect would be immediate and we know exactly what it will be. Once the social Law of Cause and Effect is properly understood, the world will become a place of perfect harmony. We will do unto others as we would have them do unto us, because we will realize that goodness is its own reward and its practice will spare us pain and suffering.

It is obvious to me that the earth is a great school or training ground for souls not yet ready to be with God. Since God is perfect, he holds us, his children, to an extremely high standard—just as we should expect of our children. We are taught that we are created in God's image, and therefore it is reasonable to believe that the human family is established as a reflection of the heavenly family. If it becomes something different through incorrect human choices, then corrections are necessary. Since God has not willed that a single soul should be lost, these corrections occur automatically, through the Law of Cause and Effect, to put us back on the proper course of return. It isn't reasonable to believe that punishments are the result of the "wrath of God," because that would attribute human failure (anger and vengeance) to God. The Bible talks about the wrath and vengeance of God, but we must remember the developmental level of the populace that received those scriptures. They were children compared to today's society, as we are tomorrow's children. We are now ready for a new message provided by the Bible Code, and, in the future, perhaps a greater message. The Bible Code verifies that the Law of Cause and Effect and Karma are the same identical law of God. The following slide (**Subject: Cause/Effect**), was found in Numbers 15:40 to 20:15.[15]

Letters	Row
י נ י כ מ א ש ר א ת מ ז נ י מ א ח ר י ה מ ל מ ע נ ת ז כ ר ו ו ע ש י ת מ א ת כ ל מ צ ו ת י ו ה י י ת מ ק ד ש י מ	215158
נ י ל ו י ה מ ע ט מ כ מ כ י ה ב ד י ל א ל ה י י ש ר א ל א ת כ מ מ ע ד ת י ש ר א ל ל ה ק ר י ב א ת כ מ א ל י ו ל	215697
ו ו י ק ח ו א י ש מ ח ת ת ו ו י ת נ ו ע ל י ה מ א ש ו י ש י מ ו ע ל י ה מ ק ט ר ת ו י ע מ ד ו פ ת ח א ה ל מ ו ע	216236
ל ה א ד מ י מ ת ו נ א ל ה ו פ ק ד ת כ ל ה א ד מ י פ ק ד ע ל י ה מ ל א י ה ו ה ש ל ח נ י ו א מ ב ר י א ה י ב ר א	216775
ש ר א ל ו י ק ח א ל ע ז ר ה כ ה נ א ת מ ח ת ו ת ה נ ח ש ת א ש ר ה ק ר י ב ו ה ש ר פ י מ ו י ר ק ע ו מ צ פ ו י ל	217314
י נ ה ח י מ ו ת ע צ ר ה מ ג פ ה ו י ה י ה מ ת י מ ב מ ג פ ה א ר ב ע ה ע ש ר א ל פ ו ש ב ע מ א ו ת מ ל ב ד ה	217853
י צ א מ ש ה א ת כ ל ה מ ט ת מ ל פ נ י י ה ו ה א ל כ ל ב נ י י ש ר א ל ו י ר א ו ו י ק ח ו א י ש מ ט ה ו ו י א מ	218392
י ש ר א ל ו א נ י ה נ ה ל ק ח ת י א ת א ח י כ מ ה ל ו י מ מ ת ו כ ב נ י י ש ר א ל ל כ מ מ ת נ ה נ ת נ י מ ל י ה	218931
כ ל ח ר מ ב י ש ר א ל ל כ י ה י ה כ ל פ ט ר ר ח מ ל כ ל ב ש ר א ש ר י ק ר י ב ו ל י ה ו ה ב א ד מ ו ב ב ה מ ה י	219470
ב ד ה ל ו י ה ו א א ת ע ב ד ת א ה ל מ ו ע ד ו ה מ י ש א ו ע ו נ מ ח ק ת ע ו ל מ ל ד ר ת י כ מ ו ב ת ו כ ב נ י י	220009
ל א ת ש א ו ע ל י ו ח ט א ב ה ר י מ כ מ א ת ח ל ב ו מ מ נ ו ו א ת ק ד ש י ב נ י י ש ר א ל ל א ת ח ל ל ו ו ל א ת	220548
ו כ ב ס ה א ס פ א ת א פ ר ה פ ר ה א ת ב ג ד י ו ו ט מ א ע ד ה ע ר ב ו ה י ת ה ל ב נ י י ש ר א ל ו ל ג ר ה ג ר ב	221087
ב ר ו ה ז ה ה ט ה ר ע ל ה ט מ א ב י ו מ ה ש ל י ש י ו ב י ו מ ה ש ב י ע י ו ח ט א ו ב י ו מ ה ש ב י ע י ו כ ב ס	221626
ו ע ד ו י פ ל ו ע ל פ נ י ה מ ו י ר א כ ב ו ד י ה ו ה א ל י ה מ ו י ד ב ר י ה ו ה א ל מ ש ה ל א מ ר ק ח א ת ה מ	222165
מ צ ר י מ ו ל א ב ת י נ ו ו נ צ ע ק א ל י ה ו ה ו י ש מ ע ק ל נ ו ו י ש ל ח מ ל א כ ו י צ א נ ו מ מ צ ר י מ ו ה	222704
ש ת מ א ת א ל ע ז ר ב נ ו ו א ה ר נ י א ס פ ו מ ת ש מ ו י ע ש מ ש ה כ א ש ר צ ו ה י ה ו ה ו י ע ל ו א ל ה ר ה ה	223243

Shape	Word	Translation	Verse	Position	Skip
ק	קרמה	karma	Numbers 15:40	215209	2683
ח	חוק	law	Numbers 16:18	216246	537
א	אותו	same	Numbers 17:4	217343	531
ז	זהה	identical	Numbers 19:19	221630	1
א	אלוה	God	Numbers 19:19	221634	-538
ס	סיבה	cause	Numbers 19:19	221646	-539
ת	תוצאה	effect	Numbers 20:15	222713	3

15, Cause/Effect: Cause and Effect, Karma, (the) same identical law (of) God

6

You Must Be Born Again

Jesus said that we must be born again to enter the Kingdom of Heaven. Those following contemporary Christian religions have not accepted this teaching literally. Christianity accepts literally scriptures that are obviously metaphor, such as the teaching that the universe was created in seven days; why, then, doesn't it accept the teaching that we must be born again? Why are we so afraid of this concept? Perhaps because we don't want to meet ourselves in another lifetime and take responsibility for all the nasty things we've done to our friends, neighbors and loved ones in this lifetime. I suppose we would like to take the easy way out. When we get older, and supposedly wiser, and we can't have much fun any more doing the things God forbids, we would like to say we're sorry and we won't do that again, and then just slip off to heaven. We think God in his mercy should forgive us all our transgressions. The idea sounds great; but what about Jesus's admonition that "he who lives by the sword, will die by the sword"—this being a statement of the Law of Cause and Effect? Suppose you murder someone, are never convicted, and do not seriously repent of your crime? You live to a ripe old age and die a natural death. How, then, if you are not born again, are you going to die by the sword? What about all the innocent people who have never committed a crime in their lives but who die by the sword anyway? Is it just bad luck? What kind of justice is this? How exactly do we accept responsibility for our actions? What about Jesus's words, "You shall give account of every idle word that you speak," which are also a part of his teachings regarding the Law of Cause and Effect?

Many believe the law changed with the coming of Jesus. Remember the words he spoke in Mat. 5:17: "Do not think that I have come to abolish the Law or the Prophets. I have come not to abolish but to fulfill." *Fulfill* means "do what is necessary to make the law effective." We are still held responsible to the Law of Cause and Effect. What we sow we shall reap, measure for measure, if not in this lifetime, then in another.

The argument goes that Jesus meant we must be born again of the spirit; I assume this is where the term "born-again Christian" comes from. If this is the case, let's look at the meaning of the word *spirit*. It is often used interchangeably with the word *soul*. But these are two totally different concepts. The Bible Code verifies that spirit is a part of us that is of God but different from the soul. Spirit is in every living being, and when spirit is removed from a living being, whether it be plant, or animal, or human, that being dies and returns to dust. Not that soul vanishes; not a sparrow falls without God's knowing it. The Bible speaks of being cut off. The prophets talked about the spirit being cut off—about physical death. The following slide (**Subject: Life/Force**), found in Genesis 9:16 to 10:12, verifies that spirit is the life force given by God at birth and is different from the soul.[16]

Our soul is an independent eternal creation, from God, of God. The soul never dies, and does not require spirit to exist. It is what makes us individuals. Originally, it was perfect. Ever since the fall (which we will discuss later), its nature has been to become what we shape it to be. It has become the sum total of all our thoughts, deeds and experiences throughout eternity. When we've learned how to shape the soul in conformance with the ideal represented by Jesus, we will once again be one with God. This is the ideal or goal of every soul. The following slide (**Subject: Eternal/Consciousness**), found in Numbers 3:3 to 3:42, verifies that the human soul and eternal consciousness are the same, identical elements of

Letters	Position
ה ה ק ש ת ב ע נ נ ו ר א י ת י ה ל ז כ ר ב ד י ת ע ו ל מ ב י נ א ל ה י מ ו ב י נ כ ל נ פ ש ח י ה ב כ ל ב ש	11004
נ ש ל ש ה א ל ה ב נ י נ ח ו מ א ל ה נ פ צ ה כ ל ה א ר צ ו י ח ל נ ח א י ש ה א ד מ ה ו י ט ע כ ר מ ו י ש ת	11165
י כ ס ו א ת ע ר ו ת א ב י ה מ ו פ נ י ה מ א ח ר נ י ת ו ע ר ו ת א ב י ה מ ל א ר א ו ו י י ק צ נ ח מ י י נ	11326
מ ו י ה י כ נ ע נ ע ב ד ל מ ו ו י ח י נ ח א ח ר ה מ ב ו ל ש ל ש מ א ו ת ש נ ה ו ח מ ש י מ ש נ ה ו י ה י כ	11487
ב נ י ג מ ר א ש כ נ ז ו ר י פ ת ו ת ג ר מ ה ו ב נ י י ו נ א ל י ש ה ו ת ר ש י ש כ ת י מ ו ד ד נ י מ מ א ל	11648
ו ד ד נ ו כ ו ש י ל ד א ת נ מ ר ד ה ו א ה ח ל ל ה י ו ת ג ב ר ב א ר צ ה ו א ה י ה ג ב ר צ י ד ל פ נ י י ה	11809
א ת כ ל ח ו א ת ר ס נ ב י נ נ י נ ו ה ו ב י נ כ ל ח ה ו א ה ע י ר ה ג ד ל ה ו מ צ ר י מ י ל ד א ת ל ו ד י	11970
י ו א ת ה ג ר ג ש י ו א ת ה ח ו י ו א ת ה ע ר ק י ו א ת ה ס י נ י ו א ת ה א ר ו ד י ו א ת ה צ מ ר י ו א ת	12131
ר צ ת מ ב ג ו י ה מ ו ל ש מ י ל ד ג מ ה ו א א ב י כ ל ב נ י ע ב ר א ח י י פ ת ה ג ד ו ל ו ב נ י ש מ ע י ל מ	12292
ו ש מ א ח י ו י ק ט נ ו י ק ט נ י ל ד א ת א ל מ ו ד ד ו א ת ש ל פ ו א ת ח צ ר מ ו ת ו א ת י ר ח ו א ת ה ד	12453
ל מ ש פ ח ת מ ל ל ש נ ת מ ב א ר צ ת מ ל ג ו י ה מ א ל ה מ ש פ ח ת ב נ י נ ח ל ת ו ל ד ת מ ב ג ו י ה מ ו מ	12614
נ ל ב נ ה ל ב נ י מ ו נ ש ר פ ה ל ש ר פ ה ו ת ה י ל ה מ ה ל ב נ ה ל א ב נ ו ה ח מ ר ה י ה ל ה מ ל ח מ ר ו	12775

Shape	Word	Translation	Verse	Position	Skip
נ	נתון	given	Genesis 9:16	11011	324
נ	נפש	soul	Genesis 9:16	11046	1
מ	מאשר	than	Genesis 9:19	11179	11
א	אחר	different	Genesis 9:23	11347	1
א	אלוה	God	Genesis 9:28	11511	-3
ח	חיים	life	Genesis 9:28	11512	-161
ר	רוח	spirit	Genesis 10:8	11824	3
ל	לידה	birth	Genesis 10:8	11832	323
כ	כוח	force	Genesis 10:12	11995	-161

16. Life/Force: Spirit, (the) life force given (by) God (at) birth, different than (the) soul.

God. The next slide (**Subject: Human/Soul**), found in Exodus 20:22 to 22:9, verifies that Saint Augustine's doctrine of the soul as not being preexistent is not the correct one. The slide states that the human soul is forever existent in the mind of God. It is like the infinite "I Am"—eternal, with no beginning or end.

Our confusion regarding being born again may be traced to the Testament of John 3. Jesus tells Nicodemus that unless we are born again, we cannot see the Kingdom of God. Nicodemus in turn asks him how a person can be born after he has become old. Jesus replies that no one can see the Kingdom of God without being born of water and spirit, that that which is born of flesh is flesh and that which is born of spirit is spirit. Jesus finally tells Nicodemus that he should not be surprised at being told that he must be born again. This lesson *is* confusing, to say the least!

There is an interesting lesson in the Holy Koran, English/Arabic Edition (Amana, 1989). Surah 2, Al Bakarah, Paragraph 28 states: "How can ye reject The faith of Allah?/Seeing that you were without life./And He gave you life; then He will cause you to die,/And will again bring you to life;/And again to Him ye will return." Perhaps this is a similar message.

The Bible Code is much clearer on the subject. In the following slide (**Subject: Born/Again**), found in Genesis 18:28 to 19:32, the Bible Code verifies that what Jesus was talking about in John 3 was indeed the rebirth on earth of spirit and *woman*.[17] Only when spirit and flesh are joined, can a soul be reborn into a human being. Rebirth is necessary to fulfill the Law of Cause and Effect, God's system of perfect justice, the Law that shapes and hones us back into the image of God. This Law is a product of God's infinite mercy. Not only are we given a second chance, but we are given as many chances as we will need to become enlightened souls. Remember that it is God's will that not one soul shall be lost. Jesus set forth this lesson in the parable of the good shepherd.

About the same time as I was learning about Edgar Cayce, I came across the writings of another great seer, Kahlil Gibran. Gibran's philosophy is relevant to this topic. Born in Bsherri, Lebanon, in 1883, Gibran was a great writer, poet and artist. Immigrat-

ת ח י ה ו ל ש ר ה ב נ ו ת כ ח ש ש ו ה ל א מ ר ל א צ ח ק ת י כ י י ר א ה ו	21150
ו ל מ ע נ א ש ר י צ ו ה א ת ב נ י ו ו א ת ב י ת ו א ח ר י ו ו ש מ ר ו ד ר	21326
ה א נ ש י מ ו י ל כ ו ס ד מ ה ו א ב ר ה מ ע ו ד נ ו ע מ ד ל פ נ י י ה ו ה	21502
ח ל ל ה ל כ ה ש פ ט כ ל ה א ר צ ל א י ע ש ה מ ש פ ט ו י א מ ר י ה ו ה א מ	21678
א מ ר ל א א ש ח י ת א מ א מ צ א ש ם א ר ב ע י מ ו ח מ ש ה ו י ס פ ע ו ד ל	21854
א ד נ י א ו ל י י מ צ א ו נ ש מ ע ש ר י מ ו י א מ ר ל א א ש ח י ת ב ע ב ו	22030
ט י ש ב ב ש ע ר ס ד מ ו י ר א ל ו ט ו י ק מ ל ק ר א ת מ ו י ש ת ח ו א פ י	22206
י א כ ל ו ט ר מ י ש כ ב ו ו א נ ש י ה ע י ר א נ ש י ס ד מ נ ס ב ו ע ל ה ב	22382
נ ו ת א ש ר ל א י ד ע ו א י ש א ו צ י א ה נ א א ת ה נ א ל י כ מ ו ע ש ו ל	22558
א ת י ד מ ו י ב י א ו א ת ל ו ט א ל י ה מ ה ב י ת ה ו א ת ה ד ל ת ס ג ר ו	22734
י ג ד ל ה צ ע ק ת מ א ת פ נ י י ה ו ה ו י ש ל ח נ ו י ה ו ה ל ש ח ת ה ו י	22910
נ מ צ א ת פ נ ת ס פ ה ב ע ו נ ה ע י ר ו י ת מ ה מ ה ו י ח ז י ק ו ה א נ ש	23086
ט א ל ה מ א ל נ א א ד נ י ה נ ה נ א מ צ א ע ב ד כ ח נ ב ע י נ י כ ו ת ג ד	23262
ת י פ נ י כ ג מ ל ד ב ר ה ז ה ל ב ל ת י ה פ כ י א ת ה ע י ר א ש ר ד ב ר ת	23438
כ כ ר ו א ת כ ל י ש ב י ה ע ר י מ ו צ מ ח ה א ד מ ה ו ת ב ט א ש ת ו מ א ח	23614
כ ר א ל ה י מ א ת א ב ר ה מ ו י ש ל ח א ת ל ו ט מ ת ו כ ה ה פ כ ה ב ה פ כ	23790
א ר צ ל כ ה נ ש ק ה א ת א ב י נ ו י י נ ו נ ש כ ב ה ע מ ו ו נ ח י ה מ א ב	23966
ח י ה מ א ב י נ ו ז ר ע ו ת ש ק י נ ג מ ב ל י ל ה ה ה ו א א ת א ב י ה נ י	24142
מ ו נ ע ד ה י ו מ ו י ס ע מ ש מ א ב ר ה מ א ר צ ה ה נ ג ב ו י ש ב ב י נ ק	24318
ל א ק ר ב א ל י ה ו י א מ ר א ד נ י ה ג ו י ג מ צ ד י ק ת ה ר ג ה ל א ה ו	24494
ל י ה ו ע ת ה ה ש ב א ש ת ה א י ש כ י נ ב י א ה ו א ו י ת פ ל ל ב ע ד כ ו	24670
מ ה ח ט א ת י ל כ כ י ה ב א ת ע ל י ו ע ל מ מ ל כ ת י ח ט א ה ג ד ל ה מ ע	24846
א מ י ו ת ה י ל י ל א ש ה ו י ה י כ א ש ר ה ת ע ו א ת י א ל ה י מ מ ב י ת	25022
י נ י כ ש ב ו ל ש ר ה א מ ר ה נ ה נ ת ת י א ל פ כ ס פ ל א ח י כ ה נ ה ה ו	25198

Shape	Word	Translation	Verse	Position	Skip
י	ישוע	Jesus	Genesis 18:28	21875	-3
ש	שלוש	three	Genesis 18:28	21881	-170
י	ילִיד	born	Genesis 19:1	22242	352
פ	פשר	meaning	Genesis 19:4	22403	-528
ש	שוב	again	Genesis 19:4	22418	-352
ג	גון	John	Genesis 19:8	22579	-359
פ	פרק	chapter	Genesis 19:15	23091	13
ה	הכרח	necessity	Genesis 19:16	23119	341
א	אומן	taught	Genesis 19:19	23278	-352
ר	רוח	spirit	Genesis 19:26	23650	-345
א	אישה	woman	Genesis 19:32	24001	174

17. Born/Again: Jesus taught (in) John, Chapter 3, (the) necessity (to be) born again, meaning (of) spirit (and) woman..

ing to the United States in 1912, he continued to write in English and Arabic. His masterpiece, *The Prophet*, first published in 1923, has sold nearly ten million copies in English alone! The work is a fictional account of an ancient philosopher and teacher named Almustafa who lived in the Middle East.

The Prophet is set in Orphalese, when Almustafa, a wise man, is leaving this village that he has lived in for many years. All the inhabitants turn out to see him off, seizing this last chance to ask him important and elusive questions about the meaning of life before his departure on a waiting ship. His answers represent one of the wisest and most concise treatises on the meaning of life that I have ever read—all in less than 100 pages! Because I knew Gibran was a Christian, Almustafa's final words to the people of Orphalese particularly astonished me: "Forget not that I shall come back to you. A little while and my longing shall gather dust and foam for another body. A little while, a moment of rest upon the wind, and another woman shall bear me." It was not until that point that I realized that the ship was a metaphor for dying.

I was so intrigued by the philosophy of Kahlil Gibran that I looked him up in the Bible Code. The following slide (**Subject: Gibran/Poet**), found in Exodus 3:5 to 4:15, tells of Kahlil Gibran, born in 1883, U.S. immigrant, a poet, writer, and prophet, an enlightened soul. His true identity will be revealed in a later slide. I will refer to the teachings of Kahlil Gibran from time to time throughout this book.

Twenty-five percent of the world's population believe in reincarnation and the law of karma. They are primarily Hindus and Buddhists. Christianity once also held a belief in reincarnation, in the early days of the Church. The Christian philosopher Origen (185-254 A.D.) taught the doctrine of "universalism" which acknowledged the preexistence of the soul as an eternal essence of God and the eventual return of all souls to God the Father.

Over 100 years later, the Christian philosopher Saint Augustine proposed a new doctrine, one holding that God created the soul separately, apart from Himself, out of nothing. This led to the belief that a new soul is created and enters the body between conception and birth. Augustine postulated that death was unnatural and must therefore be a punishment for the original sin of Adam. Soon after, in 380 A.D., the Roman Emperor Theodosius proclaimed the writings of Augustine to be the doctrine of Christianity for the Roman Empire. When Justinian became emperor in 553 A.D., the teachings of Origen regarding universalism were outlawed as heresy, and his writings were banned and destroyed. There's speculation that parts of the New Testament were expurgated during the Second (381 A.D.) and Fifth (553 A.D.) Ecumenical Councils at Constantinople, in support of the accepted theology of Augustine. Christian doctrine on the reincarnation of the soul ceased to exist during this period. The following slide **(Subject: Testament/Expurgation)** was found in Leviticus 11:44 to 13:48. It verifies that Pope John II (pope from 533 to 535 A.D.) permitted the expurgation of the New Testament of Jesus; Karma, destiny and rebirth were victims of this expurgation. Pope John II obtained a profession of orthodox faith from Justinian I, who would later call the Fifth Ecumenical Council. Perhaps that's why John 3 ("You must be born again") doesn't make sense. All of this makes you wonder what else was removed, e.g. information regarding the Tribulation that would make that doctrine easier to understand? As we shall see later, the Bible Code verifies that the Tribulation will soon occur, but that the so-called Rapture of the Church, during *this* coming Tribulation, is a myth.

One problem with current Christian doctrine is that it cannot explain the eternal soul. What is eternal is forever, infinite, without beginning and without end. It cannot be created during the conception or birth of a child. If the soul is eternal, then it must have been preexistent. Since only God is eternal, it must be a part of God. If the soul is preexistent, how can all souls be guilty of Adam's original sin? And if the soul is eternal, and the purpose of entering the world is to learn, then what can an eternal soul learn in a sojourn of 70 years?

There are groups of Hebrew scholars that adhere to the ancient mysticism of the Kabbalah. Kabbalah, meaning "a received thing," is the esoteric tradition within Judaism of things divine. It was passed down orally to the elect from the time of Moses, and it is considered the key to the hidden wisdom or inner meaning of God's plan for creation. It is basically about who we are, where we come from, why we are here, and where we are going after death.

The Kabbalah supports the doctrine of the preexistence of the soul as the essence of God. The creation is the image or reflection of God, the confirmation of God's existence in the time-space continuum. Humanity is unique because it is the only creation on earth that has free will. As I understand the kabbalistic writings of the *Zohar*, souls migrated from God in androgynous form, then split into two separate but complimentary psyches, one male, the other female. They came to Eden where they prepared to enter, through the birth process, the earth's sphere as human beings. While on earth, the twin souls have a common divine mission in support of God's creation plan. They start together, but become enmeshed in their own karma so that they do not always remain together through subsequent incarnations. Between earthly incarnations, they return to the upper worlds, where they go through a reflective cleansing process and then return to Eden for a resting period prior to being born again. At some point, these twin souls manage to incarnate together in order to jointly complete their sacred task. (The Bible Code verifies that Eden exists in the Herdsman [Bootes] constellation, on a planet in orbit around that constellation's brightest star, Arcturus. What inspired me to search on the Bootes constellation? The Book of Job. I'll have more to say about this later.)

The Bible Code validates the preexistence of the soul and also validates reincarnation and the law of karma. The next slide (**Subject: Human/Reincarnated**), found in Numbers 10:9 to 22:23, states that the Law of Karma reincarnated the human soul towards enlightenment. The following slide (**Subject: Cause/Effect**), found in Numbers 18:32 to 21:7, verifies that God's Law of Cause and Effect is a perfect system of justice.

We should take a look at two different scenarios found in the Bible Code regarding rebirth, and examine how they relate to the Law of Cause and Effect. These searches reflect actual lessons dramatized through the lives of famous individuals found in the Torah and the New Testament. We'll start with the story of Cain, first son of Eve, who killed his brother, Abel, as related in Genesis 4. Cain killed Abel in a jealous rage and tried to conceal the act from God. God knew of this crime, placed a curse on Cain, and banished him from his homeland to Nod, the land east of Eden. Later on, in Genesis 37, the Torah takes us to the land of Canaan and the House of Jacob. Jacob, called Israel, has twelve sons, one of whom he loves more than all the others. That son's name is Joseph. Joseph's brothers are jealous of him because they perceive that he is their father's favorite son. They conspire to kill him, but one brother, Judah, recommends that they sell him for 20 pieces of silver to Midianite traders. Joseph is sold, ultimately winding up in Egypt, where the saga of his adult life will begin to unfold.

Much, much later in the Bible, in Mat: 26, the story unfolds of the plot to kill Jesus Christ. Judas Iscariot, a chosen disciple of Jesus, agrees to betray him for 30 pieces of silver to the temple priests. This story and the two above seem to be isolated accounts of different biblical characters. It appears, though, that the second testament is a prophecy of the third. The following Bible Code search tells a different story. (**Subject: Judas/Iscariot**) found in Exodus 3:7 to 25:14. The search identifies Judas Iscariot, Judah and Cain as the rebirth of the same identical soul.

But this is just half the story. We have analyzed the antagonist side of this lifetime-to-lifetime drama. On the protagonist side, we need to find the soul with which Judas is constantly at odds. The following Bible Code search (**Subject: Adam/Jesus**), found also in Exodus, but in 36:12 to 36:22, identifies Jesus, Joseph and Adam as the rebirth of a single identical soul. This karmic situation started when Cain, the first born of Eve, killed Abel, Adam's beloved younger son.

Cain and Adam later return as brothers in the house of Jacob. The animosity is still there. God in his mercy is giving Cain and Adam another chance to work things out, this time as Judah and Joseph. But instead of forgiving Judah at the beginning, Joseph antagonizes him as well as his other brothers by flaunting the fact that he is his father's favorite. He even recounts a prophetic dream in which the entire family someday bows down to him. In a way, Joseph has set up his own fate which will inexorably follow him. For his part, Judah fails to reach out to his brother in love, instead feeling great jealousy towards him. He ends up selling Joseph into slavery for 20 pieces of silver. Judah doesn't kill Joseph according to the original plan, and there is some redemption here. Joseph makes the best of a bad situation; later, as a high official of Egypt, he is able to help his family as prophesied and also to forgive his brothers. Joseph passes the karmic exam; Judah does not.

The stage is set for the next karmic encounter. A relationship is again established between the two souls, with Joseph as Jesus and Judah as Judas Iscariot. God's infinite mercy is giving Judah/Judas another chance. We must assume that Jesus, being wholly enlightened, incorporated this chance for Judas into his messianic plan. Judas, out of envy, fails again. He sells his soul companion again, this time for 30 pieces of silver, and while knowing that he is condemning him to death. Though he has failed again, Judas will soon get another chance. In another of my Bible Code searches, it was made clear that Judas will return again during the end times.

We can only pray that, for the sake of all of us, Cain/Judah/Judas Iscariot will find redemption this time around. There are further incarnations of Jesus as well, and I will discuss them later.

Here, the lesson is obvious. No one circumvents the Law of Cause and Effect. Even Jesus himself, throughout his major incarnations, was tried in the court of karma. This is discussed in Romans 5:12 to19. Jesus taught and learned what it takes to pass the karmic lessons and receive grace. It is to love God above all things, love others as yourself, and forgive those who trespass against you as you would have God forgive your own trespasses.

The next karmic drama revealed by the Bible Code involves Elijah and John the Baptist. In 1 Kings 18 and 19, the story is related of how Elijah tricked the high priests of Baal by talking them into a contest to determine who the true God was. Jezebel was the wife of Ahab, at that time King of Israel. She worshipped the pagan god Baal and sponsored the priests of Baal. Probably, Ahab was desperate, because the land was divided on religious issues and a severe drought was causing dissension. In any case, he agreed to Elijah's challenge. All the people of the city assembled to watch the contest, which involved two sacrificial burnt offerings, one to Baal, the other to God. The altars were prepared, but the fires left unlit. All 450 of Jezebel's Baal priests prayed for a specified time for Baal to light their offering. When the time expired and nothing had happened, Elijah poured water on his offering and prayed to God to light it. Fire exploded within the offering, consuming everything, including the water. All of the people repented, and recognized the true God. Elijah told the people to round up the Baal priests; then he put them all to the sword. When Jezebel heard what had happened, she swore an oath to kill Elijah in like manner. Elijah escaped, and was never killed.

The next part of our story takes place when Jesus was in Israel. Baptized by John the Baptist, he acknowledged to his disciples that John was in fact Elijah returned. In Mat. 17, Jesus is returning with some of his disciples from the mountain where he has been transfigured when the following conversation takes place: "And the disciples asked Him, Why then do the scribes say that Elijah must come first? He replied, Elijah is indeed coming and will restore all things but I tell you that Elijah has already come, and they did to him whatever they pleased. So also the Son of Man is about to suffer at their hands. Then the disciples understood that He was speaking to them about John the Baptist."

The rest of the story concerns Herodias, King Herod's sister-in-law, who has been dallying with the king. John the Baptist has chided the king for consorting with his brother's wife. On Herod's birthday, Salome, Herodias's daughter, dances the dance of the seven veils before him. Herod is so pleased that he promises her he will give her anything she wants. Salome confers with her mother, then asks for the head of John the Baptist. Reluctantly, the king agrees to grant her wish. John the Baptist is beheaded, and his head is presented on a dish to Salome.

The above is the biblical account; now for the Bible Code story. The following Bible Code slide (**Subject: John/Baptist**), found in Leviticus 1:4 to 13:20, verifies what Jesus said, that John the Baptist and Elijah were the same identical soul and that he took the sword to perish by the sword, like measure. This indicates karma. The next slide (**Subject: Jezebel/Herodias**), found in Exodus 12:24 to 13:12, verifies that Jezebel and Herodias are the rebirth of the same identical soul. Now it is rather obvious what has happened.

I did not mention in my account that Jezebel had killed as many of Elijah's priests as she could before the burnt offering contest took place. This set up a revenge situation for Elijah. While he was doing God's work of converting Ahab's people, this priest of God was also planning a personal revenge on Jezebel. The Law of Cause and Effect says that if you live by the sword you will die by the sword, and Elijah was no exception. He avoided his karma during his life as Elijah, but in his life as John the Baptist the conflict with Jezebel caught up with him through her incarnation as Herodias. It's obvious also that Jezebel/Herodias failed the karmic test. She should have forgiven Elijah; but, taking revenge instead, she still has the same karma to deal with.

What can be learned from all this? First, that the soul is a pre-existent entity, a child of God, a reflection of God in the space-time continuum. As a part of God, we were initially perfect; but through free will we made ungodly choices that caused us to fall from grace. This required a rescue plan to perfect us back to our original state—which makes us gods in the re-making, so to speak, just as is related in the 82nd Psalm where it says, "I say ye are Gods, children of the Most High, all of you; nevertheless you shall die as mortals, and fall like any prince." Jesus refers to this Psalm in John 10, when he is nearly arrested for blasphemy when the Jews confront him at the temple for saying that he is the Son of God.

The rescue plan involves teaching us that we must use our free will to make godly choices—the same lesson we teach our children. The Law of Cause and Effect, mitigated by grace, brings about self-punishment when we fail and rewards us when we succeed. Being born again is necessary, because it takes many experiences, many lifetimes, to reach full enlightenment. Remember that it is the will of God that not a single soul shall be lost. We get as many chances as we need and deserve, as painful as the experiences may be. If we are cut off from God, it is by our own choice. This is the only unpardonable sin, since we ourselves circumvent God's rescue plan which is intended to save us. We can't be pardoned if we prevent the pardon from occurring. When we become fully enlightened, we are co-creators with God and share in His glorious experience. This appears to be the message of the Bible Code as we have examined it thus far.

7

The Future, Fate, and Destiny

In the previous chapter, we discussed human rebirth and the Law of Cause and Effect. That law is intertwined with the workings of what we call fate or destiny. The Bible Code verifies that karma is carried over from one life to the next as lessons to be learned on the road to enlightenment.

Imagine an innocent little boy horribly burned to death as a result of playing with matches. Can we say that this event was his divine fate, planned by a loving and merciful God? I think no rational person would believe that God would be responsible for wasting a precious human life.

Ministers of the Christian faith can't adequately address this question because they don't believe in physical rebirth. If you ask them, you will probably get an explanation like: "God works in mysterious ways, but you can be assured that this innocent child is now with God in heaven."

From what we have verified in the Bible Code about the Law of Cause and Effect, there seems to be another, more plausible explanation. Perhaps the boy's soul was part of the early Church's inquisition task force, tracking down so-called witches, torturing them for confessions, then burning them at the stake. I visited a dungeon in Austria that was once part of an early Church fortress where the Bishop of Salzburg held such inquisitions. Perhaps it was the grace of God that allowed this child's soul—that had once done similar dark deeds—to get the necessary lesson out of the way quickly so that it could be born again and resume a wiser path towards enlightenment. Kahlil Gibran tells us in *The Prophet* that "the murdered is not unaccountable for his own murder."

Under the Law of Cause and Effect, there could be a million reasons for the death of an innocent person—just as there could be a million reasons for the birth of a child prodigy like Mozart. Karma renders a strict accounting of rewards as well as punishments. Think of your own personal life. Are you rich and comfortably well off or poor and struggling to survive? According to the Bible Code, what you are now is the sum of all your thoughts and deeds since you first entered the earth plane many lifetimes ago. Most people aren't comfortable with this. They would prefer that government or society be to blame. They blame their misfortunes on others: they were discriminated against, the boss didn't like them, or they didn't have equal opportunity with others. When was the last time you heard a parent taking responsibility for the misdeed of a child? Children are given to us as a sacred trust from God. We are responsible for their proper care and upbringing, but we tend very often to abandon them for a god called greed. High school dropouts at daycare centers, who were themselves once abandoned, now raise these abandoned children, the entire system being subsidized by the government no less. To properly raise a child, parents must be willing to put the welfare of that child ahead of the desire to acquire a bigger house or an extra car.

According to the Bible Code, there is no such thing as good or bad fortune, there is only justice. We are all at various stages of enlightenment on the long road back to God. We are not on this path alone. Again, in *The Prophet*, Kahlil Gibran tells us that "you are the way and the wayfarers; when one of you falls down, he falls for those behind him, a caution against the stumbling stone. Aye, and he falls for those ahead of him, who though faster and surer of foot, yet removed not the stumbling stone." We are in truth our brother's keeper.

I did three searches on destiny in the Bible Code. The first (**Subject: Many/Futures**) was found in Genesis 38:20 to 40:8. It verified that man chooses his own many futures.[18] In other words, our destiny was chosen by our own actions, creating many futures over many lifetimes. The next slide (**Subject: Human/Destiny**), found in Deuteronomy 2:22 to 3:29, is very explicit. It verifies that human destiny is the result of our individual acts of choice, which bring about the enlightenment of the soul through the doors of rebirth. Perhaps this is what Jesus meant when he said, "Knock, and the door shall be opened unto you." The last of my three searches had to do with the destiny of the world. This slide (**Subject: Collective/Will**) was found in Genesis 45:24 to 46:17, and verified that world destiny is shaped by collective human will.[19] In other words, the inhabitants of our planet will be held accountable, through their collective actions, for what happens to the world. This scary truth leads right to the Tribulation in Revelation, the last book of the New Testament. We will discuss the Revelation in depth in a later chapter.

So it appears that fate or destiny does exist after all, but that it is not in the stars nor is it a prescribed role assigned by God at birth. Our fate is the result of all the personal choices we have made since the beginning of our sojourns on earth. This perfect system of justice has determined where we are at this very moment in our history. It is for our instruction, and leads us ultimately back to God on the path of enlightenment. The collective karma of all humans on earth at any given time determines the destiny of the world. That destiny is not set in stone, because we have moment-to-moment choices to make and therefore we remold destiny every minute of the day. It is possible to make great strides in a single lifetime or to waste a lifetime and get nowhere.

The following is an example, found in the Bible Code, of karma on a mass scale. In April, 1994, an aircraft carrying the presidents of Rwanda and Burundi crashed, killing both presidents. It is believed that Hutu extremists shot down the plane. Rwanda has always harbored deep ethnic hatred between the Hutu and the Tutsi tribes that live in the country. In the aftermath of the crash, the

Position	Letters
56207	ל ע ר ב כ ו ר ו ו ש מ ה ת מ ר ו י ה י ע ר ב כ ו ר י ה ו ד ה ר ע ב ע י נ י י ה ו ה ו י מ ת ה
56579	ל ג ז צ א נ ו ו ת ס ר ב ג ד י א ל מ נ ו ת ה מ ע ל י ה ו ת כ ס ב צ ע י פ ו ת ת ע ל פ ו ת ש ב
56951	ר ע ה ו ה ע ד ל מ י ל ק ח ת ה ע ר ב ו נ מ י ד ה א ש ה ו ל א מ צ א ה ו י ש א ל א ת א נ ש י מ
57323	ק ה מ מ נ י כ י ע ל כ נ ל א נ ת ת י ה ל ש ל ה ב נ י ו ל א י ס פ ע ו ד ל ד ע ת ה ו י ה י ב ע
57695	ס פ ח נ ב ע י נ י ו י ש ר ת א ת ו י פ ק ד ה ו ע ל ב י ת ו ו כ ל י ש ל ו נ ת נ ב י ד ו ו
58067	ו א י כ א ע ש ה ה ר ע ה ה ג ד ל ה ה ז א ת ו ח ט א ת י ל א ל ה י מ ו י ה י כ ד ב ר ה א ל י ו
58439	ד ב ר א ל י ו כ ד ב ר י מ ה א ל ה ל א מ ר ב א א ל י ה ע ב ד ה ע ב ר י א ש ר ה ב א ת ל נ ו ל
58811	ש ר ה ו א ע ש ה י ה ו ה מ צ ל י ח ו י ה י א ח ר ה ד ב ר י מ ה א ל ה ח ט א ו מ ש ק ה מ ל כ מ
59183	ה י ו מ ו י א מ ר ו א ל י ו ל ת ל ו מ ח ל מ נ ו ו פ ת ר א י נ א ת ו ו י א מ ר א ל ה מ י ו ס פ
59555	ס ד ו ה ז כ ר ת נ י א ל פ ר ע ה ו ה ו צ א ת נ י מ נ ה ב י ת ה ז ה כ י ג נ ב ג נ ב ת י מ א ר
59927	ב ד י ו י ש ב א ת ש ר ה מ ש ק י מ ע ל מ ש ק ה ו י ת נ ה כ ו ס ע ל כ פ פ ר ע ה ו א ת ש ר
60299	ל י מ ד ק ו ת ו ש ד ו פ ת ק ד י מ צ מ ח ו ת א ח ר י ה נ ו ת ב ל ע נ ה ה ש ב ל י מ ה ד ק ו ת
60671	י כ א ש ר פ ת ר ל נ ו כ נ ה י ה א ת י ה ש י ב ע ל כ נ י ו א ת ו ת ל ה ו י ש ל ח פ ר ע ה ו י

Shape	Word	Translation	Verse	Position	Skip
ש (square)	שלו	his	Genesis 38:20	56954	-388
מ (shaded)	משלו	own	Genesis 39:4	57713	-381
ע (shaded)	עתיד	future	Genesis 39:4	57720	372
ה (circle)	הרבה	many	Genesis 39:17	58465	-372
ב (diamond)	בחר	chose	Genesis 39:23	58812	-385
א (hourglass)	איש	man	Genesis 40:8	59218	365

18, Many/Future: Man chose his own many future(s)

Position	Letters
69319	ב נ י כ ו צ א נ כ ו ב ק ר כ ו כ ל א ש ר ל כ ו כ ל כ ל ת י א ת כ ש מ כ י ע ו ד ח מ ש ש נ י מ ר ע ב פ נ ת ו ר ש
69502	ב נ י מ נ א ח י ו ו י ב כ ו ב נ י מ נ ב כ ה ע ל צ ו א ר י ו ו י נ ש ק ל כ ל א ח י ו ו י ב כ ע ל ה מ ו א ח ר י
69685	א ת א ב י כ מ ו א ת ב ת י כ מ ו ב א ו א ל י ו א ת נ ה ל כ מ א ת ט ו ב א ר צ מ צ ר י מ ו א כ ל ו א ת ח ל ב ה א
69868	י ו ס פ ע ג ל ו ת ע ל פ י פ ר ע ה ו י ת נ ל ה מ צ ד ה ל ד ר כ ל כ ל מ נ ת נ ל א י ש ח ל פ ו ת ש מ ל ת ו ל ב נ
70051	ב ד ר כ ו י ע ל ו מ מ צ ר י מ ו י ב א ו א ר צ כ נ ע נ א ל י ע ק ב א ב י ה מ ו י ג ד ו ל ו ל א מ ר ע ו ד י ו ס
70234	ל ר ב ע ו ד י ו ס פ ב נ י ח י א ל כ ה ו א ר א נ ו ב ט ר מ א מ ו ת ו י ס ע י ש ר א ל ו כ ל א ש ר ל ו ו י ב א ב
70417	ש מ א נ כ י א ר ד ע מ כ מ צ ר י מ ה ו א נ כ י א ע ל כ ג מ ע ל ה ו י ו ס פ י ש י ת י ד ו ע ל ע י נ י כ ו י ק מ
70600	ע ו א ת ו ב נ י ו ו ב נ י ב נ י ו א ת ו ב נ ת י ו ר ב נ ו ח ב נ י ו ו כ ל ז ר ע ו ה ב י א א ת ו מ צ ר י מ ה ו
70783	ג ר ש ו נ ק ה ת ו מ ר ר י ו ב נ י ה ו ד ה ע ר ו א ו נ ו ש ל ה ו פ ר צ ו ז ר ח ו י מ ת ע ר ו א ו נ נ ב א ר
70966	ש ל ש י מ ו ש ל ש ו ב נ י ג ד צ פ י ו נ ו ח ג י ש ו נ י ו א צ ב נ ע ר י ו א ר ו ד י ו א ר א ל י ו ב נ י א ש ר
71149	פ ב א ר צ מ צ ר י מ א ש ר י ל ד ה ל ו א ס נ ת ב ת פ ו ט י פ ר ע כ ה נ א נ א ת מ נ ש ה ו א ת א פ ר י מ ו ב נ י
71332	נ ת נ ל ב נ ל ר ח ל ב ת ו ו ת ל ד א ת א ל ה ל י ע ק ב כ ל נ פ ש ש ב ע ה כ ל ה נ פ ש ה ב א ה ל י ע ק ב מ צ ר י
71515	נ ה ו י ב א ו א ר צ ה ג ש נ ו י א ס ר י ו ס פ מ ר כ ב ת ו ו י ע ל ל ק ר א ת י ש ר א ל א ב י ו ג ש נ ה ו י ר א
71698	א ח י ו ב י ת א ב י א ש ר ב א ר צ כ נ ע נ ב א ו א ל י ו ה א נ ש י מ ר ע י צ א נ כ י א נ ש י מ ק נ ה י ו צ
71881	י מ כ ל ר ע ה צ א נ ו י ב א י ו ס פ ו י ג ד ל פ ר ע ה ו י א מ ר א ב י ו א ח י ו צ א נ מ ו ב ק ר מ ו כ ל א ש ר
72064	ל פ ר ע ה ל ג ו ר ב א ר צ ב א נ ו כ י א י נ מ ר ע ה ל צ א נ א ש ר ל ע ב ד י כ י כ ב ד ה ר ע ב ב א ר צ כ נ ע
72247	י ל ו ש מ ת מ ש ר י מ ק נ ה ע ל א ש ר ל י ו י ב א י ו ס פ א ת י ע ק ב א ב י ו ו י ע מ ד ה ו ל פ נ י פ ר ע ה ו

Shape	Word	Translation	Verse	Position	Skip
ד (square)	דמוי	shaped	Genesis 45:24	70052	375
י (diamond)	יעוד	destiny	Genesis 45:28	70239	-380
א (shaded)	אנושי	human	Genesis 45:28	70249	188
ע (hourglass)	עולם	world	Genesis 45:28	70264	-372
ק (shaded)	קיבוצי	collective	Genesis 46:4	70466	-183
ר (circle)	רצון	will	Genesis 46:17	71016	-184

19. Collective/Will: World destiny, shaped (by) collective human will.

Hutus slaughtered 800,000 Tutsi civilians in one of the worst bloodbaths of modern history. At the time that I saw the news of this catastrophe, I could hardly believe that these events had actually occurred. I could see no reason why over three-quarters of a million innocent civilian men, women and children would deserve to die in this way. I decided to search for the answer in the Bible Code.

The following slide **(Subject: Rwanda/Holocaust)**, found in Genesis 36:19 to 37:14, verified that the holocaust of Rwanda in 1994 was the result of the punishment of souls involved in WW2 Fascism. It was suddenly clear to me. So many people were involved in atrocities during that war that karma on a mass scale was necessary to establish justice, and perfect justice it was. Fascists hated and persecuted people whom they perceived to be not as good as they were. It was necessary for those fascists to be reborn as poor black Africans on the edge of survival. Then it was necessary for them to be slaughtered as they had slaughtered others, to truly get the message across. It is a terrible way to have to learn. But that doesn't mean the karma was theirs alone. There was a United Nations contingent in the area that advised the world that the situation could get out of control, but nothing was done to help. Since there were threats of genocide, I'm surprised that Israel didn't get involved, or at least pressure the U.N. into action. The United States offered no assistance either, perhaps even blocking action to help. As it stands now, the entire world has Tutsi blood on its hands, which once more puts world destiny at risk. We have all failed the karmic lesson, and we are now doomed to repeat it. The Tribulation revealed to John in the New Testament is moving closer.

We have learned from the Bible Code that grace will remove karma only through love and forgiveness, whether it be personal or world karma. The primary responsibility for the holocaust in Rwanda lies with the Hutus and the Tutsis, who must learn to live with one another and work together to share a better life. Had the peoples done so in the past, grace would have been received. Secondary responsibility rests with the neighboring countries, who failed to establish a dialogue. Responsibility lies also with the United Nations, whose job it is to represent world interests, and who failed to do so in this case. Wise men say that history repeats itself; there will be further repercussions from the Rwanda slaughter. Perhaps there is something Palestine and Israel can learn from this saga.

Destiny exists, but can we see it before it occurs? Is there a way to look into the future and determine the final outcome? Can a visionary or a psychic—or the Bible Code, for that matter—advise us accurately of what will happen in our personal lives or world affairs? The answer to these questions is, no, only God can see the future. When Jesus was asked when he would return, he replied that only the Father knew, but that we would see the signs. Jesus did, however, know in what generation this would take place. I'll have more to say on this later.

What we get in the Bible Code are momentary glimpses of the ever-changing Akashic Records. We see the projected prospects of what may occur, based on the current status of the records. Collectively, we have the power to change those prospects, for better or for worse.

The following Bible Code search (**Subject: Knowledge/Future**), found in Numbers 32:24 to 33:16, verifies that *God alone has knowledge of the future.* The Torah Code is a teacher of future prospects.[20]

Letters	Position
ל ט פ כ מ ו ג ד ר ת ל צ נ א כ מ ו ה י צ א מ פ י כ מ ת ע ש ו ו י א מ ר ב נ י ג ד ו ב נ י	243230
ו ב נ א ת כ מ א ת ה י ר ד נ כ ל ח ל ו צ ל מ ל ח מ ה ל פ נ י י ה ו ה ו נ כ ב ש ה ה א ר צ	243481
ב נ י ו ס פ א ת מ מ ל כ ת ס י ח נ מ ל כ ה א מ ר י ו א ת מ מ ל כ ת ע ו ג מ ל כ ה ב ש נ ה	243732
ל כ ו ב נ י מ כ י ר ב נ מ נ ש ה ג ל ע ד ה ו י ל כ ד ה ו י ו ר ש א ת ה א מ ר י א ש ר ב ה	243983
א י ה מ ו י ס ע ו מ ר ע מ ס ס ב ח ד ש ה ר א ש ו נ ב ח מ ש ה ע ש ר י ו מ ל ח ד ש ה ר א ש	244234
מ פ נ י ה ח י ר ת ו י ע ב ר ו ב ת ו כ ה י מ ה מ ד ב ר ה ו י ל כ ו ד ר כ ש ל ש ת י מ י מ	244485
ע ו מ ר פ י ד מ ו י ח נ ו ב מ ד ב ר ס י נ י ו י ס ע ו מ מ ד ב ר ס י נ י ו י ח נ ו ב ק ב	244736
ה ל ת ו י ח נ ו ב ת ח ת ו י ס ע ו מ ת ח ת ר י ח נ ו ב ת ר ח ו י ס ע ו מ ת ר ח ו י ח נ ו	244987
ש ו י ח נ ו ב ה ר ה ה ר ב ק צ ה א ר צ א ד ו מ ו י ע ל א ה ר נ ה כ ה נ א ל ה ר ה ה ר ע ל	245238

Shape	Word	Translation	Verse	Position	Skip
נ	נוף	prospect	Numbers 32:24	243252	-7
א	אלוה	God	Numbers 32:29	243488	262
ת	תורה	torah	Numbers 32:29	243490	-502
מ	מורה	teacher	Numbers 32:33	243754	250
ע	עתיד	future	Numbers 32:33	243765	251
ל	לבד	alone	Numbers 32:39	244000	259
י	ידיעה	knowledge	Numbers 33:3	244267	251
ק	קוד	code	Numbers 33:16	244765	-243

20. Knowledge/Future: God alone (has) knowledge (of the) future. (The) Torah Code (is a) teacher (of) future prospects.

8

Jesus, the Guide

Who was this magnificent person, born 2,000 years ago, who established a religion that now encompasses more than one-third of the world's population? What are the odds of something of this magnitude happening as the result of the works of a single human being? I believe everyone will agree that without the intervention of God the odds would be absolutely zero. It would never have taken place. With such thoughts in my mind did I undertake my search for Jesus in the Bible Code.

Deep inside, I had never felt comfortable with the idea of the Father, the Son, and the Holy Ghost as the Trinity, as propagated by the Christian Church. I decided to begin my search with that idea. I talked to Catholic priests and Protestant ministers. The best I could get out of them was that the Trinity is a "mystery." It was described to me as similar to the identity of water, steam, and ice—all three are aspects of the same thing. I'm more inclined to believe in the concept of the Trinity as set forth by Edgar Cayce, as body, mind (soul) and spirit in all humanity as one, of God and with God. I believe we are all part of that Trinity. At the same time, I believe that Jesus was one of a kind, the only soul that ever reached perfection or enlightenment in our dimension. It is an accomplishment at which we ordinary folk can only wonder.

While I was researching the Edgar Cayce readings, I came across reading No. 5277, given by Cayce to a woman who was said to be psychically gifted. One of her questions to Cayce concerned the meaning of a message that she had apparently received during a vision several years before. The message was, "I am Gabriel, the great Head of Eden; God has heard your prayer to deliver Eden from sin. Few women are blessed as you are blessed." (I assume this woman was considered so blessed because of her psychic abilities.)

Whenever Jesus speaks in the New Testament of "His kingdom," he always declares that it is "not of this world." Similarly, the Jewish Kabbalah speaks of Eden as being a place not of this world but one where souls await rebirth. It seemed to me that, if the Archangel Gabriel was the head of Eden, and the Kingdom of Jesus was not of this world, perhaps Gabriel and Jesus were one and the same soul.

I decided to first do a search on Gabriel. The following slide quickly came together regarding this archangel: (**Subject: Angel/ Gabriel**), found in Deuteronomy 14:7 to 17:20, confirmed that Gabriel is the second Angel of God, the embodied teachers Adam, Rama, Buddha and Jesus. Furthermore, Gabriel is he who "manages the world." The next slide I encountered (**Subject: Gabriel/ Jesus**), found in Genesis 44:1 to 45:10, verified that Gabriel was the same soul in human form as Jesus.

I next decided to try to find the original Eden that was "not of this world." When God is speaking to Job, he mentions several constellations and stars and what seems to be a planet, "Mazzaroth." As far as I know, Mazzaroth, if it exists, has not yet been discovered. I searched the Bible Code on Arcturus, the brightest star in the Herdsman (Bootes) constellation. It's interesting to note that Jesus is referred to as the Good Shepherd. Perhaps this is a hint as to where his kingdom was. The following slide (**Subject: Arcturus/Mazzaroth**) was found in Numbers 26:36 to 26:59. It validates that Mazzaroth of Arcturus, in the Herdsman constellation, is the location of Eden, the Kingdom of Jesus, the home of enlightened souls.[21] This seemed to me to confirm kabbalistic teachings.

Letters	Position
ש מ ר נ י א ל ה מ ש פ ח ת י ש ש כ ר ל פ ק ד י ה מ א ר ב ע ה ו ש ש י מ א	232099
ו א פ ר י מ ב נ י מ נ ש ה ל מ כ י ר מ ש פ ח ת ה מ כ י ר י ו מ כ י ר ה ו	232262
ח פ ר י ו צ ל פ ח ד ב נ ח פ ר ל א ה י ו ל ו ב נ י מ כ י א מ ב נ ו ת ו ש	232425
ח ת ה ת ח נ י ו א ל ה ב נ י ש ו ת ל ח ל ע ר נ מ ש פ ח ת ה ע ר נ י א ל ה	232588
מ ש פ ח ת ה ש ו פ מ י ל ח ו פ מ מ ש פ ח ת ה ח ו פ מ י ו י ה י ו ב נ י ב	232751
ת מ כ ל מ ש פ ח ת ה ש ו ח מ י ל פ ק ד י ה מ א ר ב ע ה ו ש ש י מ א ל פ ו	232914
פ ח ת ב נ י א ש ר ל פ ק ד י ה מ ש ל ש ה ו ח מ ש י מ א ל פ ו א ר ב ע מ א	233077
ת א ל ה פ ק ו ד י ב נ י י ש ר א ל ש ש מ א ו ת א ל פ ו א ל פ ש ב ע מ א ו	233240
י נ ח ל ו ע ל פ י ה ג ו ר ל ת ח ל ק נ ח ל ת ו ב י נ ר ב ל מ ע ט ו א ל ה	233403
ת ה ו ל ד א ת ע מ ר מ ש ו מ א ש ת ע מ ר מ י ו כ ב ד ב ת ל ו י א ש ר י ל	233566
ד י ה מ ש ל ש ה ו ע ש ר י מ א ל פ כ ל ז כ ר מ ב נ ח ד ש ו מ ע ל ה כ י ל	233729
ר נ ה כ ה נ א ש ר פ ק ד ו א ת ב נ י י ש ר א ל ב מ ד ב ר ס י נ י כ י א מ	233892
ל ה נ ע ה ו ח ג ל ה ו מ ל כ ה ו ת ר צ ה ו ת ע מ ד נ ה ל פ נ י מ ש ה ו ל	234055
ו מ ת ו כ מ ש פ ח ת ו כ י א י נ ל ו ב נ ת נ ה ל נ ו א ח ז ה ב ת ו כ א ח	234218
א מ ר א י ש כ י י מ ו ת ו ב נ א י נ ל ו ו ה ע ב ר ת מ א ת נ ח ל ת ו ל ב	234381
א ל ל ח ק ת מ ש פ ט כ א ש ר צ ו ה י ה ו ה א ת מ ש ה ו י א מ ר י ה ו ה א	234544
מ ל ע י נ י ה מ ה מ מ י מ ר י ב ת ק ד ש מ ד ב ר צ נ ו י ד ב ר מ ש ה א ל	234707
ה ק ח ל כ א ת י ה ו ש ע ב נ נ ו נ א י ש א ש ר ר ו ח ב ו ו ס מ כ ת א ת י	234870
פ נ י י ה ו ה ע ל פ י ו י צ א ו ו ע ל פ י ו י ב א ו ה ו א ו כ ל ב נ י י	235033
ש ה ל א מ ר צ ו א ת ב נ י י ש ר א ל ו א מ ר ת א ל ה מ א ת ק ר ב נ י ל ח	235196
ה ע ר ב י מ ו ע ש י ר ת ה א י פ ה ס ל ת ל מ נ ח ה ב ל ו ל ה ב ש מ נ כ	235359
ע ש ה א ש ה ר י ח נ י ח ח ל י ה ו ה ו ב י ו מ ה ש ב ת ש נ י כ ב ש י מ ב	235522
ע ה ת מ י מ ו ש ל ש ה ע ש ר נ י מ ס ל ת מ נ ח ה ב ל ו ל ה ב ש מ נ ל פ	235685
ר ב י ע ת ה ה י נ ל כ ב ש י י נ ז א ת ע ל ת ח ד ש ב ח ד ש ו ל ח ד ש י ה	235848

Shape	Word	Translation	Verse	Position	Skip
נ	נפש	soul	Numbers 26:36	232619	646
י	ישוע	Jesus	Numbers 26:43	232939	-486
ר	רועה	herdsman	Numbers 26:47	233096	-487
א	אדן	Eden	Numbers 26:51	233260	331
ב	בית	home	Numbers 26:51	233262	-165
א	ארכתרס	Arcturus	Numbers 26:51	233274	325
מ	מלוכה	kingdom	Numbers 26:52	233289	-473
מ	מזרתה	Mazzaroth	Numbers 26:59	233584	164
נ	נאור	enlightened	Numbers 26:59	233599	-644

21. Arcturus/Mazzaroth: Herdsman (constellation), Mazzaroth (planet of) Arcturus (is) Eden, Kingdom (of) Jesus (and) home (of) enlightened soul(s).(Two letters of the word "kingdom" is hidden beyond the slide border.)

Letters	Position
כ נ י י ה ו ה ב ג ל ל כ ו י א מ ר נ ק ב ה ש כ ר כ ע ל י ו א ת נ ה ו י א מ ר א ל	42694
ה ג מ א נ כ י ל ב י ת י ו י א מ ר מ ה א ת נ ל כ ו י א מ ר י ע ק ב ל א ת ת נ ל י	42822
א ו נ ק ד ב ע ז י מ ו ה י ה ש כ ר י ו ע נ ת ה ב י צ ד ק ת י ב י ו מ מ ח ר כ י ת	42950
א א ת ה ת י ש י מ ה ע ק ד י מ ו ח ט ל א י מ ו א ת כ ל ה ע ז י מ ה נ ק ד ו ת ו ה	43078
ק ח ל ו י ע ק ב מ ק ל ל ב נ ה ל ח ו ל ו ז ו ע ר מ ו נ ו י פ צ ל ב ה נ פ צ ל ו ת	43206
ב ב א נ ל ש ת ו ת ו י ח מ ו ה צ א נ א ל ה מ ק ל ו ת ו ת ל ד נ ה צ א נ ע ק ד י מ	43334
ה ב כ ל י ח מ ה צ א נ ה מ ק ש ר ו ת ו ש מ י ע ק ב א ת ה מ ק ל ו ת ל ע י נ י ה צ	43462
ב ו ת ו ש פ ח ו ת ו ע ב ד י מ ו ג מ ל י מ ו ח מ ר י מ ו י ש מ ע א ת ד ב ר י ב נ	43590
ש ו מ ו י א מ ר י ה ו ה א ל י ע ק ב ש ו ב א ל א ר צ א ב ו ת י כ ו ל מ ו ל ד ת כ	43718
י א ב י ה י ה ע מ ד י ו א ת נ ה י ד ע ת נ כ י ב כ ל כ ח י ע ב ד ת י א ת א ב י כ	43846
י מ ו א מ כ ה י א מ ר ע ק ד י מ י ה י ה ש כ ר כ ו י ל ד ו כ ל ה צ א נ ע ק ד י מ	43974
ו ב ר ד י מ ו י א מ ר א ל י מ ל א כ ה א ל ה י מ ב ח ל ו מ י ע ק ב ו א מ ר ה נ נ	44102
א ש ר מ ש ח ת ש מ מ צ ב ה א ש ר נ ד ר ת ל י ש מ נ ד ר ע ת ה ק ו מ צ א מ נ ה א ר	44230
ו ו י א כ ל ג מ א כ ו ל א ת כ ס פ נ ו כ י כ ל ה ע ש ר א ש ר ה צ י ל א ל ה י מ מ	44358
ו ו א ת כ ל ר כ ש ו א ש ר ר כ ש מ ק נ ה ק נ י נ ו א ש ר ר כ ש ב פ ד נ א ר מ ל ב	44486
ג י ד ל ו כ י ב ר ח ה ו א ו י ב ר ח ה ו א ו כ ל א ש ר ל ו ו י ק מ ו י ע ב ר א ת	44614
ת ו ב ה ר ה ג ל ע ד ו י ב א א ל ה י מ א ל ל ב נ ה א ר מ י ב ח ל מ ה ל י ל ה ו י	44742
ב נ ל י ע ק ב מ ה ע ש י ת ו ת ג נ ב א ת ל ב ב י ו ת נ ה ג א ת ב נ ת י כ ש ב י ו	44870
ל ת ע ש ו י ש ׳ א ל י ד י ל ע ש ו ת ע מ כ מ ר ע ו א ל ה י א ב י כ מ א מ ש א מ ר	44998
ל ל ב נ כ י י ר א ת י כ י א מ ר ת י פ נ ת ג ז ל א ת ב נ ו ת י כ מ ע מ י ע מ א ש	45126
ה ל ש ת י ה א מ ה ת ו ל א מ צ א ו י צ א מ א ה ל ל א ה ו י ב א ב א ה ל ר ח ל ו ר	45254
ו כ ל ל ק ו מ מ פ נ י כ כ י ד ר כ נ ש י מ ל י ו י ח פ ש ו ל א מ צ א א ת ה ת ר פ	45382
ש י מ כ ה נ ג ד א ח ו א ח י כ ו י ו כ י ח ו ב י נ ש נ י . נ ו ז ה ע ש ר י מ ש נ	45510
ל י ל ה י ה י ת י ב י ו מ א כ ל נ י ח ר ב ו ק ר ח ב ל י ל ה ו ת ד ד ש נ ת י מ ע	45638
ב י א ל ה י א ב ר ה מ ו פ ח ד י צ ח ק ה י ה ל י כ י ע ת ה ר י ק מ ש ל ח ת נ י א	45766
ל י ה ו א ו ל ב נ ת י מ ה א ע ש ה ל א ל ה י ו מ א ו ל ב נ י ה נ א ש ר י ל ד ו	45894
א ב נ י מ ו י ע ש ו ג ל ו י א כ ל ו ש מ ע ל ה ג ל ו י ק ר א ל ו ל ב נ י ג ר ש ה	46022

Shape	Word	Translation	Verse	Position	Skip
ל	לשוב	to return	Genesis 30:27	42703	261
ש	שוב	again	Genesis 30:28	42715	510
א	אדם	Adam	Genesis 30:33	42984	-640
א	אלוה	God	Genesis 30:35	43094	-643
י	ישוע	Jesus	Genesis 30:35	43106	-640
ה	הצלה	rescue	Genesis 30:37	43239	-512
ת	תפקיד	task	Genesis 30:39	43363	-385
א	אבוד	lost	Genesis 31:8	44001	-642
נ	נפש	soul	Genesis 31:18	44516	-2
ע	עולם	world	Genesis 31:29	45036	-252
ת	תחייה	rebirth	Genesis 31:39	45641	-7

22. Task/Jesus:Task (of) Jesus, (from) world rebirth (as) Adam (to) Jesus to return again (as) Adam, (to) rescue (all) God's lost soul(s).

The real lesson of the Book of Job is of the need for patience. God must have infinite patience or the human race would have perished long ago. There can be no love without patience. I believe that's why there are so many divorces today. We all hurt those we love, for many reasons. Without patience, the hurt never really heals, and love diminishes. We have become a throwaway society of instant gratification; if something doesn't work, we throw it away and go and get another one. This tendency started with material things. Now it has moved on to families. We've become so selfish that even having children has become a matter of convenience. If our children get in the way of our career, we hand them off to sitters or to a daycare center. Sometimes, we even dispose of them before they are born. I'll have more to say on this later.

It occurred to me that if Gabriel were responsible for "managing the world," then God must have given him some special task. Since the Bible Code had identified Jesus as the embodiment of Gabriel while on earth, I decided to make a search regarding Jesus's task among men. The following search (**Subject: Task/Jesus**) was found in Genesis 30:27 to 31:39. It revealed that the task of Jesus, from rebirth in the world as Adam, to Jesus, and then as Adam again, is to rescue all of God's lost souls.[22] This corroborates 1 Corinthians 15:45. It also echoes the story of the Good Shepherd (John 10:11) and all that Jesus taught during his ministry.

One of the things the Bible Code has revealed thus far is that there are some conflicting teachings about Jesus in mainstream Christianity—including, first and foremost, the doctrine of the Trinity. In Mat.28, Jesus told His disciples that all power was given to Him in heaven and in earth [by God], and that they [the disciples] should go forth teaching all nations and baptizing them in the name of the Father, Son and Holy Ghost. *Holy* means "divine" or "godly," while *ghost* is defined as "disembodied soul." To me, Jesus's phrase means "in the name of God, Jesus the man, and Jesus, the resurrected soul." These are three different identities. Jesus also said, in John 10:30, "I and my Father are one." This means that he was of identical mind and soul with the Father, not that he was God. In Exodus 4:22, God instructs Moses to inform Pharaoh that Israel is

His *first-born son.* How often have you heard a mother say, "Look at my son and you will see his father"? This obviously doesn't mean that the son *is* the father. Also, in Acts 3:13, the disciple Peter says that "the God of Abraham, and of Isaac and Jacob, the God of our fathers, hath glorified His son Jesus." It doesn't sound as though Peter is referring to Jesus as God.

If the Archangel Gabriel incarnated as Jesus, then Jesus cannot be God. Jesus is the soul of Gabriel. He never claimed to be God; he claimed to be the son of God, and usually referred to himself as the Son of Man. As children of God, we are all sons and daughters of God. Jesus told us to pray, not to him, but to *our* Father in heaven. Jesus tells us here that God is the Father of everyone. In view of the above, to look upon Jesus as God would be to break the first commandment; it would be to commit blasphemy.

The next two slides verify the above reasoning. First, (**Subject: Christianity/Exalted**), found in Genesis 15:6 to 19:23, explains that Christianity exalted Jesus equal to God (in) Trinity, breaking the first law of God.[23] The second search on this subject, (**Subject: Trinity/Blasphemous**), found in Exodus 3.17 to 5:15, explains that the Trinity concept of Jesus/God/One is blasphemous.

I pondered the concept that Jesus was a unique human being. What could have made him so special? It came to me that a genetic change in Mary could have made Jesus unique to all human beings, different from the rest of humanity. Then I thought about the other children in the family of Joseph and Mary. There is not much information about them. Were they also special? The following search (**Subject: Conception/Jesus**), found in Exodus 36:17 to 38:5, indicates that only Jesus was unique. It turns out that the Immaculate Conception of Jesus was through a genetic DNA ovum (singular) change in Mary. Apparently, only one egg was genetically modified.

There are several theories as to how the soul, after its initial fall from grace, entered into three-dimensional density for the purpose of its long evolution back to enlightenment. Psychics like Edgar Cayce, Madame Blavatsky (author of the *Secret Doctrine,* 1888) and Rudolph Steiner (1861-1925) provide similar accounts; however,

ש מ ע א ל י ח י ה ל פ נ י כ ו י א מ ר א ל ה י מ א ב ל ש ר ה א ש ת כ י ל ד ת ל כ ב נ ו ק ר א ת א ת ש מ ו י צ ח ק ו ה ק	19984
פ ו כ ל ז כ ר ב א נ ש י ב י ת א ב ר ה מ ו י מ ל א ת ב ש ר ע ר ל ת מ ב ע צ מ ה י ו מ ה ז ה כ א ש ר ד ב ר א ת ו א ל ה י	20277
פ ת ח ה א ה ל ו י ש ת ח ו א ר צ ה ו י א מ ר א ד נ י א מ נ א מ צ א ת י ח נ ב ע י נ י כ א ל נ א ת ע ב ר מ ע ל ע ב ד כ י	20570
פ נ י ה מ ו ה ו א ע מ ד ע ל י ה מ ת ח ת ה ע צ ו י א כ ל ו ו י א מ ר ו א ל י ו א י ה ש ר ה א ש ת כ ו י א מ ר ה נ ה ב א	20863
ש ר ה ב נ ו ת כ ח ש ש ר ה ל א מ ר ל א צ ח ק ת י כ י י ר א ה ו י א מ ר ל א כ י צ ח ק ת ו י ק מ ו מ ש מ ה א נ ש י מ ו י	21156
ד ה מ א ד א ר ד ה נ א ו א ר א ה ה כ צ ע ק ת ה ה ב א ה א ל י ע ש ו כ ל ה ו א מ ל א א ד ע ה ו י פ נ ו מ ש מ ה א נ ש י מ	21449
נ ש א ת י ל כ ל ה מ ק ו מ ב ע ב ו ר מ ו י ע נ א ב ר ה מ ו י א מ ר ה נ ה נ א ה ו א ל ת י ל ד ב ר א ל א ד נ י ו א נ כ י	21742
ו ל י י מ צ א ו נ ש מ ע ש ר י מ ו י א מ ר ל א א ש ח י ת ב ע ב ו ר ה ע ש ר י מ ו י א מ ר א ל נ א י ח ר ל א ד נ י ו א ד	22035
נ ל י נ ו י פ צ ר ב מ א ד ו י ס ר ו א ל י ו י ב א ו א ל ב י ת ו ו י ע ש ל ה מ מ ש ת ה ו מ צ ו ת א פ ה ו י א כ ל ו	22328
ת ע ש ו ד ב ר כ י ע ל כ נ ב א ו ב צ ל ק ר ת י ו י א מ ר ו ג ש ה ל א ה ו י א מ ר ו ה א ח ד ב א ל ג ו ר ו י ש פ ט ש פ ו	22621
ה צ ע ק ת מ א ת פ נ י י ה ו ה ו י ש ל ח נ ו י ה ו ה ל ש ח ת ה ו י צ א ל ו ט ו י ד ב ר א ל ח ת נ י ו ל ק ח י ב נ ת י ו	22914
מ ל ט ע ל נ פ ש כ א ל ת ב י ט א ח ר י כ ו א ל ת ע מ ד ב כ ל ה כ כ ר ה ה ר ה ה מ ל ט פ נ ת ס פ ה ו י א מ ר ל ו ט א ל ה	23207
ר ע ד ב א כ ש מ ה ע ל כ נ ק ר א ש מ ה ע י ר צ ו ע ר ה ש מ ש י צ א ע ל ה א ר צ ו ל ו ט ב א צ ע ר ה ו י ה ו ה ה מ ט י ר	23500
ל ה י מ א ת א ב ר ה מ ו י ש ל ח א ת ל ו ט מ ת ו כ ה ה פ כ ה ב ה פ כ א ת ה ע ר י מ א ש ר י ש ב ב ה נ ל ו ט ו י ע ל ל ו	23793
ב כ י ר ה א ל ה צ ע י ר ה ה נ ש כ ב ת י א מ ש א ת א ב י נ ש ק נ ו י י נ ג מ ה ל י ל ה ו א ב א י ש כ ב י ע מ ו ו נ ח י ה	24086

Shape	Word	Translation	Verse	Position	Skip
ה	השילוש	trinity	Genesis 15:6	17621	-1186
א	נישא	exalted	Genesis 17:23	20323	-586
ח	חוק	law	Genesis 18:3	20605	286
נ	נצרות	Christianity	Genesis 18:3	20617	-586
ר	ראשית	first	Genesis 18:8	20882	-299
ש	שוה	equal	Genesis 18:9	20905	294
י	ישוע	Jesus	Genesis 18:21	21492	-289
א	אלוה	God	Genesis 18:27	21775	-587
ש	שבר	breaking	Genesis 19:23	23547	-293

23. Christianity/Exalted: Trinity (of) Christianity exalted Jesus equal (to) God, breaking (the) first law (of) God. (Two letters of the word "Trinity" are hiden beyond the slide border.)

Cayce disagrees with Blavatsky and Steiner regarding the number of "root race evolutions"—sentient species preceding ours, and which led up to mankind—that have gotten us to the current human race. Cayce states that we are in the fourth root race, while Blavatsky and Steiner claim we are currently in the fifth. These theories may be found throughout the works of these authors.

Since I am not a psychic, I have depended upon the Bible Code and modern science for establishing an opinion. As disclosed in the next chapter, the Bible Code identifies Cro-Magnon man as the third root race. Cro-Magnon man walked the earth approximately 40,000 to 10,000 years ago. Science has established that Neanderthal man lived from about 100,000 to 35,000 B.C. This species lived in caves or built shelters of stone, used fire and stone tools, and developed wooden spears for protection and hunting. There is evidence that Neanderthal man practiced a form of religion, was the first to bury its dead, and even performed crude surgery. This species was probably the second root race. That would make us, *Homo sapiens*, the fourth root race. This agrees with the readings of Edgar Cayce. Who the first root race was is anyone's guess, as far as I can tell.

It should be noted that Edgar Cayce, in Reading 900-227, said that man in Adam (as a group; not as an individual) entered into the world in five places at once, called Adam in one. I assume that he is talking about the sub-races of the fourth root race. In Reading 262-115, Cayce also said that the first of God's projections—not man's, but God's, projections—into the earth was Adam and Eve. This appears to mean that Adam and Eve were the first of God's rescue plan, and that the projections of the five races were those souls to be rescued.

According to Edgar Cayce, Adam was at the origin of the fourth root race of mankind. Is it possible that Jesus was at the origin of the fifth? My next search was in pursuit of that very question.

The following search (**Subject: Jesus/Nazareth**), found in Exodus 24:11 to 26:7, verified Jesus (of) Nazareth was conceived as the origin of the fifth root race.[24] It's reasonable to believe that Jesus was the example or ideal of what the human race could be at some

Letters	Position
ט ה ר ו א ל א צ י ל י ב נ י י ש ר א ל ל א ש ל ח י ד ו ו י ח ז ו א ת ה א ל ה י מ ו י א כ ל ו ו י ש ת ו ו	113023
ה א ה ר נ ו ח ו ר ע מ כ מ מ י ב ע ל ד ב ר י מ י ג ש א ל ה מ ו י ע ל מ ש ה א ל ה ה ר ו י כ ס ה ע נ נ א ת	113219
ר ב ע י מ ו י מ ו א ר ב ע י מ ל י ל ה ו י ד ב ר י ה ו ה א ל מ ש ה ל א מ ר ד ב ר א ל ב נ י י ש ר א ל ו י	113415
מ ל ש מ נ ה מ ש ח ה ו ל ק ט ר ת ה ס מ י מ א ב נ י ש ה מ ו א ב נ י מ ל א י מ ל א פ ד ו ל ח ש נ ו ע ש ו ל	113611
פ נ ו ו ע ש י ת ע ל י ו ז ר ז ה ב ס ב י ב ו י צ ק ת ל ו א ר ב ע ט ב ע ת ז ה ב ו נ ת ת ה ע ל א ר ב ע פ ע	113807
נ א ת ה ע ד ת א ש ר א ת נ א ל י כ ו ע ש י ת כ פ ר ת ז ה ב ט ה ו ר א מ ת י מ ו ח צ י א ר כ ה ו א מ ה ו ח	114003
ה מ ע ל ה כ פ ר ת ו פ נ י ה מ א י ש א ל א ח י ו א ל ה כ פ ר ת י ה י ו פ נ י ה כ ר ב י מ ו נ ת ת א ת ה כ	114199
ו ו א מ ה ר ח ב ו ו א מ ה ו ח צ י ק מ ת ו ו צ פ י ת א ת ו ז ה ב ט ה ו ר ו ע ש י ת ל ו ז ר ז ה ב ס ב י ב	114395
מ ע צ י ש ט י מ ו צ פ י ת א ת מ ז ה ב ו נ ש א ב מ א ת ה ש ל ח נ ו ע ש י ת ק ע ר ת י ו ו כ פ ת י ו ו ק ש	114591
ש ל ש ה ק נ י מ נ ר ה מ צ ד ה ה א ח ד ו ש ל ש ה ק נ י מ נ ר ה מ צ ד ה ה ש נ י ש ל ש ה ג ב ע י מ מ ש ק ד	114787
מ מ נ ה ו כ פ ת ר ת ח ת ש נ י ה ק נ י מ מ נ ה ל ש ש ת ה ק נ י מ ה י צ א י מ מ נ ה מ נ ר ה כ פ ת ר י ה	114983
ה מ ר א ה ב ה ר ו א ת ה מ ש כ נ ת ע ש ה ע ש ר י ר י ע ת ש ש מ ש ז ר ו ת כ ל ת ו א ר ג מ נ ו ת ל ע ת ש נ	115179
ל ת ע ל ש פ ת ה י ר י ע ה ה א ח ת מ ק צ ה ב ח ב ר ת ו כ נ ת ע ש ה ב ש פ ת ה י ר י ע ה ה ק י צ ו נ ה ב מ	115375
א ח ד ו ע ש י ת י ר י ע ת ע ז י מ ל א ה ל ע ל ה מ ש כ נ ש ת י ע ש ר ה י ר י ע ת ת ע ש ה א ת מ א ר כ ה	115571

Shape	Word	Translation	Verse	Position	Skip
ח	חמישי	fifth	Exodus 24:11	113052	592
מ	מקור	origin	Exodus 24:14	113206	-603
נ	נצרת	Nazareth	Exodus 25:12	113847	196
י	ישוע	Jesus	Exodus 25:24	114434	392
ג	גזע	race	Exodus 25:33	114830	381
ש	שורש	root	Exodus 25:33	114836	-191
ה	הרתה	conceived	Exodus 26:7	115594	-7

24. Jesus/Nazareth: Jesus (of) Nazareth (was) conceived (as the) origin (of the) fifth root race. (One letter of the word "origin" is hidden beyond the slide border.)

point in time. This would also explain why Jesus always seemed to be a step ahead of those around him. Probably he could read their minds through mental telepathy. The world was apparently not ready for a race change 2,000 years ago; it is therefore understandable that Jesus would not propagate the new race. His role was to present himself as the ideal towards which mankind was to aspire, to teach us that a much higher level of godliness had to be attained before we could meet the criteria of the next root-race evolution. In fact, he had to demonstrate the power that would be available to us all if we yielded up our will to that of God. According to the Bible Code, the new root race is not far away; I'll have more to say about this in a later chapter.

Was the resurrection and ascension of Jesus proof that he was of a different root race? This was the subject of my next search. That search (**Subject: Ascension/Demonstration**) was found in Exodus 22:8 to 24:2, and advises us that the ascension of Jesus was a demonstration of the power available to the race that will evolve after the Tribulation. Jesus apparently had to demonstrate the power of godliness in order to get our attention. God has embedded the essence of godliness in our consciousness, and the Ten Commandments provide us with a written definition of that essence. By observing God's Law, we yield up our will to His. It is not a matter of God's wanting to have His way like some arrogant child. There is only one path to godliness, and that is to assume the character of godliness. Apparently, the power of ascension awaits all of us in the coming new root race, if only we are ready to accept it. In fact, the Bible Code verifies that all of the godly will ascend at the end of the Golden Age, when Satan is "released for a little while" (Revelation 20:3). By then, all those souls who are worthy will have evolved to the fifth root race, from whence ascension is possible. Christianity may have confused this with the Rapture prophesied as occurring along with the coming Tribulation. The Code verifies that that Rapture is a myth. More on this later.

Ascension is possible through the attainment of godliness; it is about selflessness as opposed to selfishness. God provides for our every need, whether we accept Him or not. In essence, He acts as our servant. His is the example of selflessness (love) raised to the ultimate.

If Jesus introduced the fifth root race, then we are obviously in the fourth root race now. Who introduced the current human race? Based upon the Cayce readings, I suspected that it was also Gabriel (Jesus), under the name of Adam. This would be the subject of my next search.

The following search (**Subject: Gabriel/Initiated**) was found in Genesis 50:4 to 50:18. This search confirmed that Gabriel began the fourth root race as Adam, 10,000 years prior to his return as Jesus.

Thus far, Bible Code searches have shown us that Gabriel incarnated as Jesus and that Adam, Jesus, and Joseph (son of Jacob) were rebirths of the same soul. Since the story of Isaac (son of Abraham) appears to be a prophecy of the later sacrifice of Jesus, I decided to search for Isaac and other incarnations of Gabriel. Some of the incarnations of Gabriel (Jesus) appear in the next slide (**Subject: Rebirth/Jesus**), found in Deuteronomy 15:10 to 22:21. This slide advises us that rebirths of Jesus include Adam, Enoch, Isaac, Joseph, Joshua and Solomon. Discovering that Jesus was the incarnation of the Archangel Gabriel has led me to suspect there have been many more incarnations of Jesus.

Searching the Code further as regards the messengers of God, I discovered that there is a brotherhood of angels who have volunteered to incarnate as normal human beings in order to teach mankind the path towards enlightenment. The following slide (**Subject: Embodied/Brotherhood**), found in Exodus 13:8 to 16:15, advises us that God's angel brotherhood became messengers embodied as normal men. I'll have more to say about this in the next chapter.

9

The Fall and the Rescue Plan

According to the Bible Code, the fall from grace took place when the Archangel Lucifer rebelled against God and was banished from heaven. Lucifer had a large following of misguided disciple souls, all of whom chose to leave with him. Apparently, God confined them within the created universe in various dimensions, establishing a correction program designed to rehabilitate them to godliness.

The earth in the realm of three dimensions is part of the retraining program. Combining spirit, soul, and flesh into one unit constitutes an effective constraint on the soul. It's like our confining our children to schools and classrooms to give them an educational environment in which to capture their attention. Earth as the school, and our bodies as the classroom, would be a good comparison. Since the Bible Code verifies that we are now the fourth root race and are evolving into the fifth, there must be at least five grades to pass in this third dimension of earth. The end times as described in the Bible appear to be the graduation test from Grade Four to Grade Five. Those passing the coming end-time exam will evolve into the fifth root race, where conditions get better but standards get higher. Those souls that fail will, I assume, leave earth for retraining elsewhere, to be integrated later on or returned to repeat the fourth (fourth root race) grade. That fourth grade must have lasted 12,000 years, given that Adam introduced the current root race 10,000 years before he returned as Jesus 2,000 years ago. This was shown in a previous slide. It's interesting to note that, in the ancient Hindu traditions, 12,000 years is equal to an Age of God. It appears that the fifth grade (the fifth root race) will last 1,000 years; in the Bible Code, it is called the Golden Age, and spans the same 1,000-year period as is mentioned in John's Revelation.

The following slide (**Subject: Lucifer/Disciple**), found in Leviticus 8:20 to 11:19, confirms that Lucifer's confined disciple angels became man. The next search, entitled (**Subject: God's/ Plan**) and found in Genesis 12:2 to 14:8, confirms that God's salvation plan for Satan's lost souls is subsequent worldly embodiment as man until enlightened. The fact that we are to be embodied until enlightenment seems to imply many lifetimes, and reinforces the principle of the Law of Cause and Effect as the grading system for each lifetime or semester.

I wondered why the fourth root race lasted 12,000 years while the fifth was to last only 1,000 years. The following (**Subject: Twelve/Golden**) search, found in Numbers 7:70 to 8:3, identified twelve Golden Times of 1,000 years each in which to teach enlightenment to the human soul. The biblical Revelation mentions one Golden Age of 1,000 years, with an apparent test at the end during which Satan is turned loose again for a little while. However, as is made clear in Revelation 20:5, when the prophet speaks of those who died with the mark of the beast: "But the rest of the dead lived not again until the thousand years were finished." Perhaps each Golden Age will teach enlightenment to different populations of souls. I have not found a clear answer to this. Twenty-four thousand years, however, rounds out a complete cosmic cycle, after which school may start all over again for those dropouts who have to repeat the grade. God has not willed that one soul should be lost, and He has an eternity to achieve His goal.

Evolution is the rescue plan, according to the following search (**Subject: World/Evolvement**), found in Genesis 19:34 to 20:17, which confirms that evolution is God's universal plan for world perfection. It appears that there are two primary laws designed to implement this plan. One is the Law of the Spiral, and the other the Law of Cause and Effect. The Law of the Spiral is evident throughout creation, from the microscopic intelligence within our DNA genetic code to the development of our souls to enlightenment. This is the same law as is found throughout the natural world, where a vine will wrap itself around an object, ever spiraling itself upward towards the light. Mankind is a part of this same process. The law evolves us ever upward towards godliness, till we reach the circle of perfection from whence we started. The following search **(Subject: Spiral/Godliness)**, found in Leviticus 17:4 to 17:9, confirms that the spiral is the law that evolves the world higher and higher on its way to godliness. We have already discussed the Law of Cause and Effect, which keeps returning us to the three-dimensional world until we get it right.

Just as in our earthly schools, we are not left to do this all by ourselves. First of all, godliness is imprinted in our genetic code. It is because of this that our conscience and emotions are able to tell us what is the right way and what is the wrong way to live. We also have a direct line of communication through prayer, and guardian angels, to help us along the way. We are fragile beings in a tough world, and we would never make it far past birth if we did not get some help and protection. I know I should have been killed at least six times in my life, but something seemed to save me in each near-disaster. The following slide **(Subject: Guardian/Angel)**, found in Numbers 17:25 to 18:9, confirms that every embodied soul is given a guardian angel for protection. All of the help described above is available to everyone, whether we believe in God or not, and even if we do not practice godly behavior. But we can override our consciences so often that they become silent. We can build barriers between ourselves and God, preventing His rays of love, mercy and forgiveness from getting through. That is why, as backup, we are provided with books and teachers in life. But what do we do in the face of this? We persecute our teachers, or worship them as gods—or both—and then corrupt the contents of the teachings that they give us. However, when all else fails we have the Law of Cause and Effect to get us back on the right path. We cannot corrupt the Law, because we are not given the opportunity to do so. By the time the process of our earthly incarnations is completed, there will be few failures—but whether the learning is easy or hard is entirely our choice.

We know our earthly teachers as the founders of our basic religions and as history's great philosophers. But who are these individuals really? According to the Bible Code, they are embodied archangels—the angels who are responsible for administering God's Rescue Plan. So far I've discovered the incarnations of only four of the seven archangels, though I suspect all of them have been embodied from time to time to guide us on the path to enlightenment.

I discovered only one incarnation of the Archangel Michael. The following slide (**Subject: Melchizedek/Michael**), found in Deuteronomy 11:30 to 12:11, reveals that the Archangel Michael was embodied as Melchizedek, [who was] the same identical soul. According to the Bible Code, Michael enjoys high heavenly status; the following slide (**Subject: Michael/First**), found in Genesis 31:52 to 32:19, verifies that this archangel ranks first in God's hierarchy of angels.

The Archangel Gabriel is the great teacher, ranking second in the hierarchy of angels. We have already discussed some of the earthly fulfillments of Gabriel. This search (**Subject: Fulfillment/ Gabriel**), found in Numbers 33:26 to 35:11, verifies incarnations previously attributed in the Bible Code to Gabriel and Jesus. The fulfillments of the Archangel Gabriel include Adam, Rama, Joseph, Isaac, Solomon, Buddha and Jesus.

The next great teacher is the Archangel Raphael, who appears to rank third in the angel hierarchy. The following slide (**Subject: Fulfillment/Raphael**), found in Leviticus 18:12 to 19:2, confirms that fulfillments of the Archangel Raphael include Abel, Noah, Abraham, Jacob, Moses, David, Mohammed and Kahlil (Gibran). I also—in separate searches not included here—came across incarnations of Raphael as Daniel, Krishna and Socrates.

It's interesting to note that the holy testaments of the Kabbalah, the Torah, and the Koran were apparently all received by the soul of Raphael, embodied first as Moses, then as Mohammed. Since the Bible Code confirms that Mohammed received the Holy Koran from Gabriel, it is logical to assume that Gabriel also gave the Torah to Moses. I found a slide (**Subject: Torah/Given**), in Genesis 10:29 to 11:27, confirming that Raphael, embodied as Moses, was given the Torah in the same way as Mohammed was given the Koran, each holy book being inserted into the mind of the prophet. My next search (**Subject: Kabbalah/Word**), found in Numbers 3:4 to 3:39, confirmed that Gabriel gave Moses a different Word of God to pass on to Aaron: the secret Kabbalah. This also seems to be in accordance with the teachings of the Kabbalah.

Fourth in the angelic hierarchy, and also a great teacher, is the Archangel Chamuel. There emerged another slide (**Subject: John/ Baptist**), found in Leviticus 6:18 to 15:11, confirming that some of Chamuel's fulfillments were Seth, Elijah, Ezekiel, John (the) Baptist, Plato, Ali (son-in-law of Mohammed), Kung (Confucius) and (Edgar) Cayce.

It appears, then, that the initial fall from grace—of Lucifer and his disciples—came about long before Adam and Eve, who, as the progenitors of the new *Homo sapiens,* themselves disobeyed God. A further slide (**Subject: Homo/Sapiens**), found in Exodus 40:5 to 40:36, verifies that, 10,000 years before Jesus of Nazareth, the new *Homo sapiens* became the fourth root race. The Bible Code indicates that the Adam and Eve story, as it appears in Genesis, is a parable. The following search (**Subject: Sin/Eve**), found in Leviticus 7:9 to 8:6, confirms that the sin of Adam and Eve was to consort with the third root race in adultery which resulted in the birth of twins, Cain and Luluwa.[25] It seems that nothing changes!

Who were of the third root race? The Bible Code tells us. Another slide (**Subject: Cro-Magnon/Third**), found in Numbers 4:2 to 11:28, advises us that Cro-Magnon man was the third human root race, preexisting Adam and Eve. The next slide (**Subject: Cro-Magnon/Cain**), found in Genesis 24:5 to 24:54, revealed that a third race, Cro-Magnon man, fathered Cain and Luluwa.

ל כ ה נ ה מ ק ר י ב א ת ה ל ו ת ה י ה ו כ ל מ נ ח ה ב ל ו ל ה ב ש מ נ ו ח ר 149344
נ ו ו ה ק ר י ב ע ל ז ב ח ה ת ו ד ה ח ל ו ת מ צ ו ת ב ל ו ל ת ב ש מ נ ו ר ק 149449
ש ל מ י ו ו ה ק ר י ב מ נ ו א ח ד מ כ ל ק ר ב נ ת ר ו מ ה ל י ה ו ה ל כ ה 149554
מ נ ד ר א ו נ ד ב ה ז ב ח ק ר ב נ ו ב י ו מ ה ק ר י ב ו א ת ז ב ח ו י א כ ל 149659
ב ח ש ל מ י ו ב י ו מ ה ש ל י ש י ל א י ר צ ה ה מ ק ר י ב א ת ו ל א י ח ש ב 149764
ל ט ה ו ר י א כ ל ב ש ר ו ה נ פ ש א ש ר ת א כ ל ב ש ר מ ז ב ח ה ש ל מ י מ א 149869
מ א ה א ו ב כ ל ש ק צ ט מ א ו א כ ל מ ב ש ר ז ב ח ה ש ל מ י מ א ש ר ל י ה ו 149974
ו ע ז ל א ת א כ ל ו ו ח ל ב נ ב ל ה ו ח ל ב ט ר פ ה י ע ש ה ל כ ל מ ל א כ ה 150079
י ה ו כ ל ד מ ל א ת א כ ל ו ב כ ל מ ו ש ב ת י כ מ ל ע ו פ ו ל ב ה מ ה כ ל נ 150184
ה מ ק ר י ב א ת ז ב ח ש ל מ י ו ל י ה ו ה י ב י א א ת ק ר ב נ ו ל י ה ו ה מ 150289
נ י י ה ו ה ו ה ק ט י ר ה כ ה נ א ת ה ח ל ב ה מ ז ב ח ה ו ה י ה ה ח ז ה ל א 150394
מ ב נ י א ה ר נ ל ו ת ה י ה ש ו ק ה י מ י נ ל מ נ ה כ י א ת ח ז ה ה ת נ ו פ 150499
ל מ מ א ת ב נ י י ש ר א ל ז א ת מ ש ח ת א ה ר נ ו מ ש ח ת ב נ י ו מ א ש י י 150604
ל מ ל ד ר ת מ ז א ת ה ת ו ר ה ל ע ל ה ל מ נ ח ה ו ל ח ט א ת ו ל א ש מ ו ל מ 150709
נ י ה מ ל י ה ו ה ב מ ד ב ר ס י נ י ו י ד ב ר י ה ו ה א ל מ ש ה ל א מ ר ק ח 150814
ת ו א ת כ ל ה ע ד ה ה ק ה ל א ל פ ת ח א ה ל מ ו ע ד ו י ע ש מ ש ה כ א ש ר צ 150919
ק ר ב מ ש ה א ת א ה ר נ ו א ת ב נ י ו ו י ר ח צ א ת מ ב מ י מ ו י ת נ ע ל י 151024
י א פ ד ו ל ב ו ו י ש מ ע ל י ו א ת ה ח ש נ ו י ת נ א ל ה ח ש נ א ת ה א ו ר 151129
ש ר צ ו ה י ה ו ה א ת מ ש ה ו י ק ח מ ש ה א ת ש מ נ ה מ ש ח ה ו י מ ש ח א ת 151234
א ת ה כ י ר ו א ת כ נ ו ל ק ד ש מ ו י צ ק מ ש מ נ ה מ ש ח ה ע ל ר א ש א ה ר 151339
כ א ש ר צ ו ה י ה ו ה א ת מ ש ה ו י ג ש א ת פ ר ה ח ט א ת ו י ס מ כ א ה ר נ 151444
ו י ח ט א א ת ה מ ז ב ח ו א ת ה ד מ י צ ק א ל י ס ו ד ה מ ז ב ח ו י ק ד ש ה 151549

Shape	Word	Translation	Verse	Position	Skip
ק	קיין	Cain	Leviticus 7:9	149350	428
ה	התחבר	consort	Leviticus 7:9	149356	107
נ	נאף	adultery	Leviticus 7:12	149483	310
ת	תאום	twin	Leviticus 7:14	149579	108
מ	מין	race	Leviticus 7:16	149665	-638
ש	שורש	root	Leviticus 7:20	149901	-416
ש	שליש	third	Leviticus 7:21	149994	215
ל	לידה	birth	Leviticus 7:26	150188	323
ל	ללוה	Luluwa	Leviticus 7:29	150301	425
א	אדם	Adam	Leviticus 7:31	150417	-527
ח	חטא	sin	Leviticus 7:35	150631	105
א	איב	Eve	Leviticus 8:1	150841	105
נ	נובע	resulting	Leviticus 8:6	151035	8

25. Sin/Eve: Sin (of) Adam (and) Eve (was to) consort (with the) third root race resulting (in) adultry (and the) birth (of) twin(s), Cain (and) Luluwa.

Who was Luluwa? I will discuss that next.

In December, 2000, I came across a book called *The Lost Books of the Bible and the Forgotten Books of Eden*. The volume was made up of a number of ancient books that were never included in the Bible because it could not be reasonably determined when or by whom they were written. In this collection, the two books devoted to Adam and Eve interested me the most. Their combined length was 80 pages, and they went into great detail not only about Adam and Eve in the Garden of Eden, but about afterward, when they were expelled to another land. I'd always wondered how the new race could have been propagated through Seth and Cain alone. These books answered my question. They told me that Cain and Abel had had twin sisters. The sister of Cain was named Luluwa, and the sister of Abel was named Aklia.

According to these 'forgotten books of Eden,' Abel was murdered because Cain had been told to marry Aklia, Abel's sister, while Abel was expected to marry Luluwa, Cain's sister. However, Cain loved his own sister more and decided to kill Abel to prevent him from marrying Luluwa. After the murder, Adam banished Cain and Luluwa from the mountain where the family lived. This left Aklia without a husband, until Seth married her when he became 15. Adam forbade Seth's family to mingle with the family of Cain, predicting that a great flood would destroy them all if his command were disobeyed.

The family of Seth was called the family of God; that of Cain was called the family of Lucifer. This was likely because Cain's family was a mixture of the third and fourth root races. The previous slide showed us that Cain was an illegitimate son whose father belonged to the third root race. The families remained separated for many generations, but after about 5,000 years all of the Seth family ended up joining the Cain family in the valley below the mountain. The only people left on the slopes of the sacred mountain were the families of Methuselah, Lamech and Noah.

The fall from grace of Adam and Eve may have delayed the purification of the fourth root race for thousands of years, and even brought about the flood of Noah's time. The Bible tells us that society became so corrupt during the time of Noah that a major upheaval was necessary to return mankind to its course towards godliness. The Bible Code indicates that the Noah story, as we know it, is also a parable. The following slide (**Subject: Noah/Flood**), found in Deuteronomy 30:17 to 31:12, confirms that Noah's flood was an actual event. However, the tale is also a parable, that is, it is also metaphoric in nature. Yes, there was a great flood, and, yes, Noah (along with others) was saved; however, not all animal life on earth was destroyed, and the flood was probably a regional one, meant to purify the local race. Such a purification would be necessary for the godly development of Israel and, later on, of Islam—two major steps in God's rescue plan. The Code additionally supports recent studies by anthropologists and geologists indicating that a great flood occurred in the region approximately 7,500 years ago. The following search (**Subject: Noah/Flood**), found in Deuteronomy 30:10 to 31:7, confirms the occurrence of Noah's flood 5,500 years before the coming of Jesus of Nazareth.

I decided to search for the story of the sisters of Cain and Abel. The first search (**Subject: Cain/Adulterous**), found in Leviticus 27:26 to 27:32 and Numbers 1:1 to 1:28, confirmed that the birth of Cain and his twin sister Luluwa resulted from an adulterous relationship of Eve. In the following slide (**Subject: Abel/Aklia**), found in Leviticus 21:2 to 22:15, the Code verified that Abel and Aklia were the blessed first legitimate children of Adam and Eve.

The next slide (**Subject: Aklia/Wife**), found in Genesis 34:24 to 35:22, verified that Aklia was the wife of her brother Seth.

The original fall from grace occurred before the three-dimensional universe was created. Prior to the angels' fall, there was no need to confine souls within three-dimensional bodies. Lucifer apparently convinced us that since we were immortal souls we no longer needed God, that we were gods in our own right. Obviously, our believing him was a big mistake, one we're still paying for. We became lost, forgetting who we were and where we came from. The original fall created the necessity of the rescue plan. Thousands of years later, we're still trying to find our way back.

10

The Revelation: God's Warning

The Bible makes it clear that God always warns us before a great calamity strikes the earth. Few heed His warning, however, and most of us suffer more than is necessary. We are warned in order to convince us to choose godly behavior, thereby giving ourselves a chance to receive grace. God's grace can diminish or even wipe out collective karma built up over many generations. The problem is we don't believe this.

The coming holocaust will be so great that the entire final book of the New Testament, the Revelation to Saint John the Divine, is taken up with warning us about it. Exiled to the rocky Greek island of Patmos at the end of the first century A.D. for his vigorous defense of Christian thought, John (it is almost certain he was John the Apostle) one day finds himself engulfed in a tumultuous, mind-searing vision of an apocalyptic holocaust that will destroy the greater part of the human race. Apparently, this vision was brought to John by the fiery figure of Christ, who urged his disciple to write it down; the terrified and exalted John did so, dictating it to his assistant in the cave-grotto that they shared.

The text of the Revelation as it has come down to us falls into five sections: a prologue and four visions. The first vision is in the form of letters to seven Christian communities of Asia Minor; John upbraids these communities for falling away from the true faith. The second contains the images of seven seals, seven trumpets and seven bowls. The third leads from the judgment of sinful Babylon to the Second Coming of Christ, his battle with the Antichrist, the ultimate destruction of Satan and Death, and the New Creation; the fourth vision is of the heavenly Jerusalem.

The Revelation to Saint John is packed with symbolism, much of it an enigma to us even today, making it difficult for us to really understand what form the end times are actually going to take. I decided to see if I could clarify some of this symbolism through searches in the Bible Code. In order to ensure the continuity of the prospective events that I describe, I will discuss some of the results here, some in later chapters.

My first search focussed on the images of the seven seals. It seemed clear to me that the seals, trumpets and bowls all referred to the coming holocausts of the Tribulation—that horrific series of events leading up to the final redemption. The following slide (**Subject: Seal/Revealed**), found in Genesis 43:24 to 44:3, informed me that the seals revealed to John are the prospects for resolving world karma in the period 2005-2012.[26] Other dates are embedded in the slide, but those I have shown appear to be the most accurate. Further investigation in other areas of the Torah will be necessary to achieve a higher level of confidence regarding these extremely important dates. The presence of so many seals to be opened, with their varied, usually terrible, contents, indicates that a huge amount of negative karma has built up in humankind since the fourth root race evolved from Adam's time.

When the sixth seal comes to be opened (Rev. 7), Saint John sees a vision of four angels "standing at the four corners of the earth" and holding back the winds, but having the power to release them and cause untold devastation. Another angel, "ascending from the east, having the seal of the living God," exhorts these angels not to damage planet Earth—not to hurt "the grass of the earth, neither any green thing, neither any tree"—till the servants of the Lord have been safely "sealed;" 'sealing' seems to mean placing the identifying mark of God/Christ in the foreheads of the blessed (later,

Letters	Position
ו י ק ד ו ו י ש ת ח ו ו י ש א ע י נ י ו י ר א א ת ב נ י מ י נ א ח י ו ב נ	66645
ו ב נ א מ ו ו י א מ ר ה ז ה א ח י כ מ ה ק ט נ א ש ר א מ ר ת מ א ל י ו י א מ	66680
י א מ ר א ל ה י מ י ח נ כ ב נ י ו י מ ה ר י ו ס פ כ י נ כ מ ר ו ר ח מ י ו א	66715
י ו א ל א ח י ו ו י ב ק ש ל ב כ ו ת ו י ב א ה ח ד ר ה ו י ב כ ש מ ה ו י ר ח	66750
י ר ח צ פ נ י ו ו י צ א ו י ת א פ ק ו י א מ ר ש י מ ו ל ח מ ו י ש י מ ו ל ו	66785
ו ל ו ל ב ד ו ו ל ה מ ל ב ד מ ו ל מ צ ר י מ ה א כ ל י מ א ת ו ל ב ד מ כ י ל	66820
כ י ל א י ו כ ל ו נ ה מ צ ר י מ ל א כ ל א ת ה ע ב ר י מ ל ח מ כ י ת ו ע ב ה	66855
ע ב ה ה ו א ל מ צ ר י מ ו י ש ב ו ל פ נ י ו ה ב כ ר כ ב כ ר ת ו ו ה צ ע י ר	66890
ע י ר כ צ ע ר ת ו ו י ת מ ה ו ה א נ ש י מ א י ש א ל ר ע ה ו ו י ש א מ ש א ת	66925
ש א ת מ א ת פ נ י ו א ל ה מ ו ת ר ב מ ש א ת ב נ י מ נ מ מ ש א ת כ ל מ ח מ ש	66960
ח מ ש י ד ו ת ו י ש ת ו ו י ש כ ר ו ע מ ו ו י צ ו א ת א ש ר ע ל ב י ת ו ל א	66995
ו ל א מ ר מ ל א א ת א מ ת ח ת ה א נ ש י מ א כ ל כ א ש ר י ו כ ל ו נ ש א ת ו	67030
א ת ו ש י מ ו כ ס פ א י ש ב פ י א מ ת ח ת ו ו א ת ג ב י ע י ג ב י ע ה כ ס פ ת	67065
ס פ ת ש י מ ב פ י א מ ת ח ת ה ק ט נ ו א ת כ ס פ ש ב ר ו ו י ע ש כ ד ב ר י ו	67100
ר י ו ס פ א ש ר ד ב ר ה ב ק ר א ו ר ו ה א נ ש י מ ש ל ח ו ה מ ה ו ח מ ר י ה	67135
ר י ה מ ה מ י צ א ו א ת ה ע י ר ל א ה ר ח י ק ו ו י ו ס פ א מ ר ל א ש ר ע ל	67170
ר ע ל ב י ת ו ק ו מ ר ד פ א ח ר י ה א נ ש י מ ו ה ש ג ת מ ו א מ ר ת א ל ה מ	67205
ל ח מ ל ו ה ש ל מ ת מ ר ע ה ת ח ת ט ו ב ה ה ל ו א ז ה א ש ר י ש ת ה א ד נ י	67240
ד נ י ב ו ו ה ו א נ ח ש י נ ח ש ב ו ה ר ע ת מ א ש ר ע ש י ת מ ו י ש ג מ ו י	67275
מ ו י ד ב ר א ל ה מ א ת ה ד ב ר י מ ה א ל ה ו י א מ ר ו א ל י ו ל מ ה י ד ב	67310
י ד ב ר א ד נ י כ ד ב ר י מ ה א ל ה ח ל י ל ה ל ע ב ד י כ מ ע ש ו ת כ ד ב ר	67345
ד ב ר ה ז ה נ כ ס פ א ש ר מ צ א נ ו ב פ י א מ ת ח ת י נ ו ה ש י ב נ ו א ל	67380
ו א ל י כ מ א ר צ כ נ ע נ ו א י כ נ ג נ ב מ ב י ת א ד נ י כ כ ס פ א ו ז ה ב	67415
ז ה ב א ש ר י מ צ א א ת ו מ ע ב ד י כ ו מ ת ו ג מ א נ ח נ ו נ ה י ה ל א ד נ	67450
א ד נ י ל ע ב ד י מ ו י א מ ר ג מ ע ת ה כ ד ב ר י כ מ כ נ ה ו א א ש ר י מ צ	67485
י מ צ א א ת ו י ה י ה ל י ע ב ד ו א ת מ ת ה י ו נ ק י מ ו י מ ה ר ו ו י ו ר	67520

Shape	Word	Translation	Verse	Position	Skip
ע	עד ש	till	Genesis 43:24	66418	-356
ה	התרה	resolving	Genesis 43:27	66575	313
ק	קרמה	karma	Genesis 43:27	66609	-201
ת	תשסה	2005	Genesis 43:29	66670	34
נ	נוף	prospect	Genesis 43:33	66909	107
ג	גון	John	Genesis 43:34	66983	-245
ע	עולם	world	Genesis 43:34	66988	-65
ת	תשעב	2012	Genesis 44:1	67021	2
א	אות	seal	Genesis 44:2	67088	-105
ג	גלוי	revealed	Genesis 44:3	67158	-105

26. Seal/Revealed: (The) seal(s) revealed (to) John (are) prospect(s) (of) resolving world karma, 2005 till 2012. (One letter of each of the words "till" and "resolving" is hidden beyond the slide border.)

the 'mark of the beast' will be placed in other foreheads, for opposite reasons). John lists 144,000 as the number of those who are to be protected from the impending disasters. "And I heard the number of them, which were sealed: and there were 144,000 of all the tribes of the children of Israel." The following search (**Subject: Covenant/144,000**), found in Leviticus 27:2 to Numbers 1:24, revealed that 144,000 of God's original flock of Moses are incarnate souls of all races by 1975. These reincarnated peoples could be anyone on earth who truly loves God and has subordinated his or her will to His; these are the souls who, thousands of years ago, traveled with Moses on the Sinai and accepted God's covenant.

We are told that when the seventh seal was opened there was silence for about the space of half-an-hour. This seal intrigued me; no one seemed to have any explanation, or even a theory, as to what this obviously symbolic description could mean. I decided to search the Bible Code for the meaning of 'an hour' in the context of this prophecy. The following slide (**Subject: Revelation/Time**), found in Numbers 17:27 to 18:19, revealed that in the Revelation of John the time period of one hour, standing alone, equals one generation. Currently, a generation is three score and ten or 70 years. The seventh seal refers to a half-hour; I decided that that meant we were looking for an event that will unfold over a 35-year period. I will reveal the answer to this seventh-seal riddle in a later chapter.

The seven seals are followed by seven trumpets. In biblical times, trumpets were used to herald coming events or to provide a warning. The following slide (**Subject: Trumpet/Revealed**), found in Genesis 28:12 to 29:27, verified that seven trumpets signal to the world and reveal seven coming holocausts. The seven bowls are then described as being poured over the earth. It seems obvious that the bowls contain the holocausts. The following search (**Subject: Seven/Bowls**), found in Deuteronomy 18:9 to 18:22, verified that the seven bowls contain world-accumulated karma.

The Revelation speaks of four beasts that wreak havoc over the earth during this time. A red dragon appears as a wonder in the heavens and is cast down, its tail dragging a third of the stars of the heavens with it; this dragon has seven heads, seven crowns and ten horns. Then a beast with seven heads, ten horns and ten crowns rises out of the sea. A third beast, coming out of the earth, speaks like a dragon but resembles a lamb with two horns. The final beast is scarlet in color, with seven heads and ten horns; upon its dragon-back rides a prostitute dressed in purple and scarlet, covered with gold and precious stones, and holding a golden cup "full of abomination and filthiness." On her forehead "was a name written," saying, "Mystery, Babylon the Great, the Mother of Harlots and Abomination of the Earth."

The symbolism surrounding these beasts is so obscure that it could mean almost anything. I've read some very strange interpretations of this part of Revelation, by some very reputable religious leaders. The obscurity of these particular lines arises from the fact that we weren't supposed to understand them until the time was near. We needed only to know that a very bad time was coming, and that we must live in as godly a manner as possible in order to avoid the worst. However, now that the Bible Code is accessible, we can make some sense of these riddles as they relate to today's world.

The first two beasts have to do with particular holocausts; I'll discuss them in the following chapter having to do with the Tribulation. The meaning of the third beast is fairly obvious: Since Jesus is symbolized as the Lamb of God and the true prophet, a lamb with two horns would symbolize the lamb of Satan or the false prophet. The following slide (**Subject: Two/Horn**), found in Numbers 29:9 to 30:8, verifies that the lamb with two horns is the false prophet, teaching self-enlightenment without God. In Revelation 10:9, an angel instructs John to eat a little book that he is holding open in his hand. The angel tells him to, "Take it and eat it up, and it shall make thy belly bitter, but it shall be in thy mouth sweet as honey." I went to the Bible Code to get some sense of the meaning of this book; my next search (**Subject: Little/Book**), carried out in Leviticus 9:13 to 11:5, informed me that the little book eaten by John revealed the lie in the religion of the beast. We are being warned here to beware of a Tribulation Age religion teaching that we are gods in our own right and that with the proper training we can become self-disciplined and self-enlightened—in fact, the equal of God. This philosophy sounds good because it permits us to remain vain and selfish while at the same time becoming enlightened gods. To espouse such a philosophy would be the greatest mistake our souls could make, because our souls would then choose to cut themselves off from God's grace. Mercy is available but, tragically, it will not be accepted because it is believed to be unnecessary.

The fourth beast is the beast of Mystery Babylon. In Revelation 17, Jesus provides clues to the solution of the riddle of Mystery Babylon. Verse 7 states that the beast has seven heads and ten horns. Verse 8 says that the world will wonder when they behold the beast that *was* and *is not* and *yet is* [italics mine]. Verse 9 declares that the seven heads are seven mountains (countries?). Verse 11 says that the beast that was, and is not, even he is the eighth, and of the seventh. Verse 12 says that the ten horns are ten kings, which have received no kingdoms, but receive power as kings for one hour with the beast. Verse 13 says that they (the kings without kingdoms) have one mind and will give their power and strength unto the beast. Verse 15 says that where it sits are peoples, multitudes, and nations, and tongues. Verse 18 explains that the woman is a great city that reigns over the kings of the earth. The city of New York, with the United Nations in residence, is the only city in the world that equates to the description of Mystery Babylon in the Book of Revelation. N.Y.C. could rule the world through the power of money, commerce and U.N. military force, were the power given to it. The following slide (**Subject: Prostitute/Religion**), found in Exodus 40:16 to Leviticus 2:10, reveals that the prostitute on the beast is New York City, New Babylon of the false Tribulation Age religion of power and wealth.[27] The next slide (**Subject: Mystery/Babylon**), found in Numbers 7:36 to 8:7, advises that the beast of Mystery Babylon revealed to John is the United Nations, which became the New World Order of the Tribulation and obtained power from the beast. So it appears that N.Y.C. could be riding the beast of the United Nations, which has no king-

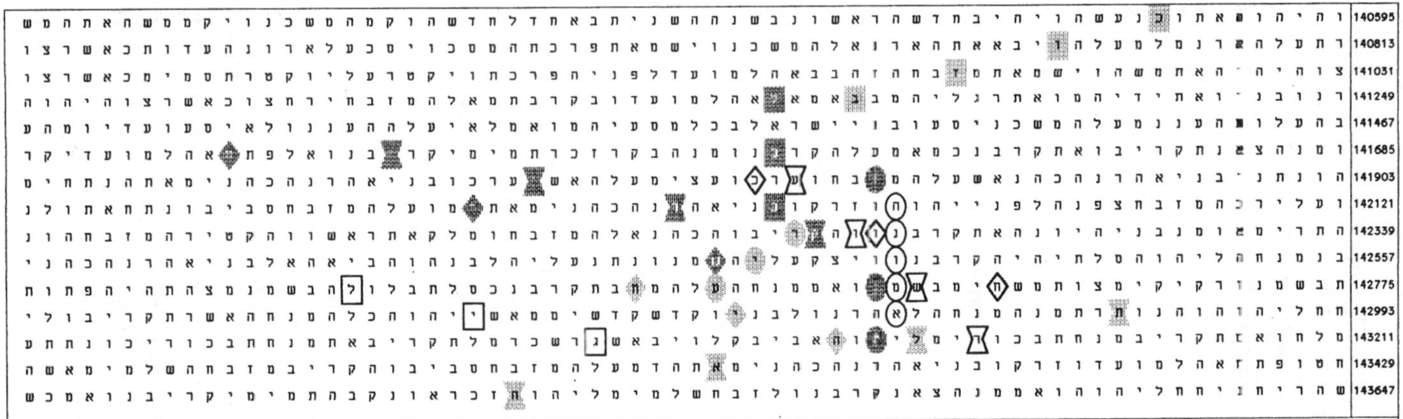

Shape	Word	Translation	Verse	Position	Skip
כ	כוזב	false	Exodus 40:16	140604	223
ב	בבל	Babylon	Exodus 40:32	141277	-436
י	יורק	York	Leviticus 1:3	141732	211
ח	חדש	new	Leviticus 1:3	141740	424
ז	זונה	prostitute	Leviticus 1:7	141926	436
ע	עושר	wealth	Leviticus 1:7	141930	433
כ	כוח	power	Leviticus 1:7	141932	430
א	אמונה	religion	Leviticus 1:11	142143	-218
ע	עיר	city	Leviticus 1:15	142366	-220
ח	חיה	beast	Leviticus 2:5	142810	213
ג	גיל	age	Leviticus 2:5	142824	-212
ת	תלאה	tribulation	Leviticus 2:10	143004	228

27. Prostitute/Religion: (The) prostitute (on the) beast (is) New York City, New Babylon (of the) Tribulation Age false religion (of) power (and) wealth.

dom but derives its power voluntarily from the other kingdoms of the world. It "was," as the League of Nations from 1919 to 1939, it "was not" during World War Two, and it "is now" since 1945, exactly as stated in Revelation 17. The U.N. controls the World Bank, the World Trade Organization, the World Court and the Security Council, and could control the armed forces of most of the world.

The next search, **(Subject: Seven/Head)**, found in Exodus 16:23 to 17:16, reveals that the seven heads of the beast of New Babylon is the G-7 (Group 7, now Group 8) of the United Nations W.T.O. (World Trade Organization), plus the eighth, Russia. An additional search **(Subject: Horn/Beast)**, found in Genesis 15:9 to 16:2, reveals that the horns of the beast of the New Babylon are ten that manage the world in secret.[28] This "ten" derives its power from the second beast, which I will discuss in a later chapter. The allusion to the "ten who rule the world in secret" remains mysterious to me, notwithstanding that secret world power conspiracy theories abound. The Trilateral Commission and the Bilderburger Group are just two of many such power groups discussed at length in *Rule by Secrecy,* by the celebrated author and journalist Jim Marrs.

According to the Bible Code, there is a prospect that the United Nations may evolve into a very dangerous and evil organization during the Tribulation. It is possible that world terrorism will become so serious over the next few years that the developed world will sacrifice too much of its liberty for safety. It has been said that those who do this deserve neither liberty nor safety. Who will be at fault if this happens? Actually, we will all share the blame, because we will not have carefully and responsibly monitored events and therefore will have voluntarily (if unknowingly) surrendered our freedom and power. The following search **(Subject: World/Order),** found in Exodus 14:9 to 15:3, reveals that the New World Order of the United Nations established tyranny toward the faithful during the Tribulation.

There is a mention in Revelation 9 of a horrific disease that breaks out during the Tribulation, causing boils to appear on every part of the bodies of those not sealed by God. It takes this disease

Letters	Row
ה ל י ע ג ל ה מ ש ל ש ת ו ע ז מ ש ל ש ת ו א י ל מ ש ל ש ו ת ר ו ג ו ז ל ו י ק ח ל ו א ת כ ל א ל ה ו י ב ת ר א	17723
ו י ש ב א ת מ א ב ר מ ו י ה י ה ש מ ש ל ב ו א ו ת ר ד מ ה נ פ ל ה ע ל א ב ר מ ו ה נ ה א י מ ה ח ש כ ה ג ד ל ה	17832
ו א ת מ א ר ב ע מ א ו ת ש נ ה ו ג מ א ת ה ג ו י א ש ר י ע ב ד ו ד נ א נ כ י ו א ח ר י כ נ י צ א ו ב ר כ ש ג ד	17941
ל א ש ל מ ע ו נ ה א מ ר י ע ד ה נ ה ו י ה י ה ש מ ש ב א ה ו ע ל ט ה ה י ה ו ה נ ה ת נ ו ר ע ש נ ו ל פ י ד א ש	18050
ת ת י א ת ה א ר צ ה ז א ת מ נ ה ר מ צ ר י מ ע ד ה נ ה ר ה ג ד ל נ ה ר פ ר ת א ת ה ק י נ י ו א ת ה ק נ ז י ו א	18159
ג ש י ו א ת ה י ב ו ס י ו ש ר י א ש ת א ב ר מ ל א י ל ד ה ל ו ו ל ה ש פ ח ה מ צ ר י ת ו ש מ ה ה ג ר ו ת א מ ר	18268
ע א ב ר מ ל ק ו ל ש ר י ו ת ק ח ש ר י א ש ת א ב ר מ א ת ה ג ר ה מ צ ר י ת ש פ ח ת ה מ ק צ ע ש ר ש נ י מ ל ש ב	18377
ה ר ת ה ו ת ק ל ג ב ר ת ה ב ע י נ י ה ו ת א מ ר ש ר י א ל א ב ר מ ח מ ס י ע ל י כ א נ כ י נ ת ת י ש פ ח ת י ב	18486
ר י ה נ ה ש פ ח ת כ ב י ד כ ע ש י ל ה ה ט ו ב ב ע י נ י כ ו ת ע נ ה ש ר י ו ת ב ר ח מ פ נ י ה ו י מ צ א ה מ ל	18595
א ת ו א נ ה ת ל כ י ו ת א מ ר מ פ נ י ש ר י ג ב ר ת י א נ כ י ב ר ח ת ו י א מ ר ל ה מ ל א כ י ה ו ה ש ו ב י א	18704
ר מ ר ב ו י א מ ר ל ה מ ל א כ י ה ו ה ה נ כ ה ר ה ו י ל ד ת ב נ ו ק ר א ת ש מ ו י ש מ ע א ל כ י ש מ ע י ה ו ה	18813
ש מ י ה ו ה ה ד ב ר א ל י ה א ת ה א ל ר א י כ י א מ ר ה ה ג מ ה ל מ ר א י ת י א ח ר י ר א י ע ל כ נ ק ר א ל ב	18922
ו א ש ר י ל ד ה ה ג ר י ש מ ע א ל ו א ב ר מ ב נ ש מ נ י מ ש נ ה ו ש ש ש נ י מ ב ל ד ת ה ג ר א ת י ש מ ע א ל ל	19031

Shape	Word	Translation	Verse	Position	Skip
ע	עולם	world	Genesis 15:9	17747	-116
ל	לנהל	manage	Genesis 15:9	17749	-212
ס	סוד	secret	Genesis 15:12	17858	-210
א	אשר	that	Genesis 15:13	17950	443
ח	חדש	new	Genesis 15:14	17981	208
ק	קרן	horn	Genesis 15:18	18173	-109
ח	חיה	beast	Genesis 15:18	18174	-109
ע	עשר	ten	Genesis 15:18	18175	-435
ב	בבל	Babylon	Genesis 16:2	18385	-110

28. Horn/Beast; (The) horn(s) (of the) beast (of) New Babylon (are) ten that manage (the) world (in) secret.

approximately five months to run its course, during which time it is so painful that those who contract it wish they could die. The following search (**Subject: Biological/Warfare**), found in Genesis 1:26 to 38:2, revealed that at the beginning of 2010 biological warfare is bringing the Tribulation boil pestilence revealed to John.

In Revelation 11, two witnesses are identified who, possessing great power, warn of the holocausts to come during the first half of the Tribulation. These two witnesses are immune from all harm till they have given their testimony; then, they are killed by Satan. Their bodies lie unburied on a Jerusalem street for three days till God resurrects them. The following search (**Subject: Zadkiel/ Chamuel**), found in Leviticus 5:10 to 6:14, identified Zadkiel and Chamuel as the two embodied angel witnesses killed in Jerusalem in 2008, as revealed to John.

Revelation 12 describes another wonder in heaven: a woman, clothed in the sun with the moon under her feet, with a crown of twelve stars on her head. "And being with child she cried, travailing in birth and pained to be delivered," reads the text. The following search (**Subject: Revelation/Twelve**), found in Genesis 25:25 to 34:28, revealed that the twelve stars in the crown of the woman in Revelation 12 are symbolic of the Bootes/Herdsman Constellation, the Edenic home of Adam and Eve. This serves to verify the many statements made by Edgar Cayce, in the course of his readings, identifying the Arcturus planetary system as a gateway of prime importance to human souls returning to earth.

In the verses following the ones I've quoted above, John tells us that a great red dragon stands before the woman, ready to devour her child as soon as it is born. Who is this child to be born? The text of Revelation tells us that it is a man-child who is to rule over all the nations with a rod of iron. The following search (**Subject: Phobos/Dragon**), found in Genesis 39:4 to 41:14, revealed that Phobos, the Red Dragon of the Tribulation, is to endanger the rebirth of Adam, the new child king. In a later chapter, I will investigate the danger inherent in this "Phobos;" the important message here is that the soul of Jesus, as Adam, is to be reborn in the second half of the Tribulation. The next slide (**Subject: Golden/**

Age), found in Genesis 30:37 to 31:21, reveals that the future prospect of a Golden Age is to start with the second birth of Adam in 2010.[29] Jesus's final teaching to John (Rev. 22:13) was, "I am the Alpha and Omega, the beginning and end, the first and the last." These words express the beginning of the root race with Adam and its ending with Adam. For the current age to end with Adam, he must be born again before the end of the Tribulation.

Everyone assumes that Jesus is coming back to be king during *this* Tribulation, in the adult body of light of the resurrected. The Bible Code tells us that his return will occur during the *next* Tribulation, at the end of the Golden Age, when Satan is turned loose once again. The following slide (**Subject: Jesus/Returning**), found in Genesis 32:30 to 34:3, reveals that Jesus is returning in a body of light as the Golden Age ends.[30]

Since Adam will be of natural birth, I wondered who would rule the world when he was a child—especially as everything will be in a state of chaos. The following search (**Subject: Covenant/144,000**), found in Leviticus 27:18 to Numbers 1:24, revealed that the 144,000 of God's covenant incarnate souls manage the world while Adam is a child. Since a previous slide told us they were reborn in all races, I assume they are where they are supposed to be right now, oblivious of who they are, but ready to assume their tasks when they are called upon to do so.

ה א ת נ ל כ ו י א מ ר י ע ק ב ל א ת ת נ ל י מ א ו מ ה א מ ת ע ש ה ל י ה ד	42840
נ ק ד ב ע ז י מ ו ה י ה ש כ ר י ו ע נ ת ה ב י צ ד ק ת י ב י ו מ מ ח ר כ י	42952
ב ר כ ו י ס ר ב י ו מ ה ה ו א א ת ה ת י ש י מ ה ע ק ד י מ ו ה ט ל א י מ ו	43064
י נ י ע ק ב ו י ע ק ב ר ע ה א ת צ א נ ל ב נ ה נ ו ת ר ת ו י ק ח ל ו י ע ק	43176
ב ר ה ט י מ ב ש ק ת ו ת ה מ י מ א ש ר ת ב א נ ה צ א נ ל ש ת ו ת ל נ כ ח ה	43288
ב ו י ת נ פ נ י ה צ א נ א ל ע ק ד ו כ ל ח ו מ ב צ א נ ל ב נ ו י ש ת ל ו ע	43400
ח מ נ ה ב מ ק ל ו ת ו ב ה ע ט י פ ה צ א נ ל א י ש י מ ו ה י ה ה ע ט פ י מ	43512
ד ב ר י ב נ י ל ב נ ל א מ ר ל ק ח י ע ק ב א ת כ ל א ש ר ל א ב י נ ו ו מ א	43624
ש ו ב א ל א ר צ א ב ו ת י כ ו ל מ ו ל ד ת כ ו א ה י ה ע מ כ ו י ש ל ח י ע	43736
ב י ה י ה ע מ ד י ו א ת נ ה י ד ע ת נ כ י ב כ ל כ ח י ע ב ד ת י א ת א ב י	43848
ו י ל ד ו כ ל ה צ א נ נ ק ד י מ ו א מ כ ה י א מ ר ע ק ד י מ י ה י ה ש כ ר	43960
ה נ ה ה ע ת ד י מ ה ע ל י מ ע ל ה צ א נ ע ק ד י מ נ ק ד י מ ו ב ר ד י מ ו	44072
מ נ ק ד י מ ו ב ר ד י מ כ י ר א י ת י א ת כ ל א ש ר ל ב נ ע ש ה ל כ א נ כ	44184
ל ו ל א ה ו ת א מ ר נ ה ל ו ה ע ו ד ל נ ו ח ל ק ו נ ח ל ה ב ב י ת א ב י נ	44296
א ו ל ב נ י נ ו ו ע ת ה כ ל א ש ר א מ ר א ל ה י מ א ל י כ ע ש ה ו י ק מ י	44408
נ א ר מ ל ב ו א א ל י צ ח ק א ב י ו א ר צ ה כ נ ע נ ו ל ב נ ה ל כ ל ג ז ז	44520
ה ו א ו כ ל א ש ר ל ו ו י ק מ ו י ע ב ר א ת ה נ ה ר ו י ש מ א ת פ נ י ו ה	44632
ב ה ר ה ג ל ע ד ו י ב א א ל ה י מ א ל ל ב נ ה א ר מ י ב ח ל מ ה ל י ל ה ו	44744
ב ה ר ה ג ל ע ד ו י א מ ר ל ב נ ל י ע ק ב מ ה ע ש י ת ו ת ג נ ב א ת ל ב ב	44856
ר ו ל א נ ט ש ת נ י ל נ ש ק ל ב נ י ו ל ב נ ת י ע ת ה ה ס כ ל ת ע ש ו י ש	44968
כ י נ כ ס פ נ כ ס פ ת ה ל ב י ת א ב י כ ל מ ה ג נ ב ת א ת א ל ה י ו י ע נ	45080
ה כ ר ל כ מ ה ע מ ד י ו ק ח ל כ ו ל א י ד ע י ע ק ב כ י ר ח ל ג נ ב ת מ ו	45192
ר פ י מ ו ת ש ח מ ב כ ר ה ג מ ל ו ת ש ב ע ל י ה מ ו י מ ש ש ל ב נ א ת כ ל	45304
א ת ה ת ר פ י מ ו י ח ר ל י ע ק ב ו י ר ב ב ל ב נ ו י ע נ י ע ק ב ו י א מ	45416
ו כ י ח ו ב י נ ש נ י נ ו ז ה ע ש ר י מ ש נ ה א נ כ י ע מ כ ר ח ל י כ ו ע	45528
ל ה ה י י ת י ב י ו מ א כ ל נ י ח ר ב ו ק ר ח ב ל י ל ה ו ת ד ד ש נ ת י מ	45640
ת מ נ י מ ל ו ל י א ל ה י א ב י א ל ה י א ב ר ה מ ו פ ח ד י צ ח ק ה י ה ל	45752
ו ה ב נ י מ ב נ י ו ה צ א נ צ א נ י ו כ ל א ש ר א ת ה ר א ה ל י ה ו א ו ל	45864

Shape	Word	Translation	Verse	Position	Skip
ע	עידן	age	Genesis 30:37	43211	444
נ	נוף	prospect	Genesis 31:12	44185	450
ת	תשעת	2010	Genesis 31:12	44213	-225
א	אדם	Adam	Genesis 31:16	44408	455
ל	להחל	to start	Genesis 31:16	44410	-122
ש	שני	second	Genesis 31:16	44438	105
ז	זהוב	golden	Genesis 31:19	44556	112
ל	לידה	birth	Genesis 31:21	44632	-231

29. Golden/Age: Prospect (of the) Golden Age to start (with the) second birth (of) Adam (in) 2010.

ח ר ו י ר א כ י ל א י כ ל ל ו ו י ג ע ב כ פ י ר כ ו ו ת ק ע כ פ י	47806
ת נ י ו י א מ ר א ל י ו מ ה ש מ כ ו י א מ ר י ע ק ב ו י א מ ר ל א	47892
ל י ע ק ב ו י א מ ר ה ג י ד ה נ א ש מ כ ו י א מ ר ל מ ה ז ה ת ש א	47978
ל פ נ י מ ו ת נ צ ל נ פ ש י ו י ז ר ח ל ו ה ש מ ש כ א ש ר ע ב ר א	48064
פ ה י ר כ ע ד ה י ו מ ה ז ה כ י נ ג ע ב כ פ י ר כ י ע ק ב ב ג י ד	48150
ל ד י מ ע ל ל א ה ו ע ל ר ח ל ו ע ל ש ת י ה ש פ ח ו ת ו י ש מ א ת	48236
ר נ י מ ו ה ו א ע ב ר ל פ נ י ה מ ו י ש ת ח ו א ר צ ה ש ב ע פ ע מ	48322
ב כ ו ו י ש א א ת ע י נ י ו ו י ר א א ת ה נ ש י מ ו א ת ה י ל ד י	48408
נ ה ו י ל ד י ה נ ו ת ש ת ח ו י נ ו ת ג ש ג מ ל א ה ו י ל ד י ה ו	48494
ת י ו י א מ ר ל מ צ א ח נ ב ע י נ י א ד נ י ו י א מ ע ר ש ו י ש ל	48580
ח ת י מ י ד י כ י ע ל כ נ ר א י ת י פ נ י כ כ ר א ת פ נ י א ל ה י	48666
ו ו י ק ח ו י א מ ר נ ס ע ה ו נ ל כ ה ו א ל כ ה ל נ ג ד כ ו י א מ	48752
ו מ ת ו כ ל ה צ א נ י ע ב ר נ א א ד נ י ל פ נ י ע ב ד ו ו א נ י א	48838
י ר ה ו י א מ ר ע ש ו א צ י ג ה נ א ע מ כ מ נ ה ע מ א ש ר א ת י ו	48924
ב נ ס ע ס כ ת ה ו י ב נ ל ו ב י ת ו ל מ ק נ ה ו ע ש ה ס כ ת ע ל כ	49010
מ ו י ח נ א ת פ נ י ה ע י ר ו י ק נ א ת ח ל ק ת ה ש ד ה א ש ר נ ט	49096
ה י י ש ר א ל ו ת צ א ד י נ ה ב ת ל א ה א ש ר י ל ד ה ל י ע ק ב ל	49182
א ת ה ו י ע נ ה ו ת ד ב ק נ פ ש ו ב ד י נ ה ב ת י ע ק ב ו י א ה ב	49268
ז א ת ל א ש ה ו י ע ק ב ש מ ע כ י ט מ א א ת ד י נ ה ב ת ו ו ב נ י	49354
א ת ו ו ב נ י י ע ק ב ב א ו מ נ ה ש ד ה כ ש מ ע מ ו י ת ע צ ב ו ה	49440
ד ב ר ח מ ו ר א ת מ ל א מ ר ש כ מ ב נ י ח ש ק ה נ פ ש ו ב ב ת כ מ	49526
מ ו א ת נ ו ת ש ב ו ו ה א ר צ ת ה י ה ל פ נ י כ מ ש ב ו ו ס ח ר ו	49612
ל י א ת נ ה ר ב ו ע ל י מ א ד מ ה ר ו מ ת נ ו א ת נ ה כ א ש ר ת א	49698
מ ה ו י ד ב ר ו א ש ר ט מ א א ת ד י נ ה א ח ת מ ו י א מ ר ו א ל י	49784
נ ו א כ ב ז א ת נ א ו ת ל כ מ א ת ה י ו כ מ נ ו ל ה מ ל כ מ כ	49870

Shape	Word	Translation	Verse	Position	Skip
ז	זהבי	golden	Genesis 32:30	48006	422
ס	סוף	ending	Genesis 33:1	48259	-252
א	אור	light	Genesis 33:5	48434	86
ג	גוף	body	Genesis 33:7	48515	518
ע	עידן	age	Genesis 34:1	49195	-91
ה	השבה	returning	Genesis 34:1	49208	-172
י	ישוע	Jesus	Genesis 34:3	49293	-172

30. Jesus/Returning: Jesus (is) returning (in a) body (of) light (at the) ending (of the) Golden Age.

11

The Tribulation: Our Future Prospects

The prophecies revealed in the Revelation to Saint John the Divine have struck terror into the hearts of Christians for almost 2,000 years, and with good reason. They describe the coming Tribulation, a prophesied period so terrible that, were God not to intervene, there would be practically nobody left alive on earth. This Tribulation will come like a thief in the night. The predictions in the text are of what appear to be shifts in the polar axis of the earth, asteroids striking our planet, earthquakes, floods, famine, plagues, tidal waves and world war. I studied all of the frightening details in the Books of Isaiah, Daniel, Mark, Matthew and the Revelation, noting the particularly vivid description of the end times holocaust which Mark ascribes to Jesus in Mark 13.

Here is how all this translates for me regarding the modern world: One of the first signs of the Tribulation is that the Christian Gospel (New Testament) will be available in every land on the earth. I believe that this has already come to pass. This was necessary because, in the Revelation, the Christian Gospel contains a warning to the end-times generation.

When will the Tribulation strike? Nobody knows, not even Jesus. We will see the signs, he has told us—but only the Father knows. Jesus was, however, aware of the generation in which the Tribulation would occur. In Matthew 24: 32-34, he relates the parable of the fig tree: "When his branch is yet tender, and putteth forth leaves, ye know that the summer is nigh: So likewise ye, when ye shall see all these things, know that it is near, even at the doors. Verily I say unto you, this generation shall not pass, till all these things are fulfilled." I believe the fig tree must represent Israel. The season in which it put forth new leaves, or came to new life, was in 1948, when Israel was reestablished as a nation. The following slide **(Subject: 1948/Generation)**, found in Exodus 37:25 to 38:24, reveals that the Tribulation Era is beginning with the generation of 1948, a depiction by Jesus in Matthew 24.[31] A follow-up slide **(Subject: 1948/Generation)**, also found in Exodus 38:15 to 38:24, advises us that the generation of 1948 is 70 years.[32] Since the Bible Code defines a generation as 70 years, the Tribulation Era should end by 2018.

According to my understanding of the Revelation, the actual Tribulation period appears to last for seven years. It will probably begin with world economic collapse and a limited war in the Middle East. Babylon is mentioned too often in the text to be ignored. It appears that a false peace will be signed with Israel at the onset of the Tribulation, and that within the next three years Solomon's Temple will be rebuilt. Natural disasters occur with increasing frequency and intensity during this period. World economic collapse will bring worldwide famine and epidemics of disease in its wake. There will be a sharp increase in crime, pornography and drug use. During this period, we will come to call good that which we normally call evil. After three-and-a-half years, the peace treaty with Israel will be broken; shortly thereafter, war will break out. A military force of 200 million is mentioned; it sounds as if this will be a Middle East/Asian alliance, aligning itself against Israel and the rest of the world. The war will become so dangerous, probably involving nuclear weapons, that divine forces committed to ensuring the integrity of planet Earth will step in with natural disasters of gigantic proportions, to bring about a stop to the war and its threat of total destruction.

These natural disasters of gigantic proportions will likely include asteroid or meteor strikes that will ultimately bring about a

Shape	Word	Translation	Verse	Position	Skip
ת	תיאור	depiction	Exodus 37:25	135959	426
ר	רישא	beginning	Exodus 38:11	136657	-241
ע	עשרים	twenty	Exodus 38:12	136733	-172
מ	מתיו	Matthew	Exodus 38:15	136895	174
ת	תלאה	tribulation	Exodus 38:18	137069	93
ע	עידן	era	Exodus 38:18	137072	10
א	ארבע	four	Exodus 38:19	137085	1
ד	דור	generation	Exodus 38:20	137152	-168
ת	תשח	1948	Exodus 38:22	137236	-168
י	ישוע	Jesus	Exodus 38:24	137389	-3

31. 1948/Generation: (The) Tribulation Era (is) beginning (with the) generation (of) 1948, (a) depiction (by) Jesus (in) Matthew: 24. (One letter of the word "depiction" is hidden beyond the slide border.

Position	Letters
136344	ש ל מ ז ב ח מ כ ב ר מ ע ש ה ר ש ת נ ח ש ת ת ח ת כ ר כ ב ו מ ל מ ט ה ע ד ח צ י ו ו י צ ק א ר ב ע ט ב ע ת ב
136428	ש א ת ה ב ד י מ ע צ י ש ט י מ ו י צ פ א ת מ נ ח ש ת ו י ב א א ת ה ב ד י מ ב ט ב ע ת ע ל צ ל ע ת ה מ ז ב ח
136512	י ו ר נ ח ש ת ו א ת כ נ ו נ ח ש ת ב מ ר א ת ה צ ב א ת א ש ר צ ב א ו פ ת ח א ה ל מ ו ע ד ו י ע ש א ת ה ח צ
136596	א מ ה ע מ ו ד י ה מ ע ש ר י מ ו א ד נ י ה מ ע ש ר י מ נ ח ש ת ו ו י ה ע מ ו ד י מ ו ח ש ק י ה מ כ ס פ ו ל
136680	ה מ ה ע ש ר י מ נ ח ש ת ו ו י ה ע מ ו ד י מ ו ח ש ק י ה מ כ ס פ ו ל פ א ת י מ ק ל ע י מ ח מ ש י מ ב א מ ה ע
136764	ח ש ו ק י ה מ כ ס פ ו ל פ א ת ק ד מ ה מ ז ר ח ה ח מ ש י מ א מ ה ק ל ע י מ ח מ ש ע ש ר ה א מ ה א ל ה כ ת פ
136848	ת מ ז ה ו מ ז ה ל ש ע ר ה ח צ ר ק ל ע י מ ח מ ש ע ש ר ה א מ ה ע מ ד י ה מ ש ל ש ה ו א ד נ י ה מ ש ל ש ה כ
136932	מ נ ח ש ת ו ו י ה ע מ ו ד י מ ו ח ש ו ק י ה מ כ ס פ ו צ פ ו י ר א ש י ה מ כ ס פ ו ה מ ח ש ק י מ כ ס פ כ
137016	ו א ר ג מ נ ת ו ל ע ת ש נ י ו ש ש מ ש ז ר ו ע ש ר י מ א מ ה א ר כ ו ק ו מ ה ב ר ח ב ח מ ש א מ ו ת ל ע מ
137100	ע ה נ ח ש ת ו ו י ה מ כ ס פ ו צ פ ו י ר א ש י ה ו מ ח ש ק י ה מ כ ס פ ו כ ל ה י ת ד ת ל מ ש כ נ ו ל ח צ ר
137184	ר פ ק ד ע ל פ י מ ש ה ע ב ד ת ה ל ו י מ ב י ד א י ת מ ר ב נ א ה ר נ ה כ ה נ ו ב צ ל א ל ב נ א ו ר י ב נ ח
137268	ש ה ו א ת ו א ה ל י א ב ב נ א ח י ס מ כ ל מ ט ה ד נ ח ר ש ו ח ש ב ו ר ק מ ב ת כ ל ת ו ב א ר ג מ נ ו ב ת ו
137352	מ ל א כ ת ה ק ד ש ו י ה י ז ה ב ה ת נ ו פ ה ת ש ע ו ע ש ר י מ כ כ ר ו ש ב ע מ א ו ת ו ש ל ש י מ ש ק ל ב ש
137436	ב ע מ א ו ת ו ח מ ש ה ו ש ב ע י מ ש ק ל ב ש ק ל ה ק ד ש ב ק ע ל ג ל ג ל ת מ ח צ י ת ה ש ק ל ב ש ק ל ה ק ד
137520	ה ל ש ש מ א ו ת א ל פ ו ש ל ש ת א ל פ י מ ו ח מ ש מ א ו ת ו ח מ ש י מ ו י ה י מ א ת כ כ ר ה כ ס פ ל צ ק ת
137604	מ א ת ה כ כ ר כ כ ר ל א ד נ ו א ת ה א ל פ ו ש ב ע ה מ א ו ת ו ח מ ש ה ו ש ב ע י מ ע ש ה ו ו י מ ל ע מ ו ד
137688	ב ע י מ כ כ ר ו א ל פ י מ ו א ר ב ע מ א ו ת ש ק ל ו י ע ש ב ה א ת א ד נ י פ ת ח א ה ל מ ו ע ד ו א ת מ ז ב
137772	ה מ ז ב ח ו א ת א ד נ י ה ח צ ר ס ב י ב ו א ת א ד נ י ש ע ר ה ח צ ר ו א ת כ ל י ת ד ת ה מ ש כ נ ו א ת כ ל

Shape	Word	Translation	Verse	Position	Skip
hourglass (ש)	שנה	year	Exodus 38:15	136894	-253
shaded circle (ד)	דור	generation	Exodus 38:20	137152	-168
circle (ת)	תשח	1948	Exodus 38:22	137236	-168
diamond (ש)	שבעים	seventy	Exodus 38:24	137352	-12

32. 1948/Generation: (The) generation (of) 1948, (is) seventy year(s).

shift in the position of our planet's poles. Before it's all over, the earth may lose up to four billion people.

While writing this chapter, I searched in the Bible Code to see if I could locate the components of the above hypothesis. To develop the scenario I've outlined, I used prophecy in the Old and New Testaments, since to be accurate Code searches must make sense in terms of what is written in the Bible. Again, it should be noted that what I found are *only prospects for the future*, not prophecy. Only God knows what the ultimate outcome will be. If the world changes—if godliness replaces selfishness—perhaps only some, or none, of the events of the Tribulation will occur. Once again, the story of Jonah and Nineveh reminds us that this possibility exists.

Even the worst-case scenario does not indicate the complete destruction of the earth and all its inhabitants. There must be survivors who give birth to the new root race. The full-blown Tribulation will probably take the earth back to the year 1930 in terms of population, when there were about two billion people on our planet. During the Tribulation, it is likely that some countries will be more severely affected than others, but all will probably suffer serious consequences. Coastal regions and islands will endure terrible tidal waves. There will be no superpowers anymore; in fact, for some time all governments will be in total disarray. Though we will probably retain aspects of our technology, society will be severely disrupted for approximately 40 years. We will be growing our own food for a time, and likely saying goodbye to our modern conveniences. Just to survive, people will have to help each other.

The coming struggle will be one between good and evil. When it's all over, the forces of selfishness, greed and lust for power that cause war, pain and destruction will be absent from the earth for 1,000 years. We will then move into the promised Golden Age. As I have indicated in earlier Code searches, as we evolve into the fifth root race the earth will experience prosperity such as it has never experienced before. One positive aspect of the destruction will be that the earth will have the opportunity to heal itself for coming generations. Lands which were contaminated by nuclear, chemical, and other industrial wastes, will probably be deep under water for thousands of years. New lands will rise from the sea to ensure the ecological balance of the earth and maintain favorable weather. We'll have the freedom to choose in all things, even to choosing our own self-destruction, but only God can destroy the earth. And He isn't finished with it yet!

My first search focussing on the above scenario concerned a global economic collapse. The following slide **(Subject: Economic/ Crash)**, found in Numbers 4:8 to 4:15, shows the prospect for a world economic crash beginning in 2002 and/or 2005. This slide is very compact, and shows the same elements of accuracy that were found in the proven historical events of Chapter Two. I would say that it is time for us to start saving and investing wisely.

My next search concerned famine, since I thought famine might be the first sign of the beginning of the Tribulation. This slide **(Subject: Year/Famine)**, found in Genesis 14:16 to 15:18, revealed the prospects for the years of famine to be 2001 to 2012. Since the Tribulation is to be seven years in duration, I decided to back up seven years, from 2012 to 2005. This latter date coincides with the second date for economic collapse and the Tribulation date prospect found in the "Seal/Revealed" slide of the previous chapter.

The following search **(Subject: Tribulation/Time)**, found in Exodus 22:18 to 23:11, confirms that the prospect for the period during which the Tribulation will unfold is, according to John, from 2005 to 2012.[33] The slide that emerged was a compact one, exhibiting every sign of accuracy. Just to be sure, I decided to search the subject matter in another location in the Torah, this time linking it to the prophecy of Daniel. The following slide **(Subject: Tribulation/2005)**, found in Deuteronomy 20:10 to 21:14, confirmed the prospect for the Tribulation according to Daniel, beginning in 2005. This search also appears to be a very accurate one. Four out of six words searched have the same skip rate of 356! One of these searches is according to the Revelation to John, the other according to the prophet Daniel. I find the date hard to dispute. Since this date is so crucial in establishing the time frame

110420 ו ש כ ב ע מ ה מ ה ר י מ ה ר נ ה ל ו ל א ש ה א מ מ א נ י מ א נ א ב י ה ל

110483 ל א ת ח י ה כ ל ש כ ב ע מ ב ה מ ה מ ו ת י ו מ ת ז ב ח ל א ל ה י מ י ח ר

110546 ל ח צ נ ו כ י ג ר י מ ה י י ת מ ב א ר צ מ צ ר י מ כ ל א ל מ נ ה ו י ת ו

110609 י צ ע ק א ל י ש מ ע א ש מ ע צ ע ק ת ו ו ח ר ה א פ י ו ה ר ג ת י א ת כ מ

110672 מ י מ א מ כ ס פ ת ל ו ה א ת ע מ י א ת ה ע נ י ע מ כ ל א ת ה י ה ל ו כ נ

110735 ל מ ת ר ע כ ע ד ב א ה ש מ ש ת ש י ב נ ו ל ו כ י ה ו א כ ס ו ת ה ל ב ד ה

110798 ע ק א ל י ו ש מ ע ת י כ י ח נ ו נ א נ י א ל ה י מ ל א ת ק ל ל ו נ ש י א

110861 ו ר ב נ י כ ת ת נ ל י כ נ ת ע ש ה ל ש ר כ ל צ א נ כ ש ב ע ת י מ י מ י ה

110924 י ק ד ש ת ה י ו נ ל י ו ב ש ר ב ש ד ה ט ר פ ה ל א ת א ל כ ו ל כ ל ב ת ש

110987 מ ר ש ע ל ה י ת ע ד ח מ ס ל א ת ה י ה א ח ר י ר ב י מ ל ר ע ת ו ל א ת ע

111050 ת ה ד ר ב ר י ב ו כ י ת פ ג ע ש ו ר א י ב כ ו א ח מ ר ו ת ע ה ה ש ב ת ש

111113 ש א ו ו ח ד ל ת מ ע ז ב ל ו ע ז ב ת ע ז ב ע מ ו ל א ת ט ה מ ש פ ט א ב י

111176 א ל ת ה ר ג כ י ל א א צ ד י ק ר ש ע ו ש ח ד ל א ת ק ח כ י ה ש ח ד י ע ו

111239 ל ח צ ו א ת מ י ד ע ת מ א ת נ פ ש ה ג ר כ י ג ר י מ ה י י ת מ ב א ר צ מ

111302 ת ת ב ו א ת ה ו ה ש ב י ע ת ת ש מ ט נ ה ו נ ט ש ת ה ו א כ ל ו א ב י נ י

111365 ר מ כ ל ז י ת כ ש ש ת י מ י מ ת ע ש ה מ ע ש י כ ו ב י ו מ ה ש ב י ע י ת

111428 א מ ת כ ו ה ג ר ו ב כ ל א ש ר א מ ר ת י א ל י כ מ ת ש מ ר ו ו ש מ א ל ה

111491 ל ש ר ג ל י מ ת ח ג ל י ב ש נ ה א ת ח ג ה מ צ ו ת ת ש מ ר ש ב ע ת י מ י

111554 א ב י ב כ י ב ו י צ א ת מ מ צ ר י מ ו ל א י ר א ו פ נ י ר י ק מ ו ח ג ה

111617 ג ה א ס פ ב צ א ת ה ש נ ה ב א ס פ כ א ת מ ע ש י כ מ נ ה ש ד ה ש ל ש פ ע

111680 י ה ו ה ל א ת ז ב ח ע ל ח מ צ ד מ ז ב ח י ו ל א י ל י נ ח ל ב ח ג י ע ד

111743 ו ה א ל ה י כ ל א ת ב ש ל ג ד י ב ח ל ב א מ ו ה נ ה א נ כ י ש ל ח מ ל א

111806 ו מ א ש ר ה כ נ ת י ה ש מ ר מ פ נ י ו ו ש מ ע ב ק ל ו א ל ת מ ר ב ו כ י

111869 ו ע ת ש מ ע ב ק ל ו ו ע ש י ת כ ל א ש ר א ד ב ר ו א י ב ת י א ת א י ב י

111932 כ ו ה ב י א כ א ל ה א מ ר י ו ה ח ת י ו ה פ ר ז י ו ה כ נ ע נ י ה ח ו י

111995 י ה מ ו ל א ת ע ב ד מ ו ל א ת ע ש ה כ מ ע ש י ה מ כ י ה ר ס ת ה ר ס מ ו

Shape	Word	Translation	Verse	Position	Skip
ת	תשעב	2012	Exodus 22:18	110496	-126
ז	זמן	time	Exodus 22:19	110507	189
ע	עד ש	till	Exodus 22:25	110748	-193
ת	תלאה	tribulation	Exodus 22:26	110759	-189
ל	לפי	according	Exodus 22:29	110878	67
ג	גון	John	Exodus 22:29	110885	-188
ת	תשסה	2005	Exodus 23:2	111002	315
נ	נוף	prospect	Exodus 23:11	111323	249

33. Tribulation/Time: Prospect (for the) tribulation time according (to) John, 2005 till 2012.

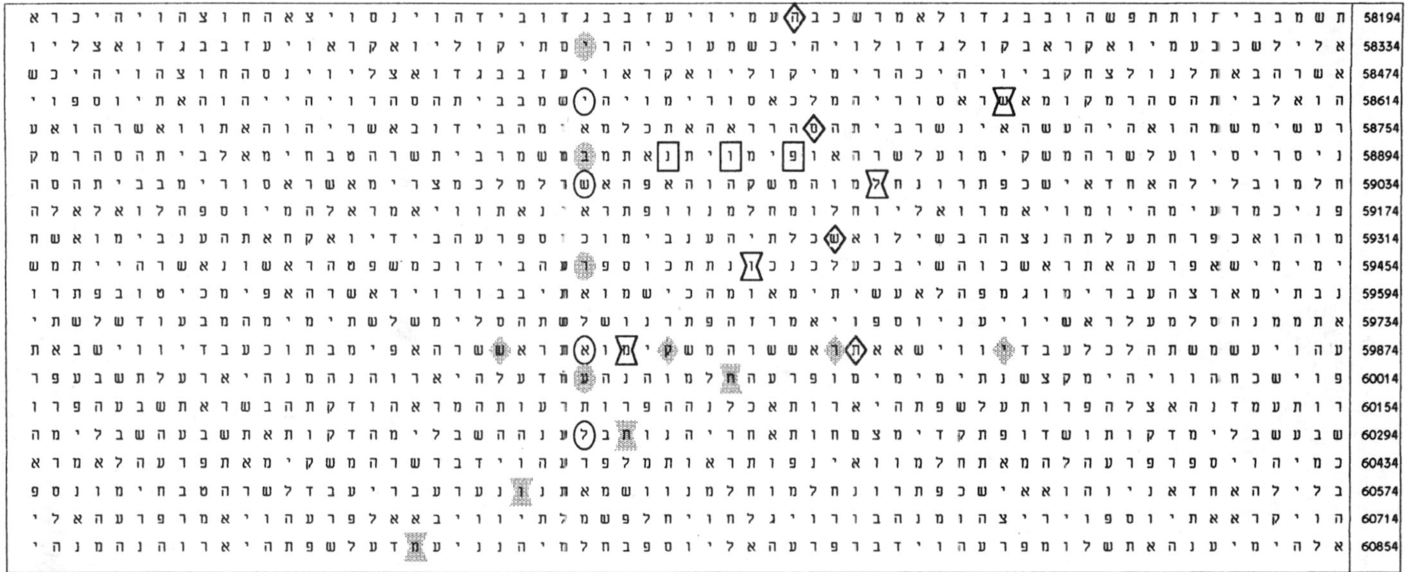

Shape	Word	Translation	Verse	Position	Skip
ת	תשסה	2005	Genesis 39:12	58220	-559
ע	ערבי	Arab	Genesis 39:15	58370	-560
ש	שלום	peace	Genesis 39:20	58630	426
י	ישראל	Israel	Genesis 39:20	58650	420
נ	נוף	prospect	Genesis 40:2	58920	-3
ש	שקרי	false	Genesis 40:20	59890	-8
ח	חתום	sealed	Genesis 41:1	60043	285

34. Arab/Israel: Prospect (that a) false Arab/Israel peace sealed (in) 2005.

for the Tribulation scenario, I decided to look for it in yet another part of the Torah. This search **(Subject: Tribulation/Era)**, found in Leviticus 14:6 to 14:37, again confirms the prospect for the Tribulation era as beginning in 2005.

The reason I had a hard time with the Tribulation period dating is that the years 1995 to 2002 also appeared in most of these searches. Additionally, Edgar Cayce predicted that pole shifts would occur from about 2000 to 2001. Nostradamus as well predicted that "the great king of terror would fall from the sky" in 1999. The confusion was finally resolved by the following two searches. The next slide **(Subject: 1995/2002)**, found in Deuteronomy 17:2 to 18:5, revealed that the prospect for the occurrence of the Tribulation from 1995 to 2002 was delayed till 2005 to 2012 by the grace of God. I wondered why. The next slide provided an answer: **(Subject: Tribulation/Delay)**, found in Numbers 21:11 to 30:16, reveals that God has given a Tribulation delay to the world because of the turnabout in the U.S.S.R. in 1991. So we can thank the Soviet Union for ten extra years, a priceless opportunity for us to wake up and get our act together and perhaps minimize the effects of the greatest calamity ever to strike the earth.

If the collective will of mankind truly resolves to change, the Tribulation could be much less severe. It could even be delayed until 2011 to 2018. It would still fall within the time span that began with the 1948 generation. Will we exercise that will and change? I pray we do!

According to the Revelation, Israel will be in a limited conflict early on, since a false peace is to be signed at the beginning of the Tribulation period. My next search **(Subject: Arab/Israel)**, found in Genesis 46:31 to 49:7, revealed the prospect of an Arab/Israeli regional armed struggle beginning 2001 or 2002. Significantly, letters in the words "beginning" and "2002" touched.

I next decided to search for a false peace agreement. The following slide **(Subject: Arab/Israel)**, found in Genesis 39:12 to 41:1, revealed the prospect of a false Arab/Israel peace sealed in 2005.[34]

At the time of this writing, Ehud Barak has just lost his bid for reelection as Prime Minister of Israel to Ariel Sharon. The Palestinian/Israeli peace talks are currently stalled, and there is frequent chaos on the streets of Israel. It appears that rebuilding Solomon's temple (destroyed by the Romans in 70 A.D.) may be a high priority of the new government of Israel. The current breakdown of order in Israel began when then-Defense Minister Sharon visited the Temple Mount in 2000.

Since resolving the temple problem seemed to be crucial for peace in Israel, I decided to do a Code search on this subject. According to Hebrew religious tradition, the Temple of Israel must be rebuilt on the Temple Mount of Jerusalem. Two Islamic holy structures currently stand there, the Dome of the Rock and the Al Aqsa Mosque. But there is still space for the temple between them, just above the Wailing Wall. The Revelation to John in Chapter 11: 1-2 states, "And there was given me a reed like unto a rod, and the angel stood saying, rise and measure the temple of God, and the altar and them that worship therein. But the court that is without the temple, leave out and measure it not, for it is given unto the Gentiles." Jesus, in the Revelation to John, prophesied hundreds of years before Islam that Islam would claim these sites and that they were not to be disturbed. In other words, Israel is told to share the Temple Mount.

The following slide (**Subject: Temple/Mount**), found in Numbers 2:1 to 3:10, advises that the Temple Mount of Salem (the old name for Jerusalem) is a test for both Israel and the Arabs, that "all shall share or all shall perish." You can't get much clearer than that. If this problem is not resolved, then war is certain and there will be no winners. According to my next search, there appears to be a good prospect that the temple will be rebuilt. This may mean that some kind of accommodation will be reached between Israel and the Palestinians regarding the Temple Mount.

The next slide (**Subject: Temple/Israel**), found in Genesis 46:4 to 47:31, indicates the prospect for rebuilding the Temple of Israel for completion in or by the year 2006. The skip rates of the words "temple" and "year" are very close, and a letter of the word "completion" shares a letter with "2006." This underlines the accuracy of the search.

If the Arabs and Israelis share the land of Israel and the Temple Mount of Jerusalem, then the severity of the prospective earth changes can probably be minimized. However, I am, as I mentioned earlier, too much of a realist to expect this. Unfortunately for the Arabs and Israelis and for the rest of the world, peace in Israel will probably not come about until after the Tribulation—if there is anything left. Too much selfishness and hatred exist in the Middle East. This is ironic because, according to the Law of Cause and Effect, the combatants may be killing their own reborn fathers and grandfathers instead of avenging them. Their enemies may be the souls of members of their own families, who have returned to experience and learn what it's like to be on the other side.

A desecration of the new temple in Israel is expected to occur soon after the temple is rebuilt. In searching for this, I got into something completely unexpected. I found the desecration of a temple in 2006, but I also found that neither Israel nor Jerusalem fitted accurately into the search. Rome suddenly came to mind—and it fit the subject of the slide perfectly. It appears that all of the religious problems may not be in the Middle East alone.

The following slide (**Subject: Anathema/Despair**), found in Genesis 18:8 to 19:25, describes the prospect that a priest, bringing anathema and despair, and serving the false prophet, is the desecrater of God's Temple of Rome during the time of 2006.

I decided to search further for the desecration of the Temple of Israel. The following slide (**Subject: Jerusalem/2008**), found in Exodus 35:22 to 36:29, reveals the prospect for blasphemy in God's Temple of Jerusalem, an abomination by Satan in 2008.[35]

The Revelation indicates that after the false peace treaty is signed and broken a full-blown world war will develop. The breaking of the treaty will occur at the "half-time"—three-and-one-half years after the beginning of the Tribulation. World War Three will probably be an Arab/Asian alliance against the United Nations. If the U.N. alliance faces opposition forces that are 200 million strong, as predicted in Revelation, it is obvious that nuclear weapons will be used.

ת ו ע ש ה ב צ ל א ל ו א ה ל י א ב ו כ ל א י ש ח כ מ ל ב א ש ר נ ת נ י ה ו ה ח כ מ ה	132672
ב ד ת ה ק ד ש ל כ ל א ש ר צ ו ה י ה ו ה ו י ק ר א מ ש ה א ל ב צ ל א ל ו א ל א ה ל י	132742
ה ב ל ב ו כ ל א ש ר נ ש א ו ל ב ו ל ק ר ב ה א ל ה מ ל א כ ה ל ע ש ת א ת ה ו י ק ח ו	132812
י י ש ר א ל ל מ ל א כ ת ע ב ד ת ה ק ד ש ל ע ש ת א ת ה ו ה מ ה ב י א ו א ל י ו ע ו ד	132882
י מ א ת כ ל מ ל א כ ת ה ק ד ש א י ש א י ש מ מ ל א כ ת ו א ש ר ה מ ה ע ש י מ ו י א מ	132952
ע ב ד ה ל מ ל א כ ה א ש ר צ ו ה י ה ו ה ל ע ש ת א ת ה ו י צ ו מ ש ה ו י ע ב י ר ו ק	133022
ל א כ ה ל ת ר ו מ ת ה ק ד ש ו י כ ל א ה ע מ מ ה ב י א ו ה מ ל א כ ה ה י ת ה ד י מ ל	133092
ח כ מ ל ב ב ע ש י ה מ ל א כ ה א ת ה מ ש כ נ ע ש ר י ר י ע ת ש ש מ ש ז ר ו ת כ ל ת ו	133162
ה א ת מ א ר כ ה י ר י ע ה ה א ח ת ש מ נ ה ו ע ש ר י מ ב א מ ה ו ר ח ב א ר ב ע ב א מ	133232
ח ב ר א ת ח מ ש ה י ר י ע ת א ח ת א ל א ח ת ו ח מ ש י ר י ע ת ח ב ר א ח ת א ל א ח ת	133302
ק צ ה ב מ ח ב ר ת כ נ ע ש ה ב ש פ ת ה י ר י ע ה ה ק י צ ו נ ה ב מ ח ב ר ת ה ש נ י ת	133372
ל ל א ת ע ש ה ב ק צ ה ה י ר י ע ה א ש ר ב מ ח ב ר ת ה ש נ י ת מ ק ב י ל ת ה ל ל א ת	133442
ר א ת ה י ר י ע ת א ח ת א ל א ח ת ב ק ר ס י מ ו י ה י ה מ ש כ נ א ח ד ו י ע ש י ר י	133512
ע ת ע ש ה א ת מ א ר כ ה י ר י ע ה ה א ח ת ש ל ש י מ ב א מ ה ו א ר ב ע א מ ו ת ר ח ב	133582
ע ת ו י ח ב ר א ת ח מ ש ה י ר י ע ת ל ב ד ו א ת ש ש ה י ר י ע ת ל ב ד ו י ע ש ל ל א	133652
ת ו ח מ ש י מ ל ל א ת ע ש ה ע ל ש פ ת ה י ר י ע ה ה ח ב ר ת ה ש נ י ת ו י ע ש ק ר ס	133722
י ע ש מ כ ס ה ל א ה ל ע ר ת א י ל מ מ א ד מ י מ ו מ כ ס ה ע ר ת ת ח ש י מ מ ל מ ע ל	133792
י מ ע ש ר א מ ת א ר כ ה ק ר ש ו א מ ה ו ח צ י ה א מ ה ר ח ב ה ק ר ש ה א ח ד ש ת י י	133862
ל כ ל ק ר ש י ה מ ש כ נ ו י ע ש א ת ה ק ר ש י מ ל מ ש כ נ ע ש ר י מ ק ר ש י מ ל פ א	133932
ת ע ש ר י מ ה ק ר ש י מ ש נ י א ד ● י מ ת ח ת ה ק ר ש ה א ח ד ל ש ת י י ד ת י ו ו ש	134002
ל צ ל ע ה מ ש כ נ ה ש נ י ת ל פ א ת צ פ ו נ ע ש ה ע ש ר י מ ק ר ש י מ ו א ר ב ע י מ	134072
ו ש נ י א ד נ י מ ת ח ת ה ק ר ש ה א ח ד ● ל י ר כ ת י ה מ ש כ נ י מ ח ע ש ח ש ש ה ק	134142
י ר כ ת י מ ו ה י ו ת ו א מ מ מ ל מ ט ה ו י ח ד ו י ה י ו ת מ י מ א ל ר א ש ו א ל ה	134212
ת ו ה י ו ש מ נ ה ק ר ש י מ ו א ד נ י ה מ כ ס ● ש ש ה ע ש ר א ד נ י מ ש נ י א ד נ י	134282
י ע צ י ש ט י מ ח מ ש ה ל ק ר ש י צ ל ע ה מ ש כ נ ה א ח ת ו ח מ ש ה ב ר י ח מ ל ק ר	134352
ש י ה מ ש כ נ ל י ר כ ת י מ י מ ה ו י ע ש א ת ה ב ר י ח ה ת י כ נ ל ב ר ח ב ת ו כ ה	134422
ה ז ה ב ו א ת ט ב ע ת מ ע ש ה ז ה ב ב ת י מ ל ב ר י ח מ ו י צ פ א ת ה ב ר י ח מ ז ה	134492
ש נ י ו ש ש מ ש ז ר מ ע ש ה ח ש ב ע ש ה א ת ה כ ר ב י מ ו י ע ש ל ה א ר ב ע ה ע מ ו	134562
מ א ר ב ע ה א ד נ י כ ס פ ו י ע ש מ ס כ ל פ ת ח ה א ה ל ת כ ל ת ו א ר ג מ נ ו ת ו ל	134632
ח מ ש ה ו א ת ו ו י ה מ ו צ פ ה ר א ש י ה מ ו ח ש ק י ה מ ז ה ב ו א ד נ י ה מ ח מ ש	134702
מ ת י מ ו ח צ י א ר כ ו ו א מ ה ו ח צ י ר ח ב ו ו א מ ה ו ח צ י ק מ ת ו ו י צ פ ה ו	134772
ב י ב ו י צ ק ל ו א ר ב ע ט ב ע ת ז ה ב ע ל א ר ב ע פ ע מ ת י ו ו ש ת י ט ב ע ת ע ל	134842
י ע ש ב ד י ע צ י ש ט י מ ו י צ פ א ת מ ז ה ב ו י ב א א ת ה ב ד י מ ב ט ב ע ת ע ל צ	134912
ט ה ו ר א מ ת י מ ו ח צ י א ר כ ה ו א מ ה ו ח צ י ר ח ב ה ו י ע ש ש נ י כ ר ב י מ ז	134982
ב א ח ד מ ק צ ה מ ז ה ו כ ר ו ב א ח ד מ ק צ ה מ ז ה מ נ ה כ פ ר ת ע ש ה א ת ה כ ר ב	135052

Shape	Word	Translation	Verse	Position	Skip
◇ נ	ניאוץ	blasphemy	Exodus 35:22	131913	773
□ ר	רקה	temple	Exodus 36:12	133461	69
● י	ירשלם	Jerusalem	Exodus 36:13	133533	210
⧗ א	אלוה	God	Exodus 36:19	133820	-416
●	נוף	prospect	Exodus 36:24	134019	143
○ ת	תשסח	2008	Exodus 36:29	134234	-70

35. Jerusalem/2008: Prospect (for) blasphemy (in) God('s) Temple (of) Jerusalem (in) 2008. (One letter of the word "blasphemy" is hidden beyond the slide border.)

The second beast of the Tribulation, described in Revelation 13, has seven heads and ten horns with ten crowns. One head has a mortal wound that was healed. This beast's power was sustained for the next three-and-one-half years, so he should be exposed to the world by the middle of 2008, assuming that the Tribulation starts in 2005. The following slide (**Subject: Arab/Seven**), found in Genesis 16:9 to 18:18, advises us that the beast revealed to John is the head of an alliance of seven Arab kings and three kings of Asia.[36] His healed mortal head wound signifies death and resurrection. At this time, the alliance leader will likely become Satan incarnated, probably in the spring of 2008.

The next slide (**Subject: Arabic/Asia**), found in Deuteronomy 32:10 to 32:28, reveals that an Arabic/Asia military alliance is expected to be established in 2006.

The following slide (**Subject: Third/War**), found in Exodus 5:10 to 6:12, confirms that in the Third World War the prospect is that great weapons of death will be employed, including hydrogen bombs.[37] Remember that the Arab/Asian alliance has 200 million troops! The next slide on the same theme (**Subject: Third/War**), found in Deuteronomy 29:4 to 30:8, reveals the prospect of a third world war to begin in 2010, the Arabian Alliance/United Nations and NATO. I did the same search in a different location of the Torah; (**Subject: United/Nations**), found in Genesis 17:12 to 18:26, revealed a probable armed world struggle in 2010, United Nations/ Arab-Asia Alliance.

As previously discussed, John is shown the contents of seven bowls that are cast down upon the earth, these contents representing the contents of the holocausts that break out during the latter part of the Tribulation. I decided to see if I could link this revelation to dates I was getting with regard to World War Three. The following slide (**Subject: Seven Bowls**), found in Exodus 8:2 to 8:22, confirmed that the seven bowls of the Tribulation revealed the prospect of holocaust after world armed struggle beginning in 2010 to 2012.

The Tribulation hypothesis stated earlier set forth the idea that it would take natural disasters of gigantic proportions to stop the

Shape	Word	Translation	Verse	Position	Skip
	גון	John	Genesis 16:9	18760	396
	ברית	alliance	Genesis 17:2	19174	627
	שבעה	seven	Genesis 17:19	20013	-418
	מלך	king	Genesis 17:26	20426	631
	ערבי	Arab	Genesis 17:26	20431	209
	חיה	beast	Genesis 18:4	20641	417
	ראש	head	Genesis 18:8	20851	1
	שלוש	three	Genesis 18:8	20856	-419
	אסיה	Asia	Genesis 18:12	21064	191
	גלוי	revealed	Genesis 18:18	21289	188

36. Arab/Seven; (The) beast revealed (to) John (is the) head (of an) alliance (of) seven Arab (region) king(s) (and) three king(s) (of) Asia. (One letter of the word "revealed" is hidden beyond the slide border.)

Letters	Position
מ ו ש ט ר י ו ר י ו י א מ ר ו א ל ה ע מ ל א מ ר כ ה א מ ר פ ר ע ה א י נ נ י	84072
ש י מ א צ י מ ל א מ ר כ ל ו מ ע ש י כ מ ד ב ר י ו מ ב י ו מ ו כ א ש ר ב	84192
ו מ ו י ב א ו ש ט ר י ב נ י י ש ר א ל ו י צ ע ק ו א ל פ ר ע ה ל א מ ר ל	84312
מ ע ל כ נ א ת מ א מ ר י מ נ ל כ ה נ ז ב ח ה ל י ה ו ה ו ע ת ה ל כ ו ע ב	84432
ע ו א ת מ ש ה ו א ת א ה ר נ נ צ ב י מ ל ק ר א ת מ ב צ א ת מ מ א ת פ ר ע	84552
מ ש ה א ל י ה ו ה ו י א מ ר א ד נ י ל מ ה ה ר ע ת ה ל ע מ ה ז ה ל מ ה ז	84672
ע ה כ י ב י ד ח ז ק ה י ש ל ח מ ו ב י ד ח ז ק ה י ג ר ש מ מ א ר צ ו ו י	84792
ת י א ת ב ר י ת י א ת מ ל ת ת ל ה מ א ת א ר צ כ נ ע נ א ת א ר צ מ ג ר י	84912
ו ה ו ה ו צ א ת י א ת כ מ מ ת ח ת ס ב ל ת מ צ ר י מ ו ה צ ל ת י א ת כ מ	85032
ל ה י כ מ ה מ ו צ י א א ת כ מ מ ת ח ת ס ב ל ו ת מ צ ר י מ ו ה ב א ת י א	85152
ש ר א ל ו ל א ש מ ע ו א ל מ ש ה מ ק צ ר ר ו ח ו מ ע ב ד ה ק ש ה ו י ד ב	85272
א ש מ ע ו א ל י ו א י כ י ש מ ע נ י פ ר ע ה ו א נ י ע ר ל ש פ ת י מ ו י	85392
א ב ת מ ב נ י ר א ו ב נ ב כ ר י ש ר א ל ח נ ו כ ו פ ל ו א ח צ ר נ ו כ ר	85512
י ל ו י ל ת ל ד ת מ ג ר ש ו נ ו ק ה ת ו מ ר י ו ש נ י ח י י ל ו י ש ב	85632
מ ו מ א ת ש נ ה ו ב נ י מ ר ר י מ ח ל י ו מ ו ש י א ל ה מ ש פ ח ת ה ל ו	85752
ר ק ר ח ו נ פ ג ו ז כ ר י ו ב נ י ע ז י א ל מ י ש א ל ו א ל צ פ נ ו ס ת	85872
ס י ר ו א ל ק נ ה ו א ב י א ס פ א ל ה מ ש פ ח ת ה ק ר ח י ו א ל ע ז ר ב	85992
ל ה מ ה ו צ י א ו א ת ב נ י י ש ר א ל מ א ר צ מ צ ר י מ ע ל צ ב א ת מ ה	86112
ו י ד ב ר י ה ו ה א ל מ ש ה ל א מ ר א נ י י ה ו ה ד ב ר א ל פ ר ע ה מ ל	86232
נ ת ת י כ א ל ה י מ ל פ ר ע ה ו א ה ר נ א ח י כ י ה י ה נ ב י א כ א ת ה	86352
ת מ ו פ ת י ב א ר צ מ צ ר י מ ו ל א י ש מ ע א ל כ מ פ ר ע ה ו נ ת ת י א	86472
ד י ע ל מ צ ר י מ ו ה ו צ א ת י א ת ב נ י י ש ר א ל מ ת ו כ מ ו י ע ש מ	86592

Shape	Word	Translation	Verse	Position	Skip
ר	רב	great	Exodus 5:10	84093	358
נ	נוף	prospect	Exodus 5:10	84105	117
ש	שליש	third	Exodus 5:15	84327	600
מ	מיתה	death	Exodus 5:17	84439	238
מ	מלחמה	war	Exodus 6:1	84807	120
נ	נשק	weapon	Exodus 6:1	84814	-472
ה	הכלה	inclusion	Exodus 6:6	85035	8
מ	מימן	hydrogen	Exodus 6:6	85044	360
פ	פצצה	bomb	Exodus 6:8	85182	-360
ש	שכיר	employed	Exodus 6:9	85273	-131
ע	עולם	world	Exodus 6:12	85418	356

37. Third/War: Third World War, prospect (of) great weapons (of) death employed (with the) inclusion (of) hydrogen bomb(s)

world from being destroyed by World War Three. With most high-tech weaponry dependent upon satellites and computers for accuracy, it would be necessary to render such facilitating hardware useless in order to stop the War. This could be brought about by a pole shift that caused a reversal of the world's magnetic pole. The magnitude of the resulting magnetic pulse would probably render most electronic equipment on earth inoperative, including automobiles. Asteroids of sufficient mass, striking the earth, could trigger off the pole shifts. The Revelation describes stars falling from the sky and the moon becoming black. A pole shift might give such an impression.

Catastrophic earthquakes, storms, floods, water the color of blood, a third of all fish dying, and the moon turning red, as described in the Revelation, could also be the after-effects of asteroid strikes. The results would render any war machine useless. The entire planet would be in total disarray. The first priority of governments still functioning would be civilian rescue operations.

Could asteroids be one of the secrets of the seven bowls of the Tribulation? I decided to check this out in the Code. My next search was to determine if it is the results of asteroid strikes that are being described in the Revelation of Saint John. The following slide (**Subject: Asteroid/Cause**), found in Exodus 10:29 to 12:28, confirms the prospect that asteroid strikes will cause three world axis shifts, commencing in 2010.[38]

My next concern was how many strikes might occur and where the impacts might take place. The following slide (**Subject: Asteroid/World**), found in Genesis 20:2 to 21:2, reveals the prospect that seven asteroids strike the world, beginning in 2010 and lasting until 2012.

My next search confirmed a previous slide with regard to the first pole shift, but also revealed the magnitude and direction of the shift: (**Subject: Pole/Shift**), found in Exodus 29:9 to 31:2, reveals the prospect that the beginning pole shift in 2010 is five degrees rotary measure southwest. My next search on this subject (**Subject: Pole/Shift**), found in Leviticus 8:25 to 9:21, reveals that the third and final world pole shift is expected in 2012.[39] Since this

י כ י ב י ו מ ר א ת כ פ נ י ת מ ו ת ו י א מ ר מ ש ה כ נ ד ב ר ת ל א א ס פ ע ו ד ר א ו ת פ נ י כ ו י א מ ר י ה ו ה א ל מ ש ה ע ו ד נ	93269
י ש מ ש ה ג ד ו ל מ א ד ב א ר צ מ צ ר י מ ב ע י נ י ע ב ד י פ ר ע ה ו ב ע י נ י ה ע מ ו י א מ ר מ ש ה כ ה א מ ר י ה ו ה כ ח צ ת ה ל	93480
ש ר א ל א י ח ר צ כ ל ב ל ש נ ו ל מ א י ש ו ע ד ב ה מ ה ל מ ע נ ת ד ע ו נ א ש ר י פ ל ה י ה ו ה ב י נ מ צ ר י מ ו ב י נ י ש ר א ל	93691
ה מ פ ת י מ ה א ל ה ל פ נ י פ ר ע ה ו י ח ז ק י ה ו ה א ת ל ב פ ר ע ה ו ל א ש ל ח א ת ב נ י י ש ר א ל מ א ר צ ו ו י א מ ר י ה ו ה א	93902
ו ש כ נ ו ה ק ר ב א ל ב י ת ו ב מ כ ס ת נ פ ש ת א י ש ל פ י א כ ל ו ת כ ס ו ע ל ה ש ה ש ה ת מ י מ ז כ ר ב נ ש נ ה י ה י ה ל כ מ מ נ	94113
ב ש ר ב ל י ל ה ה ז ה צ ל י א ש ו מ צ ו ת ע ל מ ר ר י מ י א כ ל ה ו א ל ת א כ ל ו מ מ נ ו נ א ו ב ש ל מ ב ש ל מ ב מ י מ כ י א מ צ ל י	94324
ר י מ ב ל י ל ה ה ז ה ו ה כ י ת י כ ל ב כ ו ר ב א ר צ מ צ ר י מ מ א ד מ ו ע ד ב ה מ ה ו ב כ ל א ל ה י מ צ ר י מ א ע ש ה ש פ ט י מ א	94535
ת י מ י מ מ צ ו ת ת א כ ל ו א כ ב י ו מ ה ר א ש ו נ ת ש ב י ת ו ש א ר מ ב ת י כ מ כ י כ ל א כ ל ח מ צ ו נ כ ר ת ה ה נ פ ש ה ה ו א מ	94746
ת צ ב א ו ת י כ מ מ א ר צ מ צ ר י מ ו ש מ ר ת מ א ת ה י ו מ ה ז ה ל ד ר ת י כ מ ח ק ת ע ו ל מ ב ר א ש נ ב א ר ב ע ה ע ש ר י ו מ ל ח	94957
ר א מ ש ה ל כ ל ז ק נ י י ש ר א ל ו י א מ ר א ל ה מ מ ש כ ו ו ק ח ו ל כ מ צ א נ ל מ ש פ ח ת י כ מ ו ש ח ט ו ה פ ס ח ו ל ק ח ת מ א ג	95168
ח ו ל א י ת נ ה מ ש ח י ת ל ב א א ל ב ת י כ מ ל נ ג פ ו ש מ ר ת מ א ת ה ד ב ר ה ז ה ל ח ק ל כ ו ל ב נ י כ ע ד ע ו ל מ ו ה י ה כ י ת	95379
ו ה צ י ל ו י ק ד ה ע מ ו י ש ת ח ו ו י ל כ ו ו י ע ש ו ב נ י י ש ר א ל כ א ש ר צ ו ה י ה ו ה א ת מ ש ה ו א ה ר נ כ נ ע ש ו ו י ה	95590
נ ש מ מ ת ו י ק ר א ל מ ש ה ו ל א ה ר נ ל י ל ה ו י א מ ר ק ו מ ו צ א ו מ ת ו כ ע מ י ג מ א ת מ ג מ ב נ י י ש ר א ל ו ל כ ו ע ב ד ו	95801
ר א ל ע ש ו כ ד ב ר מ ש ה ו י ש א ל ו מ מ צ ר י מ כ ל י כ ס פ ו כ ל י ז ה ב ו ש מ ל ת ו י ה ו ה נ ת נ א ת ח נ ה ע מ ב ע י נ י מ צ ר	96012
ג ר ש ו מ מ צ ר י מ ו ל א י כ ל ו ל ה ת מ ה מ ה ו ג מ צ ד ה ל א ע ש ו ל ה מ ו מ ו ש ב ב נ י י ש ר א ל א ש ר י ש ב ו ב מ צ ר י מ ש ל	96223
ר א ל ל ד ר ת מ ו י א מ ר י ה ו ה א ל מ ש ה ו א ה ר נ ז א ת ח ק ת ה פ ס ח כ ל ב נ נ כ ר ל א י א כ ל ב ו ו כ ל ע ב ד א י ש מ ק נ ת כ	96434
ו ו ה י ה כ א ז ר ח ה א ר צ ו כ ל ע ר ל ל א י א כ ל ב ו ת ו ר ה א ח ת י ה י ה ל א ז ר ח ו ל ג ר ה ג ר ב ת ו כ כ מ ו י ע ש ו כ ל ב נ	96645
ו י א מ ר מ ש ה א ל ה ע מ ז כ ו ר א ת ה י ו מ ה ז ה א ש ר י צ א ת מ מ מ צ ר י מ מ ב י ת ע ב ד י מ כ י ב ח ז ק י ד ה ו צ י א י ה ו ה	96856

Shape	Word	Translation	Verse	Position	Skip
נ	נוף	prospect	Exodus 10:29	93305	-209
ת	תשע	2010	Exodus 11:3	93502	-637
מ	מכה	strike	Exodus 11:3	93522	622
ע	עולם	world	Exodus 11:7	93726	638
כ	כוכבית	asteroid	Exodus 11:10	93930	-422
צ	ציר	axis	Exodus 11:10	93934	-204
ש	שלוש	three	Exodus 12:15	94773	418
ר	רישא	beginning	Exodus 12:15	94779	-628
ג	גורם	cause	Exodus 12:15	94786	-206
ה	הזזה	shift	Exodus 12:28	95633	414

38. Asteriod/Cause: Prospect (that) asteroid strike(s) cause three world axis shift(s) beginning (in) 2010.

year had been shown as the prospect for the end of the Tribulation, I assume the world will then be in the proper position for the start of the Golden Age of 1,000 years, as discussed in Revelation.

I was still wondering if it might be possible to find out where these asteroids would strike. I first checked out the United States. The first slide (**Subject: Asteroid/U.S.**), found in Exodus 5:22 to 9:16, uncovers the prospect that one asteroid struck the U.S. in 2010 in Utah, western Nevada, and California. I added the words "three pieces" to this search after I did the next search. The following slide (**Subject: Asteroid/Nevada**), found in Numbers 24:12 to 25:5, reveals the prospect that in 2010 a piece of an asteroid struck western Nevada, resulting in a western U.S.A. earthquake holocaust. This puzzled me for awhile, as I had originally found three strike locations and only one asteroid. Then it occurred to me that one of the asteroids might have broken up into smaller pieces before impacting the earth. Since Nevada, Utah and California are close together, it made some sense that these strikes might be three pieces of the same asteroid.

In *The Bible Code,* Michael Drosnin recounts the following story:

"There is an ancient tale, told in the Talmud, of a king who became angry with his son, and swore that he would hurl a massive stone at him. Later, he regretted it, but could not go back on his oath. So he ordered that the stone be broken up into small pebbles and that each of these be thrown, one by one, at his son." In this way, the king kept his kingly word and spared his beloved son.

Author Drosnin is telling this story in connection with the comet Shoemaker-Levy, which, impacting the planet Jupiter in 1994, caused incredible damage—but far less than it would have if it had not crumbled into 20 separate pieces before striking the surface of the planet (he says that the Bible Code foretold this encounter).

I was reminded of Drosnin's story from the Talmud when my Bible Code search suggested to me that the asteroid striking the earth would be broken into several pieces. Perhaps, the more godly we become, the smaller the asteroid pieces will be.

In *Notes from the Cosmos*, Gordon Michael Scallion describes an out-of-body-experience during which he witnesses a future near-

Shape	Word	Translation	Verse	Position	Skip
ש	שלישי	third	Leviticus 8:25	152215	482
ס	סוף	ending	Leviticus 9:7	153267	-283
ע	עולם	world	Leviticus 9:7	153279	-273
ק	קוטב	pole	Leviticus 9:9	153354	-98
ה	הזזה	shift	Leviticus 9:10	153455	91
ת	תשעב	2012	Leviticus 9:15	153645	-8
צ	צפוי	expected	Leviticus 9:21	153958	-89

39. Pole/Shift: Third (and) ending world pole shift expected (in) 2012. (One letter of the word "third" is hidden beyond the slide border.)

collision of the earth with Phobos, one of the two moons of Mars. Scallion has the impression that certain cosmic forces caused Phobos to be pulled out of its orbit around Mars, into an apparent collision course with the earth. Phobos is basically an oblong asteroid with the dimensions of 12.4, 14.3 and 17.4 miles. Could Phobos be a rock that God hurls at us if we don't change our ways? If we do change our ways, and become more godly, perhaps He will become as compassionate as the father in the parable.

In Revelation 12:3 to 4, a great red dragon with seven heads, ten horns, and seven crowns on its heads, is seen in the heavens. The tail of the dragon draws a third part of the stars with it as it is cast down to earth. The fact that the dragon was red suggested to me that it had something to do with the red planet, Mars. I wondered if the number of heads, crowns and horns had any connection with how many asteroids would strike our planet. I decided to check this out in the Code. The next search (**Subject: Phobos/ Moon**), found in Numbers 1:36 to 3:2, verifies Phobos, Mars's moon, broken apart, seven possibly struck the world in 2010-2012.

The following search (**Subject: Phobos/Piece**), found in Exodus 23:2 to 23:16, verified the prospect that a piece of Phobos is destroyed by a U.S. missile, three of four rocks hit the U.S. in 2010. This search supports the previous searches regarding asteroid strikes in the U.S.—strikes that could be responsible for the prospective five-degree pole shift of the same year.

The following searches also connect these asteroid strikes with the red dragon. The Bible Code revealed in (**Subject: Phobos/ Dragon**), found in Genesis 38:23 to 41:3, that Phobos is the red dragon beast, the Wormwood of the Tribulation as described by Jesus to John. The following search (**Subject: Phobos/Dragon**), found in Genesis 39:1 to 41:3, also reveals that Phobos, the red dragon, is seven rocks becoming ten pieces.[40] That equates to seven heads and ten horns, but it doesn't explain how the Mars moon separated out into seven pieces to begin with. The following slide (**Subject: Phobos/Moon**), found in Numbers 1:41 to 3:1, advises us of the prospect that Phobos, Mars moon, destroyed by a hydrogen bomb in 2010, ten pieces struck the world thereafter.

Position	Letters
57500	א ח י ו א ש ר ע ל י ד ו ה ש נ י ו י ק ר א ש מ ו ז ר ח ו י ו ס פ ה ו ר ד מ צ ר י מ ה ו י ק נ ה ו פ ו ט י פ ר ס ר י ס פ ר ע ה
57702	נ י ו ו י ש ר ת א ת ו ו י פ ק ד ה ו ע ל ב י ת ו ו כ ל י ש ל ו נ ת נ ב י ד ו ו י ה י מ א ז ה פ ק י ד א ת ו ב ב י ת ו ו ע ל כ
57904	י ה י א ח ר ה ד ב ר י מ ה א ל ה ו ת ש א א ש ת א ד נ י ו א ת ע י נ י ה א ל י ו ס פ ו ת א מ ר ש כ ב ה ע מ י ו י מ א נ ו י א מ
58106	ב ר ה א ל י ו ס פ י ו מ י ו מ ו ל א ש מ ע א ל י ה ל ש כ ב א צ ל ה ל ה י ו ת ע מ ה ו י ה י כ ה י ו מ ה ז ה ו י ב א ה ב י ת ה
58308	ר א ו ה ב י א ל נ ו א י ש ע ב ר י ל צ ח ק ב נ ו ב א א ל י ל ש כ ב ע מ י ו א ק ר א ב ק ו ל ג ד ו ל ו י ה י כ ש מ ע ו כ י ה ר
58510	י ע ז ב ב ג ד ו א צ ל י ו י נ ס ה ח ו צ ה ו י ה י כ ש מ ע א ד נ י ו א ת ד ב ר י א ש ת ו א ש ר ד ב ר ה א ל י ו ל א מ ר כ ד ב
58712	ב י ת ה ס ה ר ב י ד י ו ס פ א ת כ ל ה א ס י ר מ א ש ר ב ב י ת ה ס ה ר ו א ת כ ל א ש ר ע ש י מ ש מ ה ו א ה י ה ע ש ה א י נ ש
58914	ל ש ר ה א ו פ י מ ו י ת נ א ת מ ב מ ש מ ר ב י ת ש ר ה ט ב ח י מ א ל ב י ת ה ס ה ר מ ק ו מ א ש ר י ו ס פ א ס ו ר ש מ ו י פ ק
59116	י ר א א ת מ ו ה נ מ ז ע פ י מ ו י ש א ל א ת ס ר י ס י פ ר ע ה א ש ר א ת ו ב מ ש מ ר ב י ת א ד נ י ו ל א מ ר מ ד ו ע פ נ י כ
59318	א כ פ ר ח ת ע ל ת ה נ צ ה ה ב ש י ל ו א ש כ ל ת י ה ע נ ב י מ ו כ ו ס פ ר ע ה ב י ד י ו א ק ח א ת ה ע נ ב י מ ו א ש ח ט א ת
59520	כ י א מ ז כ ר ת נ י א ת כ כ א ש ר י י ט ב ל כ ו ע ש י ת נ א ע מ ד י ח ס ד ו ה ז כ ר ת נ י א ל פ ר ע ה ו ה ו צ א ת נ י מ נ ה
59722	ה א פ ה ו ה ע ו פ א כ ל א ת מ מ נ ה ס ל מ ע ל ר א ש י ו י ע נ י ו ס פ ו י א מ ר ז ה פ ת ר נ ו ש ל ש ת ה ס ל י מ ש ל ש ת י מ
59924	ו כ ע ב ד י ו ו י ש ב א ת ש ר ה מ ש ק י מ ע ל מ ש ק ה ו ו י ת נ ה כ ו ס ע ל כ פ פ ר ע ה ו א ת ש ר ה א פ י מ ת ל ה כ א ש ר פ
60126	ת א ח ר י ה נ מ נ ה י א ר ר ע ו ת מ ר א ה ו ד ק ו ת ב ש ר ו ת ע מ ד נ ה א צ ל ה פ ר ו ת ע ל ש פ ת ה י א ר ו ת א כ ל נ ה ה פ
60328	ת ב ל ע נ ה ה ש ב ל י מ ה ד ק ו ת א ת ש ב ע ה ש ב ל י מ ה ב ר י א ו ת ו ה מ ל א ו ת ו י י ק צ פ ר ע ה ו ה נ ה ח ל ו מ ו י ה
60530	ת נ א ת י ב מ ש מ ר ב י ת ש ר ה ט ב ח י מ א ת י ו א ת ש ר ה א פ י מ ו נ ח ל מ ה ח ל ו מ ב ל י ל ה א ח ד א נ י ו ה ו א א י ש
60732	ו מ נ ה ב ו ר ו י ג ל ח ו י ח ל פ ש מ ל ת י ו ו י ב א א ל פ ר ע ה ו י א מ ר פ ר ע ה א ל י ו ס פ ח ל ו מ ח ל מ ת י ו פ ת ר א
60934	ת ב ש ר ו י פ ת ת א ר ו ת ר ע י נ ה ב א ח ו ו ה נ ה ש ב ע פ ר ו ת א ח ר ו ת ע ל ו ת א ח ר י ה נ ד ל ו ת ו ר ע ו ת ת א ר מ א

Shape	Word	Translation	Verse	Position	Skip
א	אדום	red	Genesis 39:1	57536	-409
ס	סלע	rock	Genesis 39:7	57934	-391
ה	הולם	becoming	Genesis 39:14	58311	220
ש	שבע	seven	Genesis 39:14	58341	-206
ע	עשר	ten	Genesis 39:14	58347	-204
ח	חלק	piece	Genesis 40:3	58956	-210
ד	דרקון	dragon	Genesis 40:7	59163	-605
פ	פובס	Phobos	Genesis 41:3	60166	204

40. Phobos/Dragon: Phobos (the) Red Dragon (is) seven rock(s) becoming ten piece(s). (One letter of the word "dragon" is hidden beyond the slide border.)

So the prospect scenario indicates that for some reason Phobos breaks loose from its Mars orbit and enters into a collision course with our earth. It appears that first it exploded into seven pieces, with the trajectory of one piece threatening the United States. An anti-missile weapon system, to be developed in the future, likely attacks this piece.

After searching oceans, continents and countries with large landmasses, I found that the prospects for six of the remaining asteroid strikes were divided between China and Russia. The next slide (**Subject: Asteroid/Russia**), found in Numbers 31:3 to 31:21, discloses the prospect that three asteroids strike Russia in 2011, resulting in a world axis turnabout. Additionally, I found the words "ten degrees" close to the words "world" and "turnabout," though above the border of the slide. The next slide (**Subject: Asteroid/China**), found in Leviticus 23:30 to 25:1, reveals the prospect that three asteroids strike China in 2012, resulting in a ten-degree axis turnabout and a holocaust in China.

This leaves one asteroid piece still unaccounted for. I made a number of searches. Finally, the following slide (**Subject: Phobos/Tribulation**), found in Leviticus 2:2 to 4:25, revealed the prospect that one piece of Phobos known in the Tribulation as Wormwood was thrown into the Gulf of Arabia. If a world war is going on over there at this time, it will be all over in short order!

The above searches indicate that there would likely be at least a 25-degree pole shift overall. I decided to check this out in a separate search. The following slide (**Subject: Twenty/Five**), found in Deuteronomy 10:15 to 11:9, confirmed the prospect of a complete world axis turnabout by 2012 of 25 degrees.

I assume that a good astrophysicist could figure out what asteroid mass would be required to turn the earth five or ten degrees on its axis, then determine the damage that would likely cause. However, it doesn't take a genius to figure out that ten asteroid strikes and three pole shifts will cause a holocaust such as the world has never seen before. This is almost in conformance with what Jesus said, as quoted in Mark 13:19: "For in those days shall be affliction such as was not from the beginning of the creation which God created unto this time, neither shall be." In other words, it has never gotten this bad before, at least not for mankind! Jesus's statement here also verifies the Bible Code search in an earlier chapter that the flood story of Noah was basically a parable.

The rest of the Bible Code searches discussed in this chapter are an attempt to assess the damage. They pretty much confirm the Book of Revelation. The next slide (**Subject: Four/Billion**), found in Exodus 10:8 to 12:6, reveals the prospect that four billion lives could be lost as a result of the seven-year Tribulation.[41] That is two thirds of the current estimated population of the earth!

In my next series of searches, I found a troubling warning for the United States. Since there have been recent signs of racial unrest in the U.S., I decided to see if there was anything coded in the Torah regarding this problem. The first slide (**Subject: Race/War**), found in Leviticus 22:22 to 23:42, advised that the U.S.'s prospects for a race war are in 1861 and 2005.[42] Of course, 1861 is the year when the U.S. Civil War started. Note that figures in both the years "1861" and "2005" touch the word "war." I wanted to make sure I hadn't made a mistake regarding this subject, so I looked for an answer in a different location. The next search (**Subject: U.S./Racial**), found in Numbers 9:20 to 11:15, also advised armed racial warfare in the U.S. in 1861, also a great prospect in 2005. The last search in this series (**Subject: Black/Race**), found in Leviticus 14:52 to 16:15, warned of the prospect for a great black race holocaust in the U.S. in 2006. In this slide, the word "holocaust" crosses "2006" and touches letters in "great" and "race." The word "great" crosses "black," and a letter of "great" also touches "race." Unfortunately, this slide appears to be very accurate. It is time we learned to love our neighbor as ourselves, regardless of race, before it is too late. If we don't learn to forgive what happened in the past, we are bound to repeat it. This is a lesson that history teaches. Since we are not perfect, love cannot exist on earth without forgiveness.

The next slide concerns Los Angeles before the asteroids strike; (**Subject: Los/Angeles**), found in Numbers 32:2 to 33:36, reveals the prospect that the City of Los Angeles could be ruined by a great earthquake holocaust in 2006.

Shape	Word	Translation	Verse	Position	Skip
ש	שנה	year	Exodus 10:8	92046	175
ש	שבע	seven	Exodus 10:10	92196	619
נ	נוף	prospect	Exodus 10:10	92210	-759
ע	עולם	world	Exodus 10:10	92219	311
ס	סבל	tribulation	Exodus 10:14	92522	-313
ב	ביליון	billion	Exodus 11:3	93454	-152
ל	לאבד	perish	Exodus 11:7	93725	-15
ש	שואה	holocaust	Exodus 12:5	94182	15
א	ארבע	four	Exodus 12:6	94212	1

41. Four/Billion: Prospect (that) four billion (of the) world perish (from the) seven year Tribulation holocaust.

Position	Letters
173964	י פ ר מ ו ע ל כ ל נ פ ש ת מ ת ל א י ב א ל א ב י ו ו ל א מ ו ל א י ט מ א ו מ נ ה מ ק ד ש ל א י צ א ו ל
174519	נ ו א ל ב נ י ו ו א ל כ ל ב נ י י ש ר א ל ו י ד ב ר י ה ו ה א ל מ ש ה ל א מ ר ד ב ר א ל א ה ר נ ו א ל
175074	נ ה נ פ ש ק נ י נ כ ס פ ו ה ו א י א כ ל ב ו ו י ל י ד ב י ת ו ה מ י א כ ל ו ב ל ח מ ו ו ב ת כ ה נ כ י
175629	ו ע ו ר ת א ו ש ב ו ר ו א ח ר ו צ א ו י ב ל ת א ו ג ר ב א ו י ל פ ת ל א ת ק ר י ב ו א ל ה ל י ה ו ה ו
176184	ה מ מ ו ע ד י י ה ו ה א ש ר ת ק ר א ו א ת מ מ ק ר א י ק ד ש א ל ה ה מ מ ו ע ד י ש ש ת י מ י מ ת ע ש ה
176739	ה ב ש מ נ א ש ה ל י ה ו ה ר י ח נ י ח ח ו נ ס כ ה י י נ ר ב י ע ת ה ה י ו ל ח מ ו ק ל י ו כ ר מ ל ל
177294	ת י כ מ ו ב ק צ ר כ מ א ת ק צ י ר א ר צ כ מ ל א ת כ ל ה פ א ת ש ד כ ב ק צ ר כ ו ל ק ט ק צ י ר כ ל א ת
177849	מ ש ה ל א מ ר ד ב ר א ל ב נ י י ש ר א ל ל א מ ר ב ח מ ש ה ע ש ר י ו מ ל ח ד ש ה ש ב י ע י ה ז ה ח ג ה
178404	כ ת ת ש ב ו ש ב ע ת י מ י מ כ ל ה א ז ר ח ב י ש ר א ל י ש ב ו ב ס כ ת ל מ ע נ י ד ע ו ד ר ת י כ מ כ י
178959	נ א ש ה י ש ר א ל י ת ו ה ו א ב נ א י ש מ צ ר י ב ת ו כ ב נ י י ש ר א ל ו י נ צ ו ב מ ח נ ה ב נ ה י ש
179514	א ו א ת ה מ ק ל ל א ל מ ח ו צ ל מ ח נ ה ו י ר ג מ ו א ת ו א ב נ ו ב נ י י ש ר א ל ע ש ו כ א ש ר צ ו ה
180069	ב י ה י ו ב ל ה ו א ת ה י ה ל כ מ ו ש ב ת מ א י ש א ל א ח ז ת ו ו א י ש א ל מ ש פ ח ת ו ת ש ב ו י ו ב
180624	ו ז ר ע ת מ א ת ה ש נ ה ש מ י נ ת ו א כ ל ת מ מ נ ה ת ב ו א ה י ש נ ע ד ה ש נ ה ה ת ש י ע י ת ע ד ב ו
181179	י ה ל ל ו י מ ו א ש ר י ג א ל מ נ ה ל ו י מ י צ א מ מ כ ר ב י ת ו ע י ר א ח ז ת ו ב י ב ל כ י ב ת י
181734	ו ו מ מ ש פ ח ת מ א ש ר ע מ כ מ א ש ר ה ו ל י ד ו ב א ר צ כ מ ו ה י ו ל כ מ ל א ח ז ה ו ה ת נ ח ל ת מ

Shape	Word	Translation	Verse	Position	Skip
נ	נוף	prospect	Leviticus 22:22	175661	-541
מ	מלחמה	war	Leviticus 23:14	176787	555
א	ארהב	USA	Leviticus 23:14	176816	539
ת	תשסה	2005	Leviticus 23:21	177294	571
ג	גזע	race	Leviticus 23:34	177892	-3
ת	תרכא	1861	Leviticus 23:42	178405	23

42. Race/War: USA prospect(s) (for race war, 1861, 2005 (Two letters of the word "USA" and one of "1861" are hidden beyond the slide border.)

The following searches cover the period 2010-2012, that of the aftermath of the anticipated asteroid strikes. First, (**Subject: West/ Coast**), found in Numbers 31:16 to 32:14, reveals that the West Coast, U.S., possibly lost, was submerged underwater. A great quake in 2010 may have been the cause. The great quake is probably a result of the aforementioned asteroid strikes. The next searches provide the prospects for survival in the United States. First, (**Subject: Surviving/Holocaust**), found in Genesis 24:14 to 24:45, reveals the prospect that half the U.S. chose righteousness and God, surviving the holocaust between 2010 and 2012.[43] If we don't change between now and then, our chances are no better than fifty-fifty. Those who will survive probably already know it deep down inside. If you don't have that feeling, maybe it's time to change your behavior. To assure myself that the last search was correct, I did another search from the opposite point of view. The search, (**Subject: 2010/2012**), was found in the very beginning of the Bible, Genesis 1:16 to 3:6. It revealed the prospect that half the U.S. chose holocaust, rejected righteousness, therefore perishing between 2010 and 2012. This is a Bible Code warning: The more godly we become, the better our prospects for survival are.

Regarding the aftermath of the asteroid strikes, I did two more world searches. Islands will be in a precarious position during the Tribulation, so I decided to look at two of them. The first, (**Subject: Japan/Lost**), found in Numbers 1:44 to 2:27, reveals that Japan will possibly be lost to earthquakes and floods in 2010 to 2012. The final search in this area (**Subject: Philippines/Lost**), found in Exodus 18:12 to 20:5, also reveals the prospect that the Philippines may be lost to earthquakes and floods in the period 2010 to 2012.

Letters	Position
ש ר א מ ר א ל י ה ה ט י נ א כ ד כ ו א ש ת ה ו א מ ר ה ש ת ה ו ג מ ג מ ל	30078
ט ר מ כ ל ה ל ד ב ר ו ה נ ה ר ב ק ה י צ א ת א ש ר י ל ד ה ל ב ת ו א ל ב	30165
א י ש ל א י ד ע ה ו ת ר ד ה ע י נ ה ו ת מ ל א כ ד ה ו ת ע ל ו י ר צ ה ע	30252
ת ר ד כ ד ה ע ל י ד ה ו ת ש ק ה ו ו ת כ ל ל ה ש ק ת ו ו ת א מ ר ג מ ל ג	30339
ש א ב ו ת ש א ב ל כ ל ג מ ל י ו ה א י ש מ ש ת א ה ל ה מ ח ר י ש ל ד ע	30426
מ ז ה ב ב ק ע מ ש ק ל ו ו ש נ י צ מ י ד י מ ע ל י ד י ה ע ש ר ה ז ה ב מ	30513
ל י ו ב ת ב ת ו א ל א נ כ י ב נ מ ל כ ה א ש ר י ל ד ה ל נ ח ו ר ו ת א מ	30600
ה ו י א מ ר ב ר ו כ י ה ו ה א ל ה י א ד נ י א ב ר ה מ א ש ר ל א ע ז ב ח	30687
ג ד ל ב י ת א מ ה כ ד ב ר י מ ה א ל ה ו ל ר ב ק ה א ח ו ש מ ו ל ב נ ו י	30774
ח ת ו ו כ ש מ ע ו א ת ד ב ר י ר ב ק ה א ח ח ו ל א מ ר כ ה ד ב ר א ל י ה	30861
מ ה ת ע מ ד ב ח ו צ ו א נ כ י פ נ י ת י ה ב י ת ו מ ק ו ל מ ג ל י מ ו	30948
ג ל י ו ו ר ג ל י ה א נ ש י מ א ש ר א ת ו ו י ש מ ל פ נ י ו ל א כ ל ו	31035
ה ב ר כ א ת א ד נ י מ א ד ו י ג ד ל ו י ת נ ל ו צ א נ ו ב ק ר ו כ ס פ ו	31122
ק נ ת ה ו י ת נ ל ו א ת כ ל א ש ר ל ו ו י ש ב ע נ י א ד נ י ל א מ ר ל א	31209
ו א ל מ ש פ ח ת י ו ל ק ח ת א ש ה ל ב נ י ו א מ ר א ל א ד נ י א ל י ל א	31296
ה צ ל י ח ד ר כ ו ל ק ח ת א ש ה ל ב נ י מ מ ש פ ח ת י ו מ ב י ת א ב י	31383
ב א ה י ו מ א ל ה ע י נ ו א מ ר י ה ו ה א ל ה י א ד נ י א ב ר ה מ א מ י	31470
ע ל מ ה ה י צ א ת ש ל א ב ו א מ ר ת י א ל י ה ה ש ק י נ י נ א מ ע ט מ י	31557
ה ל ב נ א ד נ י א נ י ט ר מ א כ ל ה ל ד ב ר א ל ל ב י ו ה נ ה ר ב ק ה י	31644
ר ד כ ד ה מ ע ל י ה ו ת א מ ר ש ת ה ו ג מ ג מ ל י כ א ש ק ה ו א ש ת ו ג	31731
י ל ד ה ל ו מ ל כ ה ו א ש מ ה נ ז מ ע ל א פ ה ו ה צ מ י ד י מ ע ל י ד י	31818
ר כ א מ ת ל ק ח ת א ת ב ת א ח י א ד נ י ל ב נ ו ו ע ת ה א מ י ש כ מ ע ש	31905

Shape	Word	Translation	Verse	Position	Skip
א	אלוה	God	Genesis 24:14	30083	526
ב	בחר	chose	Genesis 24:16	30263	-618
מ	מחצה	half	Genesis 24:21	30454	346
ב	בין	between	Genesis 24:22	30517	358
נ	נוף	prospect	Genesis 24:24	30611	345
ר	נשאר	surviving	Genesis 24:27	30711	-174
ש	שואה	holocaust	Genesis 24:29	30798	-87
ת	תשעב	2012	Genesis 24:30	30862	185
ת	תשע	2010	Genesis 24:30	30882	524
א	ארהב	USA	Genesis 24:30	30885	2
י	יושר	righteousness	Genesis 24:45	31675	-83

43. Surviving/Holocaust: Prospect (that) half (of the) USA chose righteousness (and) God, surviving (the) holocaust between 2010 (and) 2012.

12

The Final Exam

Our holy books tell us we are to expect a judgment soon. A judgment is the same as an exam; we can either pass or fail, depending upon whether or not we have learned our lessons. Since we are children of God, we are expected to develop a character of godliness. That goal has been imprinted into our genes to help us make correct decisions. This is God's will. But we also have the freedom to choose. We can determine for ourselves what kind of character we want to develop. We can reject God's will in favor of our own. To paraphrase the 82nd Psalm, we are children of the most High and therefore may inherit godliness, but it is not an automatic birthright. Until this is understood, we will continue to die as mortals die. The problem is that we have become lost; we don't realize that we have this opportunity, and don't understand how precious it is. Long ago, Lucifer convinced us that we were immortal souls, therefore equal to God and with the ability to survive without him. We fell for the biggest lie since creation, and I believe that any religion that teaches that we are gods in our own right must be a part of that lie.

The Bible Code confirmed that we are entering into a new era following the final exam phase of the current root race. That is why there are so many souls on earth right now. All who have exhibited the potential to evolve are being given the chance to measure up. Those who fail will be removed from the earth for at least 1,000 years, while those who pass will enter into the Golden Age and evolve into a new race. The removal phase is the Tribulation period that has the prospect of starting in 2005, only a few years from now.

If you follow world news, it must be obvious to you that the warning signs are all around us. The signs include the following: global warming, severe storms, regional droughts and floods, severe earthquakes, erupting volcanoes, numerous regional wars along with social discontent, religious and race intolerance, immorality, epidemics of drug use and incurable diseases such as AIDS, famine in underdeveloped countries, the rapid spread of weapons of mass destruction, world overpopulation, regional fresh water shortages, and the threat of world economic collapse. Bible prophecy states that all of these types of events must occur simultaneously to forewarn us of the pending Tribulation. It appears that all the signs are now evident. Since World War Two, mankind has developed for the first time in recorded history the capability of destroying the earth. We are perilously close to falling into the abyss.

The Bible Code also tells us that much of this can be averted, but that this requires a tremendous change in behavior on our part. I decided to search the Bible Code regarding where we are going astray. Much of what we are doing wrong is obvious to most of us, but perhaps not to everyone. We, in the United States and in much of the world, have fallen into the trap of double-talk, political correctness, and legal maneuvering.

Killing a developing fetus is now termed a woman's "right to choose." In many countries, abortion has become legal; in China it is enforced as a means of population control. There were over 1.3 million fetuses aborted in the U.S. during 1996 alone.

Homosexuality is now called "sexual preference." AIDS has become a worldwide epidemic. Pornography is cloaked in the words "freedom of speech" and is therefore protected by the U.S. Constitution. It became a billion-dollar annual business in the U.S. in 2000, and is exported all over the world via the Internet. In fact, recent surveys indicate that over 60 percent of all Internet searches involve pornography in one fashion or another, and that 24 percent of children searching the Internet have been exposed to it.

Giving children over to daycare centers is now acceptable because mothers have the right to pursue their own careers. Over 65 million women were working in the U.S. in 2000, cutting in half the number of mothers who could be at home with their children for extended periods of time. Fathers abandon their families more frequently than ever before in history, and the number of single heads of household is increasing at an extraordinary rate. It's now easier to get out of a marriage contract than out of a contract for goods or services. Extramarital sex is no longer illegal between consenting adults, and the result is a huge increase in the number of U.S. children being born to unwed mothers. Adultery is not considered adultery if a participant doesn't define it as sex. Our children have learned this from the highest levels of the U.S. government.

Because these norms suit their lifestyle, those who choose the current path of selfishness won't admit that we have a problem. However, these are not the ideals that are presented in our holy books, nor are they the ideals upon which our nation was founded.

Since we have been warned that the coming Tribulation exam will measure the godliness of our characters, I decided to search the Bible Code to see what sort of conduct the Code identifies as necessary for us to pass the test. The first search **(Subject: Human/ Choice)**, found in Genesis 19:14 to 20:6, confirms that a great change is necessary in human choice to avoid a holocaust in 2010. What are we doing wrong? The following slide **(Subject: Deadly/Sins)**, found in Genesis 26:28 to 27:16, identifies ungodly behavior as the deadly sins of lust, jealousy, anger, judging others, intemperance, selfishness, laziness, gluttony, pride and covetousness.

It is no wonder that the prior slide told us that great change is necessary to totally avoid the Tribulation. Human nature being what it is, I don't believe we can avoid it. So what can we do to diminish it, or just to survive? I have heard evangelists say that, to be saved, all we need is faith. I decided to see if the Code confirmed this. The following slide **(Subject: Faith/Deed)**, found in Genesis

Letters	Position
ש ת ה ו י ה י ב ע ר ב ו י ק ח א ת ל א ה ב ת ו ו י ב א א ת ה א ל י ו ו י ב א	40862
ת ו ל ל א ה ב ת ו ש פ ח ה ו י ה י ב ב ק ר ו ה נ ה ה ו א ל א ה ו י א מ ר א ל	40922
ב ד ת י ע מ כ ו ל מ ה ר מ י ת נ י ו י א מ ר ל ב נ ל א י ע ש ה כ נ ב מ ק ו מ	40982
ל א ש ב ע ז א ת ו נ ת נ ה ל כ ג מ א ת ז א ת ב ע ב ד ה א ש ר ת ע ב ד ע מ ד י	41042
ב כ נ ו י מ ל א ש ב ע ז א ת ו י ת נ ל ו א ת ר ח ל ב ת ו ל ו ל א ש ה ו י ת נ	41102
ה ל ש פ ח ה ו י ב א ג מ א ל ר ח ל ו י א ה ב ג מ א ת ר ח ל מ ל א ה ו י ע ב ד	41162
י ה ו ה כ י ש נ ו א ה ל א ה ו י פ ת ח א ת ר ח מ ה ו ר ח ל ע ק ר ה ו ת ה ר ל	41222
י א מ ר ה כ י ר א ה י ה ו ה ב ע נ י י כ י ע ת ה י א ה ב נ י א י ש י ו ת ה ר	41282
ה כ י ש נ ו א ה א נ כ י ו י ת נ ל י ג מ א ת ז ה ו ת ק ר א ש מ ו ש מ ע ו נ ו	41342
ע מ י ל ו ה א י ש י א ל י כ י י ל ד ת י ל ו ש ל ש ה ב נ י מ ע ל כ נ ק ר א ש	41402
ר ה פ ע מ א ו ד ה א ת י ה ו ה ע ל כ נ ק ר א ה ש מ ו י ה ו ד ה ו ת ע מ ד מ ל	41462
ו ת ק נ א ר ח ל ב א ח ת ה ו ת א מ ר א ל י ע ק ב ה ב ה ל י ב נ י מ ו א מ א י	41522
ו י א מ ר ה ת ח ת א ל ה י מ א נ כ י א ש ר מ נ ע מ מ כ פ ר י ב ט נ ו ת א מ ר	41582
ל ב ר כ י ו א ב נ ה ג מ א נ כ י מ מ נ ה ו ת ת נ ל ו א ת ב ל ה ה ש פ ח ת ה ל	41642
ה ו ת ל ד ל י ע ק ב ב נ ו ת א מ ר ר ח ל ד נ נ י א ל ה י מ ו ג מ ש מ ע ב ק ל	41702
ו ת ה ר ע ו ד ו ת ל ד ב ל ה ה ש פ ח ת ר ח ל ב נ ש נ י ל י ע ק ב ו ת א מ ר ר	41762
ח ת י ג מ י כ ל ת י ו ת ק ר א ש מ ו נ פ ת ל י ו ת ר א ל א ה כ י ע מ ד ה מ ל	41822
ת ה ל י ע ק ב ל א ש ה ו ת ל ד ז ל פ ה ש פ ח ת ל א ה ל י ע ק ב ב נ ו ת א מ ר	41882
ז ל פ ה ש פ ח ת ל א ה ב נ ש נ י ל י ע ק ב ו ת א מ ר ל א ה ב א ש ר י כ י א ש	41942
י ל כ ר א ו ב נ ב י מ י ק צ י ר ח ט י מ ו י מ צ א ד ו ד א י מ ב ש ד ה ו י ב	42002
ל א ה ת נ י נ א ל י מ ד ו ד א י ב נ כ ו ת א מ ר ל ה ה מ ע ט ק ח ת כ א ת א י	42062
מ ר ר ח ל ל כ נ י ש כ ב ע מ כ ה ל י ל ה ת ח ת ד ו ד א י ב נ כ ו י ב א י ע ק	42122
ת ו ו ת א מ ר א ל י ת ב ו א כ י ש כ ר ש כ ר ת י כ ב ד ו ד א י ב נ י ו י ש כ	42182
א ל ל א ה ו ת ה ר ו ת ל ד ל י ע ק ב ב נ ח מ י ש י ו ת א מ ר ל א ה נ ת נ א ל	42242
ש י ו ת ק ר א ש מ ו י ש ש כ ר ו ת ה ר ע ו ד ל א ה ו ת ל ד ב נ ש ש י ל י ע ק	42302
ז ב ד ט ו ב ה פ ע מ י ז ב ל נ י א י ש י כ י י ל ד ת י ל ו ש ש ה ב נ י מ ו ת	42362
ת ו ת ק ר א א ת ש מ ה ד י נ ה ו י ז כ ר א ל ה י מ א ת ר ח ל ו י ש מ ע א ל י	42422
ת ל ד ב נ ו ת א מ ר א ס פ א ל ה י מ א ת ח ר פ ת י ו ת ק ר א א ת ש מ ו י ו ס	42482
י כ א ש ר י ל ד ה ר ח ל א ת י ו ס פ ו י א מ ר י ע ק ב א ל ל ב נ ש ל ח נ י ו	42542
נ ש י ו א ת י ל ד י א ש ר ע ב ד ת י א ת כ ב ה נ ו א ל כ ה כ י א ת ה י ד ע ת	42602
ל י ו ל ב נ א מ נ א מ צ א ת י ח נ ב ע י נ י כ נ ח ש ת י ו י ב ר כ נ י י ה ו	42662
ו א ת נ ה ו י א מ ר א ל י ו א ת ה י ד ע ת א ת א ש ר ע ב ד ת י כ ו א ת א ש ר	42722

Shape	Word	Translation	Verse	Position	Skip
מ	מלאכה	work	Genesis 29:26	41019	111
מ	מעשה	deed	Genesis 29:31	41225	-120
א	אמונה	faith	Genesis 29:32	41286	-60
ב	בלי	without	Genesis 29:34	41409	-120
ע	עקר	futile	Genesis 29:35	41477	537
ט	טוב	good	Genesis 30:3	41649	-358

44. Faith/Deed; Faith without good work(s) (or) deed(s) (is) futile.

29:26 to 30:3, declares that faith without good works or deeds is futile.[44] In the next two searches, I found out why. First (**Subject: Surviving/Holocaust**), found in Genesis 24:18 to 24:31, advises us that you must subordinate your will to God's to survive the prospect of holocaust in 2010 to 2012. This echoes the prayer given to us by Jesus that says, "Thy will be done." This doesn't just mean that we must accept the will of God. It also means that our conduct and character must be in accordance with God's will. The second slide (**Subject: Surviving/Holocaust**), also found in Genesis 24:16 to 24:50, advises us that in order to survive the Tribulation holocaust you must also love God above yourself and all souls as yourself. I believe this represents a personal commitment that, if truly followed, will allow us to escape tragedy during the Tribulation. It is a summation of the Ten Commandments and the teachings of Jesus, as well as of the teachings of all God-given testaments throughout the ages.

It is apparent that many Christians believe they will be caught up in what is called the "Rapture" and be removed from the earth before the Tribulation begins. This belief, grounded in hopelessness, is based upon 1 Thessalonians 4:16 to 4:18. I decided to check this out as well. The next search (**Subject: Rapture/Church**), found in Numbers 30: 7 to 32:40, advises us that the prospect for a 'Faithful Church Rapture' during the 2005 to 2012 Tribulation is a myth.[45] Notice how the word "myth" directly crosses the word "rapture." However, it appears that during this dangerous period the faithful will be protected. The following search (**Subject: Tribulation/ Era**), Leviticus 13:59 to 15:3, tells us that during the Tribulation era the Archangel Michael is the protector of all God's faithful on earth. Descriptions in 1 Corinthians 15:51-52 of how the faithful will be changed could be describing the transition to the new root race.

I believe there is a confusion between the coming Tribulation and the one said to occur after the 1,000 years of the Golden Age have ended. We saw earlier that during the Golden Age mankind evolves into the fifth root race, the race that Jesus introduced. Christ was able to resurrect and ascend. It's logical to believe that, before

Shape	Word	Translation	Verse	Position	Skip
ת	תשעב	2012	Numbers 30:7	238800	7
ת	תלאה	tribulation	Numbers 30:7	238817	-1164
ש	שלהוב	rapture	Numbers 31:1	239399	1746
ב	במשך	during	Numbers 31:12	239948	602
נ	נוף	prospect	Numbers 31:36	241138	-597
כ	כנסייה	church	Numbers 32:17	242891	-581
ת	תשסה	2005	Numbers 32:28	243436	596
א	אמון	faithful	Numbers 32:40	244047	-594
ב	בדיה	myth	Numbers 32:40	244057	-581

45. Rapture/Church: Prospect (of a) Faithful Church Rapture during (the) 2005 (to) 2012 Tribulation (is a) myth.

the start of the final Tribulation, those souls that are faithful to God will be allowed to ascend before Satan is turned loose again on earth. This idea was confirmed to me in the next search. The following slide (**Subject: Golden/Ascension**), found in Genesis 21:13 to 22:5, confirmed that the prospect of the ascension of the faithful at the end of the 1,000-year Golden Era is factual.[46]

The first resurrection is described in Revelation 20:6, and states, "Blessed and holy is he that hath part in the first resurrection; on such the *second death hath no power* [italics mine], but they shall be priests of God and of Christ, and shall reign with him 1,000 years." The following search (**Subject: First/Resurrection**), found in Leviticus 23:16 to 25:6, revealed that the first resurrection included souls born in the Golden Age. The assertion that "the second death hath no power"—meaning that there will be no physical death after the rebirth in the Golden Age—strongly supports the idea that there will be an ascension of the faithful at the end of 1,000 years. These are the souls of the faithful who died prior to the Tribulation period and deserve to be reincarnated in the Golden Age.

I mentioned in an earlier chapter that I don't use the Internet. Like all scientific inventions, it has the potential to be used for good or evil both. A friend of mine signed up for a security-type newsletter through the Internet. One day, he received an e-mail that stated, "If you want to know who you are, click here." The newsletter attachment that he subsequently opened revealed an unbelievable amount of personal information about himself and also listed all the Internet sites he had visited over the past several months. This happened despite the fact that he is very security-conscious and uses an alias and fictitious address on the Net. When I heard about this, I realized how dangerous the Internet really is. The Book of Revelation discloses that during the Tribulation the beast will attempt to rule the world by controlling all commerce. It says that the mark of the beast will be 6-6-6, and that no one will be able to buy or sell without accepting its mark. It's not too great a stretch of the imagination to say that the Internet is rapidly moving in this direction. I also believe that a false religion may well spring up before the Tribulation starts. It will probably spread rapidly and

Letters	Position
ק ר א ל כ ז ר ע ו ג מ א ת ב נ ה א מ ה ל ג ו י א ש י מ נ ו כ י ז ר ע כ ה ו א ו י ש כ מ	25882
ת ל כ ו ת ת ע ב מ ד ב ר ב א ר ש ב ע ו י כ ל ו ה מ י מ מ נ ה ח מ ת ו ת ש ל כ א ת ה י ל	25979
ת ה י ל ד ו ת ש ב מ נ ג ד ו ת ש א א ת ק ל ה ו ת ב כ ו י ש מ ע א ל ה י מ א ת ק ו ל ה נ	26076
א ל ה י מ א ל ק ו ל ה נ ע ר ב א ש ר ה ו א ש מ ק ו מ י ש א י א ת ה נ ע ר ו ה ח ז י ק י	26173
ו ת מ ל א א ת ה ח מ ת מ י מ ו ת ש ק א ת ה נ ע ר ו י ה י א ל ה י מ א ת ה נ ע ר ו י ג ד	26270
ו י ה י ב ע ת ה ה ו א ו י א מ ר א ב י מ ל כ ו פ י כ ל ש ר צ ב א ו א ל א ב ר ה מ ל א מ	26367
י ו ל נ כ ד י כ ח ס ד א ש ר ע ש י ת י ע מ כ ת ע ש ה ע מ ד י ו ע מ ה א ר צ א ש ר ג ר ת	26464
ר ג ז ל ו ע ב ד י א ב י מ ל כ ו י א מ ר א ב י מ ל כ ל א י ד ע ת י מ י ע ש ה א ת ה ד ב	26561
ק ר ו י ת נ ל א ב י מ ל כ ו י כ ר ת ו ש נ י ה מ ב ר י ת ו י צ ב א ב ר ה מ א ת ש ב ע כ	26658
ב ד נ ה ו י א מ ר כ י א ת ש ב ע כ ב ש ת ת ק ח מ י ד י ב ע ב ו ר ת ה י ה ל י ל ע ד ה כ	26755
כ ר ת ו ב ר י ת ב ב א ר ש ב ע ו י ק מ א ב י מ ל כ ו פ י כ ל ש ר צ ב א ו ו י ש ב ו א ל	26852
ר צ פ ל ש ת י מ י מ י מ ר ב י מ ו י ה י א ח ר ה ד ב ר י מ ה א ל ה ו ה א ל ה י מ נ ס ה	26949
א ה ב ת א ת י צ ח ק ו ל כ ל כ א ל א ר צ ה מ ר י ה ו ה ע ל ה ו ש מ ל ע ל ה ע ל א ח ד ה	27046
ת ו ו א ת י צ ח ק ב נ ו ו י ב ק ע ע צ י ע ל ה ו י ק מ ו י ל כ א ל ה מ ק ו מ א ש ר א מ	27143
ר א ב ר ה מ א ל נ ע ר י ו ש ב ו ל כ מ פ ה ע מ ה ח מ ו ר ו א נ י ו ה נ ע ר נ ל כ ה ע ד	27240
ח ב י ד ו א ת ה א ש ו א ת ה מ א כ ל ת ו י ל כ ו ש נ י ה מ י ח ד ו ו י א מ ר י צ ח ק א	27337
ל ע ל ה ו י א מ ר א ב ר ה מ א ל ה י מ י ר א ה ל ו ה ש ה ל ע ל ה ב נ י ו י ל כ ו ש נ י	27434
כ א ת ה ע צ י מ ו י ע ק ד א ת י צ ח ק ב נ ו ו י ש מ א ת ו ע ל ה מ ז ב ח מ מ ע ל ל ע צ	27531
ה מ נ ה ש מ י מ ו י א מ ר א ב ר ה מ א ב ר ה מ ו י א מ ר ה נ נ י ו י א מ ר א ל ת ש ל ח	27628
ב נ כ א ת י ח י ד כ מ מ נ י ו י ש א א ב ר ה מ א ת ע י נ י ו ו י ר א ו ה נ ה א י ל א ח	27725
א א ב ר ה מ ש מ ה מ ק ו מ ה ה ו א י ה ו ה י ר א ה א ש ר י א מ ר ה י ו מ ב ה ר י ה ו ה	27822
ה כ י י ע נ א ש ר ע ש י ת א ת ה ד ב ר ה ז ה ו ל א ח ש כ ת א ת ב נ כ א ת י ח י ד כ כ י	27919
ז ר ע כ א ת ש ע ר א י ב י ו ו ה ת ב ר כ ו ב ז ר ע כ כ ל ג ו י י ה א ר צ ע ק ב א ש ר ש	28016
ב ב א ר ש ב ע ו י ה י א ח ר י ה ד ב ר י מ ה א ל ה ו י ג ד ל א ב ר ה מ ל א מ ר ה נ ה י	28113
י א ר מ ו א ת כ ש ד ו א ת ח ז ו ו א ת פ ל ד ש ו א ת י ד ל פ ו א ת ב ת ו א ל ו ב ת ו א	28210
ו ת ל ד ג מ ה ו א א ת ט ב ח ו א ת ג ח מ ו א ת ת ח ש ו א ת מ ע כ ה ו י ה י ו ח י י ש ר	28307
ר ו נ ב א ר צ כ נ ע נ ו י ב א א ב ר ה מ ל ס פ ד ל ש ר ה ו ל ב כ ת ה ו י ק מ א ב ר ה מ	28404
כ מ ו א ק ב ר ה מ ת י מ ל פ נ י ו י ע נ ו ב נ י ח ת א ת א ב ר ה מ ל א מ ר ל ו ש מ ע נ	28501
ו ל א י כ ל ה מ מ כ מ ק ב ר מ ת כ ו י ק מ א ב ר ה מ ו י ש ת ח ו ל ע מ ה א ר צ ל ב נ י	28598
פ ר ו נ ב נ צ ח ר ו י ת נ ל י א ת מ ע ר ת ה מ כ פ ל ה א ש ר ל ו א ש ר ב ק צ ה ש ד ה ו	28695
נ ה ח ת י א ת א ב ר ה מ ב א ז נ י ב נ י ח ת ל כ ל ב א י ש ע ר ע י ר ו ל א מ ר ל א א ד	28792

Shape	Word	Translation	Verse	Position	Skip
מ	משלם	absolute	Genesis 21:13	25892	102
מ	ממשי	factual	Genesis 21:15	26010	95
ע	עלייה	ascension	Genesis 21:18	26207	194
ש	שנה	year	Genesis 21:19	26286	5
א	אלף	thousand	Genesis 21:22	26390	-491
ז	זהוב	golden	Genesis 21:28	26691	-291
נ	נוף	prospect	Genesis 21:32	26878	-198
ק	קצה	end	Genesis 22:1	26972	-93
ע	עידן	age	Genesis 22:2	27073	579
א	אמון	faithful	Genesis 22:5	27248	-7

46. Golden/Ascension: Ascension prospect (of the) faithful (at the) end (of the) thousand-year Golden Age (is) factual (and) absolute.

become very powerful through the Internet. By 2005, the Internet could evolve into a network that will control our lives. The less information it contains about me, the better!

In Hebrew, letters of the alphabet are also used as numbers. If you look at the translated dates on the slides throughout this book, you will notice that they consist of a series of three or four Hebrew letters. The Hebrew letter equivalent to the English "w" has a numeric value of six. Isn't it interesting that every Internet address begins with WWW—or, in Hebrew, "6-6-6"? I decided to do a Bible Code search on this 'coincidence.' The following slide (**Subject: World/Web**), found in Deuteronomy 21:8 to 23:7, verifies that the World Wide Web, 6-6-6, computer-connected network is the mark of the beast, a depiction to John.[47] Before you become a serious participant in the Internet, you may want to reread the Revelation to John. I'm not implying that the Internet is *the* mark of the beast. But I believe it is probably one of many tools of the beast to implement an unholy plan. The mark of the beast will be further discussed in the next chapter.

If you believe in a woman's right to choose an abortion, you may want to consider the repercussions of making that choice. The Bible Code verifies the Kabbalah that when souls leave the earth they go back to Eden to evaluate their life and plan the next one. The planning process is a very complex one, because you have to plan your next life as a learning experience in the light of mistakes you made in previous lives. For example, suppose that at some time in a previous lifetime you were responsible for painfully destroying the life of someone. You may have to return to life along with that soul, in order to work things out in a godly manner. You may have to choose the genes to predispose you to develop a painfully destructive disease as self-punishing justice in case you fail in your previously planned mission. That means you will have to choose your own mother and father. Moreover, most of us have a lot to work out with regard to the many soul mates with whom we normally incarnate. All of these souls will be in the process of reincarnating at around about the same time as us. To ensure that learning progresses, some of these souls have planned to help each

Letters	Position
ו א א ל י ה ו ב ע ל ת ה ו ה י ת ה ל כ ל א ש ה ו ה י ה א מ ל א ח פ צ ת ב ה ו ש ל ח ת ה ל נ פ ש ה ו מ כ ר ל א ת מ כ ר נ	283309
נ ו ל ו מ ש פ ט ה ב כ ר ה כ י י ה י ה ל א י ש ב נ ס ו ר ר ו מ ו ר ה א י נ נ ו ש מ ע ב ק ו ל א ב י ו ו ב ק ו ל א מ ו ו	283593
י ק ב ו ר ת ק ב ר נ ו ב י ו מ ה ה ו א כ י ק ל ל ת א ל ה י מ ת ל ו י ו ל א ת ט מ א א ת א ד מ ת כ א ש ר י ה ו ה א ל ה י	283877
מ ב ד ר כ ו ה ת ע ל מ ת מ ה מ ה ק מ ת ק י מ ע מ ו ל א י ה י ה כ ל י ג ב ר ע ל א ש ה ו ל א י ל ב ש ג ב ר ש מ ל ת א ש ה	284161
י מ פ נ ת ק ד ש ה מ ל א ה ה ז ר ע א ש ר ת ז ר ע ו ת ב ו א ת ה כ ר מ ל א ת ח ר ש ב ש ו ר ו ב ח מ ר י ח ד ו ל א ת ל ב ש	284445
ל א י ש ה ז ה ל א ש ה ו י ש נ א ה ו ה נ ה ה ו א ש מ ע ל י ל ת ד ב ר י מ ל א מ ר ל א מ צ א ת י ל ב ת כ ב ת ו ל י מ ו א	284729
י ע ש ת ה נ ב ל ה ב י ש ר א ל ל ז נ ו ת ב י ת א ב י ה ו ב ע ר ת ה ר ע מ ק ר ב כ כ י י מ צ א א י ש ש כ ב ע מ א ש ה ב ע	285013
ר ש ה ו ה ח ז י ק ב ה ה א י ש ו ש כ ב ע מ ה ו מ ת ה א י ש א ש ר ש כ ב ע מ ה ל ב ד ו ו ל נ ע ר ל א ת ע ש ה ד ב ר א י נ	285297
י ב א פ צ ו ע ד כ ה ו כ ר ו ת ש פ כ ה ב ק ה ל י ה ו ה ל א י ב א מ מ ז ר ב ק ה ל י ה ו ה ג מ ד ו ר ע ש י ר י ל א י ב א	285581
ל מ מ ו ט ב ת מ כ ל י מ י כ ל ע ו ל מ ל א ת ת ע ב א ד מ י כ י א ח י כ ה ו א ל א ת ת ע ב מ צ ר י כ י ג ר ה י י ת ב א ר	285865
כ ח ו צ ו ח פ ר ת ה ב ה ו ש ב ת ו כ ס י ת א ת צ א ת כ כ י י ה ו ה א ל ה י כ מ ת ה ל כ ב ק ר ב מ ח נ כ ל ה צ י ל כ ו ל	286149
כ ג מ ש נ י ה מ ל א ת ש י כ ל א ח י כ נ ש כ כ ס פ נ ש כ א כ ל נ ש כ כ ל ד ב ר א ש ר י ש כ ל נ כ ר י ת ש י כ ו ל א ח י	286433
ל כ ל י כ ל א ת ת נ כ י ת ב א ב ק מ ת ר ע כ ו ק ט פ ת מ ל י ל ת ב י ד כ ו ח ר מ ש ל א ת נ י פ ע ל ק מ ת ר ע כ כ י י ק	286717

Shape	Word	Translation	Verse	Position	Skip
ר	רשת	network	Deuteronomy 21:8	283056	-274
ו	ווו	6-6-6	Deuteronomy 21:14	283346	563
ת	תיאור	depiction	Deuteronomy 21:14	283366	-276
כ	כתם	mark	Deuteronomy 21:23	283896	5
מ	מחשב	computer	Deuteronomy 22:4	284162	-570
ג	גון	John	Deuteronomy 22:5	284195	274
ק	קשר	connected	Deuteronomy 22:21	285025	-288
ח	חיה	beast	Deuteronomy 22:25	285301	-574
ר	רחב	wide	Deuteronomy 23:2	285600	-297
ע	עולם	world	Deuteronomy 23:7	285880	1
מ	מסכת	web	Deuteronomy 23:7	285883	284

47. World/Web: World Wide Web, 6-6-6, computer-connected network, (a) mark (of the) beast, (a) depiction (to) John.

other out, usually as spouses, family members, or close friends. In order to help its parents in their own soul development, a soul may have planned to sacrifice its new life by returning to earth in some abnormal form. Only God knows the future, so these incarnating souls don't know how their plan will interact with choices made here on earth. Suppose some parents decide to abort the child who has a complex, loving plan to join them and is depending upon them to help it fulfill its earthly mission. The repercussions could be staggering when you consider all the other souls who will also be adversely affected. Abortion ultimately disrupts the evolution of all souls.

The search I found on abortion did not surprise me. The following slide (**Subject: Baby/Abortion**), found in Exodus 8:24 to 9:13, advises that for every baby abortion the guilty receive identical punishment as murder under the Law of Karma.[48]

We've all recently heard in the news that plans are being made by some scientific groups to experiment with human cloning. As previously mentioned, all science is a two-edged sword that can be used for good or evil. In the Edgar Cayce readings on Atlantis, it is explained that during that period ungodly "thought projections" resulted in mixed human/animal monstrosities. The reading is unclear to me but all human deeds are the result of thought projections. The mixing of genes from two different species, however it occurred, must have been involved. It was one of the reasons Atlantis was destroyed. Some of the godly souls that escaped from Atlantis migrated to the Nile where, according to the Bible Code, they built the Sphinx to remind the world of the repercussions of such evil science. The following slide (**Subject: Sphinx/Reminder**), found in Numbers 5:27 to 7:25, confirms that the Sphinx was built 10,000 years before Jesus and is a reminder of prior evil gene science.

The Bible Code has a warning about human genome experimentation. The following slide (**Subject: Human Genome**), found in Numbers 24:12 to 24:23, warns that the evil in human genome science leads to the prospect of death, chaos and affliction in 2010.[49]

Letters	Position
ח א ת כ מ ו ז ב ח ת מ ל י ה ו ה א ל ה י כ מ ב מ ד ב ר ר ק ה ר ח ק ל א ת ר ח י ק	89330
מ ר מ ש ה ה נ ה א נ כ י י ו צ א מ ע מ כ ו ה ע ת ר ת י א ל י ה ו ה ו ס ר ה ע ר ב	89388
ר ר ק א ל י ס פ פ ר ע ה ה ת ל ל ב ל ת י ש ל ח א ת ה ע מ ל ז ב ח ל י ה ו ה ו י צ	89446
י ה ו ה ו י ע ש י ה ו ה כ ד ב ר מ ש ה ו י ס ר ה ע ר ב מ פ ר ע ה מ ע ב ד י ו ו מ	89504
ר ע ה א ת ל ב ו ג מ ב פ ע מ ה ז א ת ו ל א ש ל ח א ת ה ע מ ו י א מ ר י ה ו ה א ל	89562
י ו כ ה א מ ר י ה ו ה א ל ה י ה ע ב ר י מ ש ל ח א ת ע מ י ו י ע ב ד נ י כ י א מ	89620
י ק ב מ ה נ ה י ד י ה ו ה ה ו י ה ב מ ק נ כ א ש ר ב ש ד ה ב ס ו ס י מ ב ח מ ר י	89678
ר כ ב ד מ א ד ו ה פ ל ה י ה ו ה ב י נ מ ק נ ה י ש ר א ל ו ב י נ מ ק נ ה מ צ ר י	89736
א ל ד ב ר ו י ש מ י ה ו ה מ ו ע ד ל א מ ר מ ח ר י ע ש ה י ה ו ה ה ד ב ר ה ז ה ב	89794
ז ה מ מ ח ר ת ו י מ ת כ ל מ ק נ ה מ צ ר י מ ו מ מ ק נ ה ב נ י י ש ר א ל ל א מ ת	89852
מ ת מ מ ק נ ה י ש ר א ל ע ד א ח ד ו י כ ב ד ל ב פ ר ע ה ו ל א ש ל ח א ת ה ע מ ו	89910
ר נ ק ח ו ל כ מ מ ל א ח פ נ י כ מ פ י ח כ ב ש נ ו ז ר ק ו מ ש ה ה ש מ י מ ה ל ע	89968
ל א ר צ מ צ ר י מ ו ה י ה ע ל ה א ד מ ו ע ל ה ב ה מ ה ל ש ח י נ פ ר ח א ב ע ב ע	90026
ת פ י ח ה כ ב ש נ ו י ע מ ד ו ל פ נ י פ ר ע ה ו י ז ר ק א ת ו מ ש ה ה ש מ י מ ה	90084
א ד מ ו ב ב ה מ ה ו ל א י כ ל ו ה ח ר ט מ י מ ל ע מ ד ל פ נ י מ ש ה מ פ נ י ה ש	90142
מ ו ב כ ל מ צ ר י מ ו י ח ז ק י ה ו ה א ת ל ב פ ר ע ה ו ל א ש מ ע א ל ה מ כ א ש	90200
י ה ו ה א ל מ ש ה ה ש כ מ ב ב ק ר ו ה ת י צ ב ל פ נ י פ ר ע ה ו א מ ר ת א ל י ו	90258
מ ש ל ח א ת ע מ י ו י ע ב ד נ י כ י ב פ ע מ ה ז א ת א נ י ש ל ח א ת כ ל מ ג פ ת	90316
ב ע ב ו ר ת ד ע כ י א י נ כ מ נ י ב כ ל ה א ר צ כ י ע ת ה ש ל ח ת י א ת י ד י ו	90374
כ ח ד מ נ ה א ר צ ו א ו ל מ ב ע ב ו ר ז א ת ה ע מ ד ת י כ ב ע ב ו ר ה ר א ת כ א	90432
ה א ר צ ע ו ד כ מ ס ת ו ל ל ב ע מ י ל ב ל ת י ש ל ח מ ה נ נ י מ מ ט י ר כ ע ת מ	90490
ה כ מ ה ו ב מ צ ר י מ ל מ נ ה י ו מ ה ו ס ד ה ו ע ד ע ת ה ו ע ת ה ש ל ח ה ע ז א	90548
ה כ ל ה א ד מ ו ה ב ה מ ה א ש ר י מ צ א ב ש ד ה ו ל א י א ס פ ה ב י ת ה ו י ר ד	90606
ד ב ר י ה ו ה מ ע ב ד י פ ר ע ה ה נ י ס א ת ע ב ד י ו ו א ת מ ק נ ה ו א ל ה ב ת	90664
י ה ו ה ו י ע ז ב א ת ע ב ד י ו ו א ת מ ק נ ה ו ב ש ד ה ו י א מ ר י ה ו ה א ל ח	90722
י ה י ב ר ד ב כ ל א ר צ מ צ ר י מ ע ל ה א ד מ ו ע ל ה ב ה מ ה ו ע ל כ ל ע ש ב ה	90780
א ת מ ט ה ו ע ל ה ש מ י מ ו י ה ו ה נ ת נ ק ל ת ו ב ר ד ו ת ה ל כ א ש א ר צ ה ו	90838
ר י מ ו י ה י ב ר ד ו א ש מ ת ל ק ח ת ב ת ו כ ה ב ר ד כ ב ד מ א ד א ש ר ל א ה י	90896
ז ה י ת ה ל ג ו י ו י כ ה ב ר ד ב כ ל א ר צ מ צ ר י מ א ת כ ל א ש ר ב ש ד ה מ א	90954

Shape	Word	Translation	Verse	Position	Skip
ק	קרמכ	karmic	Exodus 8:24	89362	167
ל	לקבל	receive	Exodus 8:25	89461	236
א	אשמ	guilty	Exodus 8:25	89469	172
ז	זהה	identical	Exodus 8:28	89577	639
ב	בכל	every	Exodus 9:1	89637	292
ר	רצה	murder	Exodus 9:3	89694	-585
ד	דינ	justice	Exodus 9:3	89698	-465
ה	הפלה	abortion	Exodus 9:5	89821	-232
ת	תינוק	baby	Exodus 9:10	90111	-116
ק	קנס	punishment	Exodus 9:13	90273	113

48. Baby/Abortion: (For) every baby abortion, the guilty receive identical punishment (as) murder (under) karmic justice.

ה מ נ ע כ י ה ו ה מ כ ב ו ד ו י א מ ר ב ל ע מ א ל ב ל ק ה ל א ג מ א ל מ ל א	229535
ר ש ל ח ת א ל י ד ב ר ת י ל א מ ר א מ י ת נ ל י ב ל ק מ ל א ב י ת ו כ ס פ ו	229578
א ו כ ל ל ע ב ר א ת פ י י ה ו ה ל ע ש ו ת ט ו ב ה א ו ר ע ה מ ל ב י א ש ר י	229621
ו ה א ת ו א ד ב ר ו ע ת ה ה נ נ י ה ו ל כ ל ע מ י ל כ ה א י ע צ כ א ש ר י ע	229664
ה ז ה ל ע מ כ ב א ח ר י ת ה י מ י מ ו י ש א מ ש ל ו ו י א מ ר נ א מ ב ל ע מ	229707
ר ו נ א מ ה ג ב ר ש ת מ ה ע י נ נ א מ ש מ ע א מ ר י א ל ו י ד ע ד ע ת ע ל י	229750
ה ש ד י י ח ז ה נ פ ל ו ג ל ו י ע י נ י מ א ר א נ ו ו ל א ע ת ה א ש ו ר נ ו	229793
ו ב ד ר כ כ ו כ ב מ י ע ק ב ו ק מ ש ב ט מ י ש ר א ל ו מ ח צ פ א ת י מ ו א ב	229836
כ ל ב נ י ש ת ו ה י ה א ד ו מ י ר ש ה ו ה י ה י ר ש ה ש ע י ר א י ב י ו ו י	229879
ש ה ח י ל ו י ר ד מ י ע ק ב ו ה א ב י ד ש ר י ד מ ע י ר ו י ר א א ת ע מ ל ק	229922
ש ל ו ו י א מ ר ר א ש י ת ג ו י מ ע מ ל ק ו א ח ר י ת ו ע ד י א ב ד ו י ר א	229965
נ י ו י ש א מ ש ל ו ו י א מ ר א י ת נ מ ו ש ב כ ו ש י מ ב ס ל ע ק נ כ כ י א	230008
ל ב ע ר ק י נ ע ד מ ה א ש ו ר ת ש ב כ ו י ש א מ ש ל ו ו י א מ ר א ו י מ י י	230051
מ ו א ל ו צ י מ מ י ד כ ת י מ ו ע נ ו א ש ו ר ו ע נ ו ע ב ר ו ג מ ה ו א ע ד	230094
י ק מ ב ל ע מ ו י ל כ ו י ש ב ל מ ק מ ו ו ג מ ב ל ק ה ל כ ל ד ר כ ו ו י ש ב	230137
ב ש ט י מ ו י ח ל ה ע מ ל ז נ ו ת א ל ב נ ו ת מ ו א ב ו ת ק ר א נ ל ע מ ל ז	230180
ה י ה נ ו י א כ ל ה ע מ ו י ש ת ח ו ו ל א ל ה י ה נ ו י צ מ ד י ש ר א ל ל ב	230223
ר ו י ח ר א פ י ה ו ה ב י ש ר א ל ו י א מ ר י ה ו ה א ל מ ש ה ק ח א ת כ ל ר	230266
מ ו ה ו ק ע א ו ת מ ל י ה ו ה נ ג ד ה ש מ ש ו י ש ב ח ר ו נ א פ י ה ו ה מ י	230309
י א מ ר מ ש ה א ל ש פ ט י י ש ר א ל ה ר ג ו א י ש א נ ש י ו ה נ צ מ ד י מ ל	230352
ו ר ו ה נ ה א י ש מ ב נ י י ש ר א ל ב א ו י ק ר ב א ל א ח י ו א ת ה מ ד י נ	230395
נ י מ ש ה ו ל ע י נ י כ ל ע ד ת ב נ י י ש ר א ל ו ה מ ה ב כ י מ פ ת ח א ה ל	230438
י ר א פ י נ ח ס ב נ א ל ע ז ר ב נ א ה ר נ ה כ ה נ ו י ק מ מ ת ו כ ה ע ד ה ו	230481
ח ב י ד ו ו י ב א א ח ר א י ש י ש ר א ל א ל ה ק ב ה ו י ד ק ר א ת ש נ י ה מ	230524
י ש ר א ל ו א ת ה א ש ה א ל ק ב ת ה ו ת ע צ ר ה מ ג פ ה מ ע ל ב נ י י ש ר א	230567
ו ה מ ת י מ ב מ ג פ ה א ר ב ע ה ו ע ש ר י מ א ל פ ו י ד ב ר י ה ו ה א ל מ ש	230610

Shape	Word	Translation	Verse	Position	Skip
ר	רשע	evil	Numbers 24:12	229553	177
מ	מוות	death	Numbers 24:13	229598	-42
ת	תשע	2010	Numbers 24:13	229598	260
נ	נוף	prospect	Numbers 24:14	229678	478
ר	ראשי	leading	Numbers 24:16	229774	42
ג	גנום	genome	Numbers 24:17	229856	-172
מ	מדע	science	Numbers 24:18	229907	-38
נ	נגע	affliction	Numbers 24:21	230026	299
ק	קאוס	chaos	Numbers 24:21	230037	-170
א	אנושי	human	Numbers 24:23	230071	-43

49. Human/Genome: Evil (in) human genome science (is) leading (to the) prospect (of) death, chaos, (and) affliction, (in the year) 2010.

13

Transition into the Golden Age

Modern science cannot fully explain why we grow old and die. Our body cells replace themselves perfectly for many years, but after a while cell replacement starts to become imperfect. Soon, more and more defective cells replace perfect cells and bodily aging sets in; we start to deteriorate, and ultimately we die. Some scientists believe we have a biological clock programmed into our genes.

The Torah shows us in great detail, family by family, that the life span during the era from Adam to Noah was nearly 1,000 years. Then, a strange phenomenon set in for the generation that came after the great flood: The human life span was shortened to approximately one-seventh of what it had been prior to the flood. That time span dropped even further, then stabilized at approximately 70 years. I believe that when the Bible dwells upon a subject such as this, there is a lesson to be learned. I decided to investigate the subject in the Bible Code.

One hypothesis put forth by medical science is that our growth, our ability to fight disease, and our life span, are regulated primarily by a system of glands in our bodies called the endocrine system. After puberty, some of these glands slow down to a quiescent stage, providing minimal hormonal output to sustain what we consider to be a normal life. What I haven't been able to find in layman's books on this subject is any suggestion that perhaps these glands might be regulated by the body's resonant electrical frequencies. I'm referring to the electrical energy by which our body operates. I imagine it to be somewhat like the modulated output of a chemical battery. It sets up the rhythm of our body systems. The following search (**Subject: Endocrine/Gland**), found in Numbers 5:27 to 6:23, revealed that body frequency regulates endocrine glands.[50] The next slide (**Subject: Human/Life**), found in Numbers 34:4 to 36:5, reveals that the human life span is established by body frequency to regulate pineal and thymus gland output.

If we could change our resonant frequency, perhaps we could extend our life span. After the great flood of Noah's time, something must have happened to alter our body's resonant frequency in such a way as to cause the human life span to dramatically decrease. Revelation 20:4 states that those who did not receive the mark of the beast during the Tribulation lived 1,000 years with Christ. This must mean that our body frequency changes during the Golden Age. I decided to search this subject further. The following slide (**Subject: Golden/Era**), found in Numbers 7:71 to 8:4, revealed that the Golden Era life span is 300 years. This falls far short of 1,000 years, but I decided to search further to determine what caused the increase to 300 years.

On February 24, 1987, some 160,000 light-years distant from our earth's solar system, a supernova exploded in the satellite galaxy of our Milky Way galaxy known as the Large Magellanic Cloud. A supernova is basically an exploding super-hot star (usually a "Red Giant" but in this case a Blue Giant) that can subsequently implode into a very dense neutron star called a pulsar. When the star becomes a pulsar, it radiates radio waves at precise intervals. This supernova was named SN 1987A, and it went on to exhibit such unusual traits that it is currently under intense scrutiny by the world astronomical community. The U.S., Japan and Russia recorded bursts of neutrinos in deep underground detectors at the time the supernova was observed. Neutrinos are massless neutral particles that travel at the speed of light. Since we rarely observe a supernova, I decided to search the Bible Code to determine if radiation

Letters	Position
כ צ ב ה ו ב א ו ה מ י מ ה מ א ר ר י מ ה א ל ה ב מ ע י כ ל צ ב ו ת ב ט נ ו ל נ פ ל י ר כ ו	196441
ה א ש ה א ת ה מ י מ ו ה ש ק ה א ת ה מ י מ ו ה י ת ה א מ נ ט מ א ה ת מ ע ל מ ע ל ב א י ש	196691
ז א ת ו נ ק ה ה א י ש מ ע ו נ ו ה א ש ה ה ו א ת ש א א ת ע ו נ ה ו י ד ב ר י ה ו ה א ל מ	196941
ו ע ד מ ל א ת ה י מ מ א ש ר י ז י ר ל י ה ו ה ק ד ש י ה י ה ג ד ל פ ר ע ש ע ר ר א ש ו כ ל	197191
ה ל מ ו ע ד ו ע ש ה ה כ ה נ א ח ד ל ח ט א ת ו א ח ד ל ע ל ה ו כ פ ר ע ל י ו מ א ש ר ח ט א	197441
י מ ל ש ל מ י מ ו ס ל מ צ ו ת ס ל ת ח ל ת ב ל ו ל ת ב ש מ נ ו ר ק י ק י מ צ ו ת מ ש ח י מ	197691
צ ה א ח ת מ נ ה ס ל ו ר ק י ק מ צ ה א ח ד ו נ ת נ ע ל כ פ י ה נ ז י ר א ח ר ה ת ג ל ח ו א	197941
נ י י ש ר א ל א מ ו ר ל ה מ י ב ר כ כ י ה ו ה ו י ש מ ר כ י א ר י ה ו ה פ נ י ו א ל י כ ו	198191
ב נ מ ל פ נ י י ה ו ה ש ש ע ג ל ת צ ב ו ש נ י ע ש ר ב ק ר ע ג ל ה ע ל ש נ י ה נ ש א י מ ו	198441
ב נ י מ ר ר י כ פ י ע ב ד ת מ ב י ד א י ת מ ר ב נ א ה ר נ ה כ ה נ ו ל ב נ י ק ה ת ל א נ ת	198691
כ ס פ א ח ת ש ל ש י מ ו א מ ה מ ש ק ל ה מ ז ר ק א ח ד כ ס פ ש ב ע י מ ש ק ל ב ש ק ל ה ק ד	198941
ק ר ב נ ו ק ע ר ת כ ס פ א ח ת ש ל ש י מ ו מ א ה מ ש ק ל ה מ ז ר ק א ח ד כ ס פ ש ב ע י מ ש	199191
ק ר ב נ ו ק ע ר ת כ ס פ א ח ת ש ל ש י מ ו מ א ה מ ש ק ל ה מ ז ר ק א ח ד כ ס פ ש ב ע י מ ש	199441
א ו ר ק ר ב נ ו ק ע ר ת כ ס פ א ח ת ש ל ש י מ ו מ א ה מ ש ק ל ה מ ז ר ק א ח ד כ ס פ ש ב ע	199691

Shape	Word	Translation	Verse	Position	Skip
ב	בלוטה	gland	Numbers 5:27	196716	-4
א	אנדכרנ	endocrine	Numbers 5:27	196722	250
ל	לכוון	regulate	Numbers 6:11	197476	492
ג	גוף	body	Numbers 6:19	197969	-243
ת	תדר	frequency	Numbers 6:23	198201	-502

50. Endocrine/Gland: Body frequency regulate(s) endocrine gland(s).

from this supernova may have had some impact on our body frequency.

My first search on this **(Subject: Human/Life)**, found in Numbers 34:14 to 35:20, revealed that the human life span is increased by the blue nova cosmic ray in the Golden Age. The follow-up search **(Subject: Blue/Star)**, found in Genesis 28:28 to 31:25, revealed that a cosmic ray from the blue star supernova of 1987 is beginning a new race in 2011.[51] I didn't understand how a ray from the 1987 supernova could initiate a new race 24 years later. Seven is referred to as a "time" in the Bible. Daniel 12:7 refers to a prophetic period of "times" regarding the Tribulation, which would be multiples of seven. Perhaps this supernova was emitting a very powerful radiation burst every seven years. I started to search the Bible Code, using intervals of seven years, to see if I could make this connection. I made my first connection with the year 2001, 14 years, or two intervals of seven years, after the explosion was observed. The following search **(Subject: Fifth/Root)**, found in Leviticus 25:55 to 27:18, revealed that the fifth root race is beginning on 02/26/2001 when 144,000 are irradiated by the blue star. Taking the International Date Line (+ or - one day) and leap days into account, this appears to be exactly two intervals of seven years, to the day! The next amazing thing is that this event involves 144,000 people. Revelation 7:3-4 relates an angel saying, "Hurt not the earth, neither the sea, nor the trees till we have sealed the servants of our God in their foreheads. And I heard the number of them, which were sealed: and they were sealed a hundred and forty and four thousand of all the tribes of the children of Israel." This was promised to occur before the Tribulation could begin. Not only had I found the mechanism for the race transition, but I had also found that the seal of God in the forehead of the faithful appeared to have been received from the radiation of a blue star supernova! The following search **(Subject: Transition/Fifth)**, found in Genesis 21:29 to 24:32, verified that transition to the fifth root race is the seal of God within the forehead of the faithful, as revealed to John. This may have a parallel meaning, also referring to the single eye of enlightenment, of which Jesus spoke.

Shape	Word	Translation	Verse	Position	Skip
	זיק	ray	Genesis 29:28	41101	-624
	מין	race	Genesis 29:28	41104	-313
	תשעא	2011	Genesis 29:34	41420	6
	הדף	explosion	Genesis 30:5	41701	334
	חדש	new	Genesis 30:6	41720	307
	יקום	cosmos	Genesis 30:6	41729	610
	רישא	beginning	Genesis 30:20	42347	-617
	תשמז	1987	Genesis 30:32	42957	-308
	כוכב	star	Genesis 30:32	42965	620
	תכלת	blue	Genesis 30:38	43275	-620
	נובה	nova	Genesis 31:25	44837	-3

51. Blue/Star: (A) cosmic ray (from the) Blue Star Nova explosion (of) 1987 (is) beginning (a) new race (in) 2011.

It would probably be catastrophic to the human system if our body frequency were to change abruptly. I decided to look for a transition time. The following slide **(Subject: Root/Transition)**, found in Genesis 11:10 to 12:3, revealed that three years are necessary for complete root race transition. If this is the case, then the 144,000 of God's faithful should be fully sealed by 2004. This would be prior to the prospective beginning of the Tribulation in 2005, just as the Revelation promised. The following search **(Subject: 144,000/God)**, found in Genesis 1:5 to 13:14, verified that 144,000 are marked by God and transfigured by 2/28/2004. Again, another leap day is taken into account.

We saw in an earlier Bible Code search that the Rapture of the faithful during this Tribulation was a myth. In a further search, we found that the Archangel Michael protects the faithful during the Tribulation. I wondered if the blue star ray sealed *all* of God's faithful. Revelation 9:4 states, "And it was commanded them that they should not hurt the grass of the earth, neither any green thing, neither any tree; but only those men which have not the seal of God in their foreheads." This was *not* a reference to the 144,000 discussed in Revelation 7.

The next interval of seven years after 2001 takes us to 2008. If you add a three-year transition period, this brings us to 2011, the date that the first slide of this series stated would see the beginning of the fifth root race. The next search **(Subject: Feb 29/2008)**, found in Leviticus 15:19 to 16:34, verified that Feb. 29, 2008, is the final prospect for our being given God's seal of salvation.[52] Another leap day is again taken into account. So it is clear that *all* of God's faithful will receive the seal, 144,000 first, in 2001, and the rest, in 2008.

So we have found the mark of God. But what about the mark of the beast? This latter was the subject of the following two searches. The first search **(Subject: Mark/Beast)**, found in Gen esis 6:16 to 7:8, revealed that *all remnant* of the fourth root race took the mark of the beast. As Jesus said, there would be only hot or cold, pass or fail, no partial godliness, accepted at the judgment. We will receive God's seal or we will not. If we are not sealed, we

Letters	Position
ה ע ר ב ו א ש ה כ י ת ה י ה ז ב ה ד מ י ה י ה ז ב ה ב ב ש ר ה ש ב ע ת י מ י מ ת ה י ה ב	165145
ו ו ר ת צ ב מ י מ ו ט מ א ע ד ה ע ר ב ו כ ל ה נ ג ע ב כ ל כ ל י א ש ר ת ש ב ע ל י ו י כ	165273
ש כ ב א י ש א ת ה ו ת ה י נ ד ת ה ע ל י ו ו ט מ א ש ב ע ת י מ י מ ו כ ל ה מ ש כ ב א ש ר	165401
ט מ א ה ה ו א כ ל ה מ ש כ ב א ש ר ת ש כ ב ע ל י ו כ ל י מ י ז ו ב ה כ מ ש כ ב נ ד ת ה י	165529
ר ה מ ז ו ב ה ו ס פ ר ה ל ה ש ב ע ת י מ י מ ו א ח ר ת ט ה ר ו ב י ו מ ה ש מ י נ י ת ק ח	165657
ה ה כ ה נ ל פ נ י י ה ו ה מ ז ו ב ט מ א ת ה ו ה ז ר ת מ א ת ב נ י י ש ר א ל מ ט מ א ת מ	165785
ז ו ב ו ל ז כ ר ו ל נ ק ב ה ו ל א י ש א ש ר י ש כ ב ע מ ט מ א ה ו י ד ב ר י ה ו ה א ל מ	165913
י ת ל פ ר כ ת א ל פ נ י ה כ פ ר ת א ש ר ע ל ה א ר נ ו ל א י מ ו ת כ י ב ע נ נ א ר א ה ע	166041
ח ג ר ו ב מ צ נ פ ת ב ד י צ נ פ ב ג ד י ק ד ש ה מ ו ר ח צ ב מ י מ א ת ב ש ר ו ו ל ב ש מ	166169
ת ו ו ל ק ח א ת ש נ י ה ש ע י ר מ ה ע מ י ד א ת מ ל פ נ י י ה ו ה פ ת ח א ה ל מ ו ע ד	166297
ה ו ה ו ע ש ה ו ח ט א ת ו ה ש ע י ר א ש ר ע ל ה ע ל י ו ה ג ו ר ל ל ע ז א ז ל י ע מ ד ח	166425
ה ח ט א ת א ש ר ל ו ו ל ק ח מ ל א ה מ ח ת ה ג ח ל י א ש מ ע ל ה מ ז ב ח מ ל פ נ י י ה ו	166553
ע ד ו ת ו ל א י מ ו ת ו ל ק ח מ ד מ ה פ ר ו ה ז ה ב א צ ב ע ו ע ל פ נ י ה כ פ ר ת ק ד מ	166681
כ א ש ר ע ש ה ל ד מ ה פ ר ו ה ז ה א ת ו ע ל ה כ פ ר ת ו ל פ נ י ה כ פ ר ת ו כ פ ר ע ל ה	166809
ב א ו ל כ פ ר ב ק ד ש ע ד צ א ת ו ו כ פ ר ב ע ד ו ו ב ע ד ב י ת ו ו ב ע ד כ ל ק ה ל י ש	166937
מ ב א צ ב ע ו ש ב ע פ ע מ י מ ו ט ה ר ו ו ק ד ש ו מ ט מ א ת ב נ י י ש ר א ל ו כ ל ה מ כ	167065
ל ע ו נ ת ב נ י י ש ר א ל ו א ת כ ל פ ש ע י ה מ ל כ ל ח ט א ת מ ו נ ת נ א ת מ ע ל ר א ש	167193
ו ע ד ו פ ש ט א ת ב ג ד י ה ב ד א ש ר ל ב ש ב ב א ו א ל ה ק ד ש ו ה נ י ח מ ש מ ו ר ח צ	167321
ה מ ז ב ח ה ו ה מ ש ל ח א ת ה ש ע י ר ל ע ז א ז ל י כ ב ס ב ג ד י ו ו ר ח צ א ת ב ש ר ו	167449
ו ב א ש א ת ע ר ת מ ו א ת ב ש ר מ ו א ת פ ר ש מ ו ה ש ר פ א ת מ י כ ב ס ב ג ד י ו ו ר ח	167577
ה ל א ת ע ש ו ה א ז ר ח ו ה ג ר ה ג ר ב ת ו כ כ מ כ י ב י ו מ ה ז ה י כ פ ר ע ל י כ מ ל	167705
ו א ש ר י מ ל א א ת י ד ו ל כ ה נ ת ח ת א ב י ו ו ל ב ש א ת ב ג ד י ה ב ד ב ג ד י ה ק ד	167833
ע ל ב נ י י ש ר א ל מ כ ל ח ט א ת מ א ח ת ב ש נ ה ו י ע ש כ א ש ר צ ו ה י ה ו ה א ת מ ש	167961
מ ב י ת י ש ר א ל א ש ר י ש ח ט ש ו ר א ו כ ש ב א ו ע ז ב מ ח נ ה א ו א ש ר י ש ח ט מ ח	168089
ו א מ ק ר ב ע מ ו ל מ ע נ א ש ר י ב י א ו ב נ י י ש ר א ל א ת ז ב ח י ה מ א ש ר ה מ ז ב	168217
ה ו ה פ ת ח א ה ל מ ו ע ד ו ה ק ט י ר ה ח ל ב ל ר י ח נ י ח ח ל י ה ו ה ו ל א י ז ב ח ו	168345
א ש ר י ג ו ר ב ת ו כ מ א ש ר י ע ל ה ע ל ה א ו ז ב ח ו א ל פ ת ח א ה ל מ ו ע ד ל א י ב	168473
ב נ פ ש ה א כ ל ת א ת ה ד מ ו ה כ ר ת י א ת ה מ ק ר ב ע מ ה כ י נ פ ש ה ב ש ר ב ד מ ה ו	168601
ה ג ר ה ג ר ב ת ו כ כ מ ל א י א כ ל ד מ ו א י ש א י ש מ ב נ י י ש ר א ל ו מ נ ה ג ר ה ג	168729
מ כ ל ב ש ר ל א ת א כ ל ו כ י נ פ ש כ ל ב ש ר ד מ ו ה ו א כ ל א כ ל י ו י כ ר ת ו כ ל נ	168857
נ ו ו י ד ב ר י ה ו ה א ל מ ש ה ל א מ ר ד ב ר א ל ב נ י י ש ר א ל ו א מ ר ת א ל ה מ א נ	168985
ל א ת ל כ ו א ת מ ש פ ט י ת ע ש ו ו א ת ח ק ת י ת ש מ ר ו ל ל כ ת ב ה מ א נ י י ה ו ה א	169113
ה א נ י י ה ו ה ע ר ו ת א ב י כ ו ע ר ו ת א מ כ ל א ת ג ל ה א מ כ ה ו א ל א ת ג ל ה ע ר	169241
ו ת ב ת ב נ כ א ו ב ת ב ת כ ל א ת ג ל ה ע ר ו ת נ כ י ע ר ו ת כ ה נ ה ע ר ו ת ב ת א ש ת	169369
כ ה ו א ע ר ו ת א ח י א ב י כ ל א ת ג ל ה א ל א ש ת ו ל א ת ק ר ב ד ד ת כ ה ו א ע ר ו ת	169497

Shape	Word	Translation	Verse	Position	Skip
א	אות	mark	Leviticus 15:19	165150	514
א	אלוה	God	Leviticus 15:24	165409	-905
ת	תשסת	2008	Leviticus 15:28	165683	897
נ	נתון	given	Leviticus 15:29	165696	-756
נ	נוף	prospect	Leviticus 16:2	166066	386
ס	סופי	final	Leviticus 16:10	166451	-387
י	ישועה	salvation	Leviticus 16:15	166825	-388
כ	כג אדר א	2/29	Leviticus 16:34	167979	-384

52. Feb 29/2008: Feb. 29, 2008 (is the) final prospect (to be) given God('s) mark (of) salvation. (One letter of the word "Feb, 29" are hidden beyond the slide border.)

will be among the remnant of the fourth race. The next slide (**Subject: Mark/Beast**), again found in Genesis 6:19 to 7:4, revealed that the mark of the beast on the forehead and/or hand stood for ungodly mind and/or deeds.[53] Again, it takes more than just faith to be sealed by God; it takes godly character that results in godly deeds. There is no free ride through the Tribulation. In Revelation 22:12, Jesus states in his vision to John, "And behold I come quickly and my reward is with me, to give every man according as his *work* shall be."

I wondered what happens to the remnant. Revelation 20:5 states, "But the rest of the dead lived not again until the 1,000 years were finished." The following slide (**Subject: Remnant/Race**), found in Exodus 27:9 to 27:18, revealed the remnant of the fourth race as returning to Eden and other places for 1,000 years. Eden may not be so bad; it's the *other places* that I'd be worried about.

I wondered how the godly would be distinguished from the ungodly regarding the seal of God or the mark of the beast. It has long been understood that we are a complex integration of body, mind and spirit. The modern world, however, has a tendency to segregate the physical, the mental and the spiritual parts of us. Has a doctor ever asked you if you felt guilty about something when you complained of an illness? It is harmonious integration that makes us happy, healthy, unique human beings. I felt that this harmony, or lack of it, must be the key or receptor of the seal. The following search (**Subject: Seal/Receptor**), found in Deuteronomy 22:21 to 23:16, revealed that the receptor of the seal of God is the color blue in the human aura.[54] We've known for thousands of years that an aura, invisible to us, surrounds the human body. Early artists painted auras as halos around angels and holy people. Some gifted psychics, such as Edgar Cayce, can see the aura; Cayce described it as a hue of colors that indicate our mood, health and spirituality. Our aura changes as we change. It is like a constantly changing barcode that registers the character of our soul. It disappears from the body at death, so it must be an extension of our soul. The light spectrum is a multitude of frequencies. It is possible that the blue aura frequency acts as the filter that is necessary

Letters	Position
מ כ ל ב ש ר ש נ י מ מ כ ל ת ב י א א ל ה ת ב ה ל ה ח י ת א ת כ ז כ ר ו נ ק ב ה י ה י ו מ ה ע ו פ ל מ י נ ה ו ו מ נ ה	7748
ה ו ו מ נ ה ב ה מ ה ל מ י נ ה מ כ ל ר מ ש ה א ד מ ה ל מ י נ ה ו ש נ י מ מ כ ל י ב א ו א ל י כ ל ה ח י ו ת ו א ת ה ק	7800
ת ו א ת ה ק ח ל כ מ כ ל מ א כ ל א ש ר י א כ ל ו א ס פ ת א ל י כ ו ה י ה ל כ ו ל ה מ ל א כ ל ה ו י ע ש נ ח כ כ ל א ש	7852
ח כ כ ל א ש ר צ ו ה א ת ו א ל ה י מ כ נ ע ש ה ו י א מ ר י ה ו ה ל נ ח ב א א ת ה ו כ ל ב י ת כ א ל ה ת ב ה כ י א ת כ	7904
ה כ י א ת כ ר א י ת י צ ד י ק ל פ נ י ב ד ו ר ה ז ה מ כ ל ה ב ה מ ה ה ט ה ו ר ה ת ק ח ל כ ש ב ע ה ש ב ע ה א י ש ו א	7956
ה א י ש ו א ש ת ו ו מ נ ה ב ה מ ה א ש ר ל א ט ה ר ה ה ו א ש נ י מ א י ש ו א ש ת ו ג מ מ ע ו פ ה ש מ י מ ש ב ע ה ש ב	8008
ש ב ע ה ש ב ע ה ז כ ר ו נ ק ב ה ל ח י ו ת ז ר ע ע ל פ נ י כ ל ה א ר צ כ י ל י מ י מ ע ו ד ש ב ע ה א נ כ י מ מ ט י ר	8060
י מ מ ט י ר ע ל ה א ר צ א ר ב ע י מ י ו מ ו א ר ב ע י מ ל י ל ה ו מ ח י ת י א ת כ ל ה י ק ו מ א ש ר ע ש י ת י מ ע ל	8112
י ת י מ ע ל פ נ י ה א ד מ ה ו י ע ש נ ח כ כ ל א ש ר צ ו ה ו י ה ו ה ו נ ח ב נ ש ש. מ א ו ת ש נ ה ו ה מ ב ו ל ה י ה מ	8164
ו ל ה י ה מ י מ ע ל ה א ר צ ו י ב א נ ח ו ב נ י ו ו א ש ת ו ו נ ש י ב נ י ו א ת ו א ל ה ת ב ה מ פ נ י מ י ה מ ב ו ל	8216
י ה מ ב ו ל מ נ ה ב ה מ ה ה ט ה ר ר ה ו מ נ ה ב ה מ ה א ש ר א י נ נ ה ט ה ר ה ו מ נ ה ע ו פ ו כ ל א ש ר ר מ ש ע ל ה	8268
ר מ ש ע ל ה א ד מ ה ש נ י מ ש נ י מ ב א ו א ל נ ח א ל ה ת ב ה ז כ ר ו נ ק ב ה כ א ש ר צ ו ה א ל ה י מ א ת נ ח ו י ה	8320
ת נ ח ו י ה י ל ש ב ע ת ה י מ י מ ו מ י ה מ ב ו ל ה י ו ע ל ה א ר צ ב ש נ ת ש ש מ א ו ת ש נ ה ל ח י י נ ח ב ח ד ש ה	8372
ח ב ח ד ש ה ש נ י ב ש ב ע ה ע ש ר י ו מ ל ח ד ש ב י ו מ ה ז ה נ ב ק ע ו כ ל מ ע י נ ו ת ת ה ו מ ר ב ה ו א ר ב ת ה ש	8424
א ר ב ת ה ש מ י מ נ פ ת ח ו ו י ה י ה ג ש מ ע ל ה א ר צ א ר ב ע י מ י ו מ ו א ר ב ע י מ ל י ל ה ב ע צ מ ה י ו מ ה ז	8476
ה י ו מ ה ז ה ב א נ ח ו ש מ ו ח מ ו י פ ת ב נ י נ ח ו א ש ת נ ח ו ש ל ש ת נ ש י ב נ י ו א ת מ א ל ה ת ב ה ה מ ה ו כ	8528

Shape	Word	Translation	Verse	Position	Skip
ח	חומא	ungodly	Genesis 6:19	7776	-254
א	אות	mark	Genesis 7:1	7940	104
פ	פשר	meaning	Genesis 7:1	7972	216
מ	מצח	forehead	Genesis 7:2	7988	106
מ	מעשה	deed	Genesis 7:2	7990	-56
ח	חיה	beast	Genesis 7:2	7992	-104
י	יד	hand	Genesis 7:4	8104	-148
ר	רצון	mind	Genesis 7:4	8135	55

53. Mark/Beast; The mark (of the) beast (in) forehead (and/or) hand meaning ungodly mind (and/or) deed(s).

ס ק ל ו ה א נ ש י ע י ר ה ב א ב נ י מ ו מ ת ה כ י ע ש ת ה נ ב ל ה ב י ש ר א ל ל ז נ ו ת ב י ת א ב י ה ו ב ע ר ת	284989
כ ב ע מ ה א ש ה ו ה א ש ה ו ב ע ר ת ה ר ע מ י ש ר א ל כ י י ה י ה נ ע ר ב ת ו ל ה מ א ר ש ה ל א י ש ו מ צ א ה א	285094
ב א ב נ י מ ו מ ת ו א ת ה נ ע ר ע ל ד ב ר א ש ר ל א צ ע ק ה ב ע י ר ו א ת ה א י ש ע ל ד ב ר א ש ר ע נ ה א ת א ש	285199
י ק ב ה ה א י ש ו ש כ ב ע מ ה ו מ ת ה א י ש א ש ר ש כ ב ע מ ה ל ב ד ו ו ל נ ע ר ל א ת ע ש ה ד ב ר א י נ ל נ ע ר	285304
צ א ה צ ע ק ה ה נ ע ר ה מ א ר ש ה ו א י נ מ ו ש י ע ל ה כ י י מ צ א א י ש נ ע ר ב ת ו ל ה א ש ר ל א א ר ש ה ו ת	285409
ו ת ה י ה ל א ש ה ת ח ת א ש ר ע נ ה ל א י ו כ ל ש ל ח ה כ ל י מ י ו ל א י ק ח א י ש א ת א ש ת א ב י ו ו ל א י ג	285514
ה ל י ה ו ה ג מ ד ו ר ע ש י ר י ל א י ב א ל ו ב ק ה ל י ה ו ה ל א י ב א ע מ ו נ י ו מ ו א ב י ב ק ה ל י ה ו ה ג	285619
ב ל ח מ ו ב מ י מ ב ד ר כ ב צ א ת כ מ מ מ צ ר י מ ו א ש ר ש כ ר ע ל י כ א ת ב ל ע מ ב נ ב ע ו ר מ פ ת ו ר א ר מ	285724
ל כ א ת ה ק ל ל ה ל ב ר כ ה כ י א ה ב כ י ה ו ה א ל ה י כ ל א ת ד ר ש ש ל מ מ ו ט ב ת מ כ ל י מ י כ ל ע ו ל מ ל	285829
ו ל ד ו ל ה מ ד ו ר ש ל י ש י י ב א ל ה מ ב ק ה ל י ה ו ה כ י ת צ א מ ח נ ה ע ל א י ב י כ ו נ ש מ ר ת מ כ ל ד ב	285934
ה ל א י ב א א ל ת ו כ ה מ ח נ ה ו ה י ה ל פ נ ו ת ע ר ב י ר ח צ ב מ י מ ו כ ב א ה ש מ ש י ב א א ל ת ו כ ה מ ח נ	286039
ה ב ש ב ת כ ח ו צ ו ח פ ר ת ה ב ה ו ש ב ת ו כ ס י ת א ת צ א ת כ כ י י ה ו ה א ל ה י כ מ ת ה ל כ ב ק ר ב מ ח נ כ	286144
ו ש ב מ א ח ר י כ ל א ת ס ג י ר ע ב ד א ל א ד נ י ו א ש ר י נ צ ל א ל י כ מ ע מ א ד נ י ו ע מ כ י ש ב ב ק ר ב כ	286249
י ש ר א ל ו ל א י ה י ה ק ד ש מ ב נ י י ש ר א ל ל א ת ב י א א ת נ נ ז ו נ ה ו מ ח י ר כ ל ב ב י ת י ה ו ה א ל ה	286354
ש כ א כ ל נ ש כ כ ל ד ב ר א ש ר י ש כ ל נ כ ר י ת ש י כ ו ל א ח י כ ל א ת ש י כ ל מ ע נ י ב ר כ כ י ה ו ה א ל ה	286459
ה י כ ל א ת א ח ר ל ש ל מ ו כ י ד ר ש י ד ר ש נ ו י ה ו ה א ל ה י כ מ ע מ כ ו ה י ה ב כ ח ט א ו כ י ת ח ד ל ל נ	286564

Shape	Word	Translation	Verse	Position	Skip
כ	כחל	blue	Deuteronomy 22:21	285028	-524
צ	צבע	color	Deuteronomy 22:24	285225	111
א	אוירה	aura	Deuteronomy 22:25	285323	318
א	אלוה	God	Deuteronomy 22:29	285522	-13
ק	קולט	receptor	Deuteronomy 23:1	285551	106
א	אות	seal	Deuteronomy 23:1	285553	104
א	אנושי	human	Deuteronomy 23:16	286270	2

54. Seal/Receptor: (The) receptor (of the) seal (of) God (is the) color blue (in the) human aura.

to let the blue star radiation wavelength pass, enabling that wavelength to energize our endocrine system. It is not unlike tuning a radio receiver to a specific station by turning a dial that controls a filter. When the filter is properly tuned to the wavelength of the signal, it lets the frequency pass and you can hear the desired station. Apparently, the absence of blue in the aura of an ungodly person would result in that person's being passed over for God's seal.

It appears from earlier Bible Code searches that the worst part of the Tribulation will start in 2010. Since God's faithful will be irradiated in February of 2008, and fully sealed by February of 2011, I wondered how the filter could offer protection in 2010. The following slide (**Subject: Fifth/Transition**), found in Genesis 21:29 to 24:14, revealed that one-half of the fifth race changeover is established in the leading year of the transition time. This would make the transition time non-linear. By February of 2010, we would be approximately 85 percent through the transition process, which would probably provide us with sufficient protection for this period.

I next decided to see if I could determine how much of a change in resonant body frequency was necessary to initiate the new root race. The following slide (**Subject: Doubling/Resonant**), found in Genesis 22:13 to 24:9, revealed that doubling resonant body frequency in the new era stretched our life span by a factor of four-and-one-half. Four-and-one-half times our current life span of 70 years equals 315 years, and corroborates the earlier search which advised that the Golden Era life span is 300 years.

We still have to make it through the Tribulation, and I wondered how doubling our body frequency would protect us during this period. The next slide (**Subject: Virus/Bacterium**), found in Exodus 22:25 to 23:8, revealed that unfriendly viruses and bacteria die at a higher body frequency. The Revelation describes many plagues that will be unleashed during the Tribulation. The friendly bacteria in our bodies that help us survive will probably transition with us and become compatible with our new body frequency. It took thousands of years of evolution, however, for foreign viruses and bacteria to become compatible with our present physiological system, and it will probably require thousands of years more for them to readjust.

The final question troubling me was a prophecy by Jesus in Revelation 20:4, repeated again in 20:6, that the faithful would live with Christ for 1,000 years. So far, I had found that the blue star would extend the human life span to around 300 years. Did this mean that we would die and then be reborn at 300-year intervals? Was I missing something? I have reason to believe that all the prophecies made by Jesus can be verified in the Bible Code, so I decided to continue my search. The following search (**Subject: Golden/Rejuvenation**), found in Leviticus 13:51 to 14:9, revealed that rejuvenation in the Golden Age prolonged the life of the faithful to 1,000 years.[55] This search corroborates Revelation 20:4 to 20:6, but contradicts the earlier search (**Subject: Golden/Era**) stating that the Golden Era life span is 300 years. I found the answer in a follow-up search using the same subject. The next search (**Subject: Golden/Rejuvenation**), found in Leviticus 13:2 to 14:9, revealed that rejuvenation is given to the faithful as needed in the Golden Age, at seven earth grid cities at seven-year intervals.

So, this is how it appears to me. The faithful are irradiated by the blue star in 2008 and are rejuvenated during a transition period of three years. The human life span will then be extended to 300 years. As we have learned, however, we must have a godly blue aura for this to occur.

From the time of Adam to that of Noah, the human life span, or so the Torah tells us, was almost 1,000 years. I wondered why it wouldn't be the same during the Golden Age. During the days of Adam to Noah, however, most people were ungodly, and the times were worse than they are now. Jesus promised that only the godly would be on earth during the Golden Age. I believe that a life span of 300 years is a safety factor to ensure that this occurs. We will still have free choice during the Golden Era, because God never takes that away from us. But suppose we were to go back to our old selfish ways? If we must rejuvenate to remain on earth, we will have to maintain our commitment to godliness; otherwise, our aura

Letters	Position
ר ב ש ר א י ש צ ר ו ע ה ו א ט מ א ה ו א ט מ א י ט מ א נ ו ה כ ה נ ב ר א ש ו נ ג ע ו ו ה צ ר ו ע א ש ר ב ו ה	160302
צ מ ר א ו ב ב ג ד פ ש ת י מ א ו ב ש ת י א ו ב ע ר ב ל פ ש ת י מ ו ל צ מ ר א ו ב ע ו ר א ו ב כ ל מ ל א כ ת ע	160475
ע ב י ו מ ה ש ב י ע י כ י פ ש ה ה נ ג ע ב ב ג ד א ו ב ש ת י א ו ב ע ר ב א ו ב ע ו ר ל כ ל א ש ר י ע ש ה ה ע	160648
ה כ ה נ ו ה נ ה ל א פ ש ה ה נ ג ע ב ב ג ד א ו ב ש ת י א ו ב ע ר ב א ו ב כ ל כ ל י ע ו ר ו צ ו ה ה כ ה נ ו כ	160821
ו א מ ר א ה ה כ ה נ ו ה נ ה כ ה ה ה נ ג ע א ח ר י ה כ ב ס א ת ו ו ק ר ע א ת ו מ נ ה ב ג ד א ו מ נ ה ע ו ר	160994
ה מ ה נ ג ע ו כ ב ס ש נ י ת ו ט ה ר ז א ת ת ו ר ת נ ג ע צ ר ע ת ב ג ד ה צ מ ר א ו ה פ ש ת י מ א ו ה ש ת י א	161167
ה צ ר ע ת מ נ ה צ ר ו ע ו צ ו ה ה כ ה נ ו ל ק ח ל מ ט ה ר ש ת י צ פ ר י מ ח י ו ת ט ה ר ו ת ו ע צ א ר ז ו ש	161340
פ ר ה ש ח ט ה ע ל ה מ י מ ה ח י י מ ו ה ז ה ע ל ה מ ט ה ר מ נ ה צ ר ע ת ש ב ע פ ע מ י מ ו ט ה ר ו ו ש ל ח א	161513
ו א ת ר א ש ו ו א ת ז ק נ ו ו א ת ג ב ת ע י נ י ו ו א ת כ ל ש ע ר ו י ג ל ח ו כ ב ס א ת ב ג ד י ו ו ר ח צ א	161686
ה ר ו א ת מ ל פ נ י י ה ו ה פ ת ח א ה ל מ ו ע ד ו ל ק ח ה כ ה נ א ת ה כ ב ש ה א ח ד ו ה ק ר י ב א ת ו ל א ש	161859
מ ו נ ת נ ה כ ה נ ע ל ת נ ו כ א ז נ ה מ ט ה ר ה י מ נ י ת ו ע ל ב ה נ י ד ו ה י מ נ י ת ו ע ל ב ה נ ר ג ל ו	162032
ה ש מ נ א ש ר ע ל כ פ ו י ת נ ה כ ה נ ע ל ת נ ו כ א ז נ ה מ ט ה ר ה י מ נ י ת ו ע ל ב ה נ י ד ו ה י מ נ י ת	162205
ת ה ע ל ה ו ה ע ל ה ה כ ה נ א ת ה ע ל ה ו א ת ה מ נ ח ה ה מ ז ב ח ה ו כ פ ר ע ל י ו ה כ ה נ ו ט ה ר ו א מ ד	162378

Shape	Word	Translation	Verse	Position	Skip
ש	שנה	year	Leviticus 13:51	160654	173
מ	משוך	prolonged	Leviticus 13:56	161009	-341
ז	זהוב	golden	Leviticus 13:59	161185	173
א	אלף	thousand	Leviticus 13:59	161206	330
ה	הצערה	rejuvenation	Leviticus 14:3	161347	-2
ח	חיים	life	Leviticus 14:6	161527	1
א	אמון	faithful	Leviticus 14:7	161543	-168
ע	עידן	age	Leviticus 14:9	161717	357

55. Golden/Rejuvenation; Rejuvenation (in the) Golden Age prolonged life (of the) faithful (to a) thousand years.(One letter of the word "age" is hidden beyond the slide border.)

will not let the rejuvenation frequency pass, and we will die. The key word in the previous two slides is *faithful*. We must remain faithful, or we will join those with the mark of the beast who left during the Tribulation.

The last slide indicates that cities will be built on the new vortex grid. The earth's vortex grid contains locations where cosmic radiation is strongest. The Great Pyramid and the Sphinx are built on a current vortex location in Egypt. Of course, if there were to be a pole shift, these vortex locations would all change. Since the word "cities" in the last slide touches the word "seven," this probably means that cities will be built on seven of these vortex grid locations that would be used as rejuvenation centers.

We've learned that the blue star seal of God will rejuvenate health and protect the faithful from disease during the Tribulation. I wondered about all the other tragic events that are predicted to occur during this period. Asteroid strikes, horrendous storms, earthquakes, fires, tidal waves, crime, famine and world war—all these things are expected during the Tribulation. An earlier search advised that the Archangel Michael would protect all of the faithful during the Tribulation. The following search (**Subject: Guardian/Angel**), found in Numbers 18:7 to 18:31, reveals that guardian angels protect the faithful during the Tribulation.

I mentioned earlier that I am convinced that my guardian angel has saved my life on at least six occasions, and perhaps many other times that I am not even aware of. One time I missed an airline flight, which is extremely rare for me. The plane ended up crashing due to an ice buildup on its wings. Nearly half the people on board were killed. Based upon the Law of Cause and Effect, accidents and serious diseases that are planned karmic events for our learning are allowed to occur. If they are not planned, or if we deserve mercy, then guardian angels will protect us. There must be millions of people in the air on flights throughout the world everyday. Have you ever wondered why so very few of these flights ever crash? I doubt that it is due to our great technology. According to karmic law, everyone on the plane would have to be scheduled for a catastrophe at the exact same moment! One godly person, or even one sincere prayer, could protect everyone on board, since everyone's fate hangs together in such circumstances. It is said that there are no accidents in God's universe. I am convinced that, during the Tribulation, the faithful will be where they are supposed to be in order to survive. They will be needed in the Golden Age.

14

The Golden Age

According to the Bible, horrific times lie ahead. Like every life experience in our soul's eons of existence, this will be a learning process. When these horrific times are over, those who have passed the test will believe it was all well worth it. Survivors will evolve into a world of love, because all those who survive will be committed to godliness. People won't have to lock their doors anymore, because all will treat their neighbors as they themselves would like to be treated. There will be opportunity for everyone, because there will be plenty of work to do. Everyone will trust and help each other; therefore, all peoples will move up the social ladder together, making homelessness and slum neighborhoods a thing of the past.

Unlike the case of Atlantis, modern technology will probably be retained. The new race, quickly rebounding, will soon far surpass current living standards. There will be no need to expend vast resources on gigantic war machines, because the threat of war will no longer exist. Those resources will instead go toward research, education, the healing sciences and human services. Clean energy cells will power homes and automobiles. Mass transit will probably be the favored form of transportation; it will be fast, safe and luxurious.

Once the dust settles, the air will be clean and the climate of the world will be healthier than ever. Farms will produce great quantities of organic food, and no one will ever need go hungry again. The population will become much healthier, and the human life span will expand by many hundreds of years. Machines will replace most manual labor. The world will see the greatest economic expansion ever. Does this sound like some hypothetical utopia? It should, because that's what the Revelation promises. Let's see if it can be confirmed in the Bible Code.

My first search involved world peace. The following slide (**Subject: World/Peace**), found in Genesis 30:31 to 31:2, revealed that we will have world peace for 1,000 years after the Tribulation.[56] This supports the idea that when governments are reestablished, prior military budgets will be diverted to science, medicine, education and social services.

The next slide (**Subject: Prison/Close**), found in Leviticus 4:29 to 5:18, revealed that all prisons of the world close for 1,000 years after the Tribulation. Again, great resources will be diverted from worldwide law enforcement to advancing a utopia-style society.

The next two searches involve the problem of clean, abundant energy. The exploitation of polluting fuels is, in part, bringing about the Tribulation. Expected earth changes are necessary to reestablish the ecological balance that the earth has lost over the last 100 years. Humanity would probably be extinct within a few generations if nothing were to change, so the Tribulation may be a blessing in disguise. The first search (**Subject: Heating/Cooling**), found in Deuteronomy 32:51 to 33:14, revealed that the heating and cooling of homes in the new age is by hydrogen fuel. This will probably be accomplished by using hydrogen fuel cells. Such a technology is currently being developed. The next search on this subject (**Subject: Automobile/Powered**), found in Genesis 47:15 to 47:25, revealed that the automobile is powered by a hydrogen fuel motor in the new age. I imagine this will also be a hydrogen fuel cell, producing electricity for an electric motor that powers the wheels. This technology for automobiles is also currently being developed. I believe we would be wise to invest heavily in fuel

Position	Letters
42827	כ י ל ב י ת י ו י א מ ר מ ה א ת נ ל כ ו י א מ ר י ע ק ב ל א ת ת נ ל י מ א ו מ ה א מ ת ע ש ה
42951	ו נ ק ד ב ע ז י מ ו ה י ה ש כ ר י ו ע נ ת ה ב י צ ד ק ת י ב י ו מ מ ח ר כ י ת ב ו א ע ל ש כ
43075	ה ה ו א א ת ה ת י ש י מ ה ע ק ד י מ ו ה ט ל א י מ ו א ת כ ל ה ע ז י מ ה נ ק ד ו ת ו ה ט ל א
43199	נ ו ת ר ת ו י ק ח ל ו י ע ק ב מ ק ל ל ב נ ה ל ח ו ל ו ז ו ע ר מ ו נ ו י פ צ ל ב ה נ פ צ ל ו
43323	ח ה צ א נ ו י ח מ נ ה ב ב א נ ל ש ת ו ת ו י ח מ ו ה צ א נ א ל ה מ ק ל ו ת ו ת ל ד נ ה צ א נ
43447	א ש ת מ ע ל צ א נ ל ב נ ו ה י ה ב כ ל י ח מ ה צ א נ ה מ ק ש ר ו ת ו ש מ י ע ק ב א ת ה מ ק ל
43571	א י ש מ א ד מ א ד ו י ה י ל ו צ א נ ר ב ו ת ו ש פ ח ו ת ו ע ב ד י מ ו ג מ ל י מ ו ח מ ר י מ
43695	י ל ב נ ו ה נ ה א י נ נ ו ע מ ו כ ת מ ו ל ש ל ש ו מ ו י א מ ר י ה ו ה א ל י ע ק ב ש ו ב א ל
43819	א ב י כ נ כ י א י נ נ ו א ל י כ ת מ ל ש ל ש מ ו א ל ה י א ב י ה י ה ע מ ד י ו א ת נ ה י ד ע
43943	י א מ ר נ ק ד י מ י ה י ה ש כ ר כ ו י ל ד ו כ ל ה צ א נ נ ק ד י מ ו א מ כ ה י א מ ר ע ק ד י
44067	ח ל ו מ ו ה נ ה ה ע ת ד י מ ה ע ל י מ ע ל ה צ א נ ע ק ד י מ נ ק ד י מ ו ב ר ד י מ ו י א מ ר
44191	ב ר ד י מ כ י ר א י ת י א ת כ ל א ש ר ל ב נ ע ש ה ל כ א נ כ י ה א ל ב י ת א ל א ש ר מ ש ח ת
44315	נ ו ח ל ק ו נ ח ל ה ב ב י ת א ב י נ ו ה ל ו א נ כ ר י ו ת נ ח ש ב נ ו ל ו כ י מ כ ר נ ו ו י

Shape	Word	Translation	Verse	Position	Skip
ת	תלאה	tribulation	Genesis 30:31	42840	-496
א	אחרי	after	Genesis 30:35	43101	244
ש	שלום	peace	Genesis 30:35	43109	-124
ע	עולם	world	Genesis 30:35	43109	-248
א	אלף	thousand	Genesis 30:37	43235	-118
ש	שנה	year	Genesis 31:2	43718	252

56. World/Peace: World peace (for a) thousand year(s) after (the) Tribulation.

cell technology over the next few years, because our vast electrical, gas and petroleum distribution systems will undoubtedly be destroyed during the last half of the Tribulation.

I can't believe that every one of the faithful who evolves or is born into the new race will be totally karma-free, so accidents and disease will probably continue to be a problem for some time. This problem should diminish, however, because serious new karma will not be developing. The following search (**Subject: Disease/To diminish**), found in Genesis 2:18 to 4:8, revealed that disease is to diminish for 1,000 years in the new age. Funds committed to medical research will probably find cures for the diseases that plague mankind today.

Since greed and jealousy will be a thing of the past, there should be little in the way of class differentiation in the Golden Age. The next search (**Subject: Equal/Wealth**), found in Exodus 26:5 to 26:19, reveals the abundance of equal wealth for all in the new age of 1,000 years.

I have always believed that the male ego prevents many men from subordinating their will to that of God. Men tend to be more selfish than women, often losing themselves in pursuit of the gods of wealth and power. For this reason, a greater number of men than women may be passed over during the transition into the Golden Age. My next search supports that belief. The following slide (**Subject: Polygamy/Practiced**), found in Genesis 47:22 to 48:16, reveals that, since there will be more women than men, polygamy will be practiced in the new age.

The seventh seal described in the Revelation to Saint John states simply that, "There was silence in heaven for about the space of half-an-hour." In Chapter Ten, we discovered that an hour standing alone in the Revelation symbolizes a generation of 70 years; therefore, "the space of half-an-hour" indicates that something happens in heaven over a period of 35 years. This was a mystery that I pondered for some time. After I had discovered how extensive the earth changes might be during the Tribulation, it became clear to me that it would take some time for civilization to be reestablished. This is when it occurred to me why heaven might be silent for 35 years. The following slide (**Subject: Heaven/Silent**), found in Genesis 39:19 to 41:3, regarding the silence of heaven for half-an-hour, revealed that rebirth will be suspended from 2010 to 2045.[57] Apparently, souls waiting to join the new age will not be allowed to reincarnate until the earth is stable and civilization has been reestablished.

Since one of the seven seals is involved, this must be a description of world karma. As far as I can tell, we are talking here about the only Tribulation karma that extends beyond the seven-year Tribulation period. It may be the hardest karma to bear. I had been wondering why the world would have to suffer without children for so long. The following slide (**Subject: Eden/Silent**), found in Genesis 1:29 to 3:24, on 'the silence of Eden,' revealed that world abortion karma suspended soul rebirth from 2010 till 2045. I should have known. Karma is just as we have been taught: an eye for an eye and a tooth for a tooth.

The next search is so disturbing that I almost didn't include it. I had wondered if ovulation in women would simply cease for 35 years, or if, perhaps, men would become temporarily sterile. According to some medical reports, sperm counts in our own generation are alarmingly low. The future prospect scenario turned out to be much worse. The following slide (**Subject: Children/Born**), found in Genesis 20:9 to 21:3, revealed that all the children for one-half a generation are born dead, from 2010 till 2045, when Eden is "still." We learned earlier that it takes spirit and flesh, joined by a reincarnating soul, to produce a living human baby. Apparently, souls will not be incarnating during this period. For the past 30 years, as we have chosen to abort millions of fetuses, the world has denied human bodies to souls. Now it appears that human bodies will be denied souls. Remember that this is accumulated world karma. Each soul involved in abortion also has personal karma to deal with. I searched on Eden instead of heaven in the previous two slides, because the Kabbalah views Eden as a level of heaven. Apparently, it is.

The last search of this series of slides in a way confirms the others. The following slide (**Subject: Last/Child**), found in

א מ ר כ ד ב ר י מ ח א ל ה ע ש ה ל י ע ב ד כ ו י ח ר א פ ו ו י ק ח א ד נ י	58566
ש מ ב ב י ת ה ס ה ר ו י ח י י ה ו ה א ת י ו ס פ ו י ט א ל י ו ח ס ד ו י ת	58651
א ש ר ב ב י ת ה ס ה ר ו א ת כ ל א ש ר ע ש י מ ש מ ה ו א ה י ה ע ש ה א י נ	58736
ו ה מ צ ל י ח ו י ה י א ח ר ה ד ב ר י מ ה א ל ה ח ט א ו מ ש ק ה מ ל כ מ צ	58821
ה מ ש ק י מ ו ע ל ש ר ה א ו פ י מ ו י ת נ א ת מ ב מ ש מ ר ב י ת ש ר ה ט ב	58906
א ת מ ו י ש ר ת א ת מ ו י ה י ו י מ י מ ב מ ש מ ר ו י ח ל מ ו ח ל ו מ ש נ	58991
מ צ ר י מ א ש ר א ס ו ר י מ ב ב י ת ה ס ה ר ו י ב א א ל י ה מ י ו ס פ ב ב	59076
א ד נ י ו ל א מ ר מ ד ו ע פ נ י כ מ ר ע י מ ה י ו מ ו י א מ ר ו א ל י ו ח	59161
פ ר ו נ א ל י ו י ס פ ר ש ר ה מ ש ק י מ א ת ח ל מ ו ל י ו ס פ ו י א מ ר ל	59246
ה ב ש י ל ו א ש כ ל ת י ה ע נ ב י מ ו כ ו ס פ ר ע ה ב י ד י ו א ק ח א ת ה	59331
ו ס פ ז ה פ ת ר נ ו ש ל ש ת ה ש ר ג י מ ש ל ש ת י מ י מ ה מ ב ע ו ד ש ל ש	59416
ט ה ר א ש ו נ א ש ר ה י י ת מ ש ק ה ו כ י א מ ז כ ר ת נ י א ת כ כ א ש ר י	59501
ז ה כ י ג נ ב ג נ ב ת י מ א ר צ ה ע ב ר י מ ו ג מ פ ה ל א ע ש י ת י מ א ו	59586
י ב ח ל ו מ י ו ה נ ה ש ל ש ה ס ל י ח ר י ע ל ר א ש י ו ב ס ל ה ע ל י ו נ	59671
פ ו י א מ ר ז ה פ ת ר נ ו ש ל ש ת ה ס ל י מ ש ל ש ת י מ י מ ה מ ב ע ו ד ש	59756
ש ר כ מ ע ל י כ ו י ה י ב י ו מ ה ש ל י ש י י ו מ ה ל ד ת א ת פ ר ע ה ו י	59841
ע ב ד י ו ו י ש ב א ת ש ר ה מ ש ק י מ ע ל מ ש ק ה ו ו י ת נ ה כ ו ס ע ל כ	59926
י ו ס פ ו י ש כ ח ה ו ו י ה י מ ק צ ש נ ת י מ י מ י מ ו פ ר ע ה ח ל מ ו ה	60011
ו ת ר ע י נ ה ב א ח ו ו ה נ ה ש ב ע פ ר ו ת א ח ר ו ת ע ל ו ת א ח ר י ה נ	60096
א כ ל נ ה ה פ ר ו ת ר ע ו ת ה מ ר א ה ו ד ק ת ה ב ש ר א ת ש ב ע ה פ ר ו ת	60181
י מ ע ל ו ת ב ק נ ה א ח ד ב ר י א ו ת ו ט ב ו ת ו ה נ ה ש ב ע ש ב ל י מ ד	60266
ש ב ל י מ ה ב ר י א ו ת ו ה מ ל א ו ת ו י י ק צ פ ר ע ה ו ה נ ה ח ל ו מ ו	60351
י ה ו י ס פ ר פ ר ע ה ל ה מ א ת ח ל מ ו ו א י נ פ ו ת ר א ו ת מ ל פ ר ע ה	60436
ע ל ע ב ד י ו ו י ת נ א ת י ב מ ש מ ר ב י ת ש ר ה ט ב ח י מ א ת י ו א ת ש	60521
ו ו ש מ א ת נ ו נ ע ר ע ב ר י ע ב ד ל ש ר ה ט ב ח י מ ו נ ס פ ר ל ו ו י פ	60606
ש י ב ע ל כ נ י ו ת א ו ת ל ה ו י ש ל ח פ ר ע ה ו י ק ר א א ת י ו ס פ ו י	60691

Shape	Word	Translation	Verse	Position	Skip
ש	שעה	hour	Genesis 39:19	58575	-598
ת	תשע	2010	Genesis 39:19	58584	-172
ת	תחייה	rebirth	Genesis 39:21	58663	-342
ש	שותק	silent	Genesis 39:22	58753	170
ר	רקיע	Heaven	Genesis 40:1	58838	425
ת	תלוי	suspended	Genesis 40:1	58839	-510
ת	תתה	2045	Genesis 40:9	59260	-512
ג	גלוי	revealed	Genesis 40:15	59609	337
ע	עד ש	till	Genesis 40:21	59941	-337
ח	חצי	half	Genesis 41:3	60128	246

57. Heaven/Silent: Heaven (is) silent (for a) half-hour... revealed (that) rebirth (will be) suspended (from) 2010 till 2045.

Shape	Word	Translation	Verse	Position	Skip
ת (diamond)	תשע	2010	Leviticus 22:6	174869	-117
א (hourglass)	אדם	Adam	Leviticus 22:11	175108	362
י (shaded)	ילד	child	Leviticus 22:16	175347	119
א (circle)	אחרון	last	Leviticus 22:18	175469	-119
י (shaded hourglass)	יליד	born	Leviticus 22:18	175470	-353
ת (square)	תלאה	tribulation	Leviticus 22:25	175830	-352
ב (shaded diamond)	במשך	during	Leviticus 23:6	176410	125

58. Last/Child: (The) last child born during (the) Tribulation (was) Adam (in) 2010.

Leviticus 22:6 to 23:6, reveals that the last child born during the Tribulation was Adam, in 2010.[58] This reaffirms what Jesus told us in Revelation 20:13, that "I am the alpha and omega, the beginning and the end, the first and the last."

15

An Overview

Over the past 100 years, there has been a growing divergence between science and religion. People with logical minds became confused when their religious leaders held on to old-fashioned views regarding the literal interpretation of their holy books. As the level of education has increased around the world, people have become more and more disillusioned with religion because it no longer makes sense to them.

One of the greatest difficulties confronting Christianity was the theory of evolution. The Church couldn't accept that the universe was not literally created in six earth days as appears to be presented in Genesis. On the other hand scientists, supporting the big bang theory of creation, estimate that the universe must be between seven and 20 billion years old. The following Bible Code search supports this scientific conclusion. (**Subject: Genesis/Billion**), found in Genesis 27:24 to 27:41, reveals that one day equals one billion years at the beginning of Genesis.[59] This would make the universe seven billion years old. In Genesis 1:16 to 19, there is a description of how God made two great lights, the greater to rule by day and the lesser to rule by night. "And the evening and morning were the fourth day." This is a description of the earth's being

Letters	Position
י א מ ר א ל י ו י צ ח ק א ב י ו ג ש ה נ א ו ש ק ה ל י ב נ י ו י ג ש ו י ש ק ל ו ו י ר ח א ת ר י ח ב ג ד י	37385
ש מ י מ ו מ ש מ נ י ה א ר צ ו ר ב ד ג נ ו ת י ר ש י ע ב ד ו כ ע מ י מ ו י ש ת ח ו ל כ ל א מ י מ ה ו ה ג ב	37494
ק ל ב ר כ א ת י ע ק ב ו י ה י א כ י צ א י צ א י ע ק ב מ א ת פ נ י י צ ח ק א ב י ו ו ע ש ו א ח י ו ב א מ צ	37603
ע ב ר ת ב ר כ נ י נ פ ש כ ו י א מ ר ל ו י צ ח ק א ב י ו מ י א ת ה ו י א מ ר א נ י ב נ כ ב כ ר כ ע ש ו ו י	37712
מ ת ב ו א ו א ב ר כ ה ו ג מ ב ר ו כ י ה י ה כ ש מ ע ע ש ו א ת ד ב ר י א ב י ו ו י צ ע ק צ ע ק ה ג ד ל ה ו	37821
ו י א מ ר ה כ י ק ר א ש מ ו י ע ק ב ו י ע ק ב נ י ז ה פ ע מ י מ א ת ב כ ר ת י ל ק ח ו ה נ ה ע ת ה ל ק ח ב	37930
ל א ח י ו נ ת ת י ל ו ל ע ב ד י מ ו ד ג נ ו ת י ר ש ס מ כ ת י ו ו ל כ ה א פ ו א מ ה א ע ש ה ב נ י ו י א מ	38039
נ י צ ח ק א ב י ו ו י א מ ר א ל י ו ה נ ה מ ש מ נ י ה א ר צ י ה י ה מ ו ש ב כ ו מ ט ל ה ש מ י מ מ ע ל ו ע	38148
א ת י ע ק ב ע ל ה ב ר כ ה א ש ר ב ר כ ו א ב י ו ו י א מ ר ע ש ו ב ל ב ו י ק ר ב ו י מ י א ב ל א ב י ו א ה	38257
ק ט נ ו ת א מ ר א ל י ו ה נ ה ע ש ו א ח י כ מ ת נ ח מ ל כ ל ה ר ג כ ו ע ת ה ב נ י ש מ ע ב ק ל י ו ק ו מ ב	38366
א ח י כ מ כ ו ש כ ח א ת א ש ר ע ש י ת ל ו ו ש ל ח ת י ו ל ק ח ת י כ מ ש מ ל מ ה א ש כ ל ג מ ש נ י כ מ י	38475
ת כ א ל ה מ ב נ ו ת ה א ר צ ל מ ה ל י ח י י מ ו י ק ר א י צ ח ק א ל י ע ק ב ו י ב ר כ א ת ו ו י צ ו ה ו	38584
ש מ א ש ה מ ב נ ו ת ל ב נ א ח י א מ כ ו א ל ש ד י י ב ר כ א ת כ ו י פ ר כ ו י ר ב כ ו ה י י ת ל ק ה ל ע מ	38693
ל א ב ר ה מ ו י ש ל ח י צ ח ק א ת י ע ק ב ו י ל כ פ ד נ ה א ר מ א ל ל ב נ ב נ ב ת ו א ל ה א ר מ י א ח י ר	38802
ש מ א ש ה ב ב ר כ ו א ת ו ו י צ ו ע ל י ו ל א מ ר ל א ת ק ח א ש ה מ ב נ ו ת כ נ ע נ ו י ש מ ע י ע ק ב א ל	38911

Shape	Word	Translation	Verse	Position	Skip
ר	רישא	beginning	Genesis 27:24	37304	107
ש	שווה	equal	Genesis 27:26	37407	332
ש	שנה	year	Genesis 27:28	37518	541
י	יום	day	Genesis 27:32	37732	328
ב	בראשית	Genesis	Genesis 27:34	37857	109
א	אחד	one	Genesis 27:37	38057	-328
ב	ביליון	billion	Genesis 27:41	38273	113

59. Genesis/Billion: One day equal(s) one billion year(s) (in the) beginning (of) Genesis.

placed in orbit around the sun and the moon's being placed in orbit around the earth on the fourth day—or, according to the Bible Code, at the end of four billion years. Science currently estimates the age of the earth at from four to 4.65 billion years.

It was a great mistake on the part of religious leaders not to readily accept the fact that the time frame of creation as depicted in Genesis is a metaphor. The real lesson of Genesis is that God created the universe, not how long it took. Religion's conflicting views in regard to science opened the door to world communism and a greater acceptance of atheism. Many who didn't accept atheism became increasingly liberal and selfish in their views of how society should be organized. They considered religion as outdated and constraining. These permissive views had a devastating effect on our society. Extramarital sex between consenting adults soon became quite acceptable. That is one reason why, today, one-third of all families in the U.S. are single-parent families. It is a reason why 76 percent of teenage mothers are unmarried, and why the national divorce rate more than doubled in the U.S. between 1960 and 1997. As the result of the 1973 decision of the U.S. Supreme Court, abortion became legal; since then, more than 35 million abortions have been carried out in this country. The social behavior enumerated above, compounded worldwide, has in part created a great collective karmic debt, bringing us closer to the coming Tribulation.

The Bible Code has sounded a warning. Code searches in this book indicate a strong prospect for the Tribulation to occur between 2005 and 2012. The worst is to occur in the latter half of that period, which gives us ample time to change our behavior. I believe that, through the mediation of God's grace, it is possible to avert much or possibly all of this bad karma, in the same way as we saw its being averted in the case of the biblical Nineveh. But it will take a great change in human behavior to turn things around. Unselfish religious and racial tolerance is absolutely essential in these times.

I hope this book brings with it the realization that we are all viewed equally in the eyes of God. It makes little difference whether we are Christians, Jews, Muslims, Hindus, Buddhists or whatever.

We are all part of the whole. The prayer given to the world by Jesus starts in the plural with, "*Our* Father," not with the singular "*My.*" Even if we pray alone, we still say, "Our Father." This salutation is intended to remind us that we are all part of the divine creation. We are more than just brothers and sisters; we are part of the whole of mankind, just as our fingers are part of our hand. If we hurt one of our fingers, our entire hand is hurt. The laws of creation are based upon the collective nature of mankind, that is, our collective consciousness resulting in collective karma. We all share in the good and the evil choices made by man. The Elizabethan poet-preacher John Donne understood this well when he wrote in his seventeenth *Devotion*, "No man is an island, entire of itself...any man's death diminishes me, because I am involved in mankind; And therefore never send to know for whom the bell tolls; It tolls for thee."

Our fall from grace came about when we took on the "*I*" consciousness of selfishness. We became convinced that individually we were gods. When we examine any of mankind's problems, we can trace its origins back to the single root cause of selfishness. The Ten Commandments forbade selfishness. If you commit a crime, the motive is necessarily a selfish one; you have wanted something at the expense of someone else. Love is the opposite of selfishness; it is the "we" consciousness of self*less*ness. It is the difference between good and evil. We are confined to our human bodies here on earth for the purpose of learning to choose the selfless path back to the enlightened state that we have lost. It is an evolutionary process encompassing all of mankind, but each soul proceeds at its own pace.

We are now apparently coming to a fork of decision in the road, and we are to be tested as to which path we will choose to follow. We have seen the prospect put forth by the Bible Code that only one-third of mankind will choose the path of enlightenment. Let's review that decision-time scenario as it is presented in the Bible Code. In 2008, mankind will be irradiated by a cosmic ray coming from the 1987 blue star supernova which became a periodic signal emitter. The Bible Code refers to the radiation of this star as the Seal of God, and this is perhaps the meaning of the star depicted in Surah eighty-six, Al Tariq, in the Holy Koran. The following search **(Subject: Al Tariq)**, found in Exodus 29:3 to 29:13, advises that Al Tariq of the Koran is the Blue Star ray, Tribulation salvation seal of God for the faithful on 2/27/2001 and in 2008.[60] The color blue in the aura of the faithful soul will act as a filter to let pass the frequency of a signal that initiates a bodily transfiguration. Sometime within the three years of the emission, these souls will transition into the fifth root race of mankind. They are destined to enter earth's coming Golden Age, as promised in Chapter 20 of the Revelation. If these souls remain faithful, they will live for 1,000 years and never suffer human death again. They will ascend at the end of the Golden Age to a much higher realm of existence.

Revelation 20:4 to 6 describes this event as the first resurrection: "Blessed and holy is he that hath part in the first resurrection: on such the second death hath no power but they shall be priests of God and of Christ, and shall reign with him a thousand years."

The following Bible Code searches explain the meaning of the first resurrection and the second death. **(Subject: Revelation/ Twenty)**, found in Numbers 20:16 to 22:19, advised that the second death revealed in Revelation 20 is resulting from being born again. In other words, the second death is the reincarnation cycle of rebirth and death that fulfills the Law of Cause and Effect. **(Subject: Golden/Faithful)**, found in Leviticus 20:11 to 21:18, advised that, as revealed in Revelation 20, the second death is to have no power for the faithful of the Golden Age. This apparently means that the reincarnation cycle will end for the faithful in this age. **(Subject: Death/Nevermore)**, found in Exodus 27:7 to 28:2, revealed death nevermore for the faithful souls of the Golden Age.[61] This search confirms the prior search. **(Subject: Resurrection/ Fifth)**, found in Leviticus 25:19 to 27:15, revealed that the first resurrection is the Tribulation transition to the fifth root race, the second death becoming suspended. This search confirms that the transfiguration from the fourth to the fifth root race is a resurrection process and that it is the first to occur in the fourth root race.

Position	Letters
120679	ת מ ו נ ת ת א ו ת מ ע ל ס ל א ח ד ו ה ק ר ב ת א ת מ ב ס ל ו א ת ה פ ר ו א ת ש נ
120726	א ת א ה ר נ ו א ת ב נ י ו ת ק ר י ב א ל פ ת ח א ה ל מ ו ע ד ו ר ח צ ת א ת מ ב מ
120773	א ת ה ב ג ד י מ ו ה ל ב ש ת א ת א ה ר נ א ת ה כ ת נ ת ו א ת מ ע י ל ה א פ ד ו א
120820	ת ה ח ש נ ו א פ ד ת ל ו ב ח ש ב ה א פ ד ו ש מ ת ה מ צ נ פ ת ע ל ר א ש ו ו נ ת ת
120867	ד ש ע ל ה מ צ נ פ ת ו ל ק ח ת א ת ש מ נ ה מ ש ח ה ו י צ ק ת ע ל ר א ש ו ו מ ש ח
120914	ב נ י ו ת ק ר י ב ו ה ל ב ש ת מ כ ת נ ת ו ח ג ר ת א ת מ א ב נ ט א ה ר נ ו ב נ י
120961	ה מ מ ג ב ע ת ו ה י ת ה ל ה מ כ ה נ ה ל ח ק ת ע ו ל מ ו מ ל א ת י ד א ה ר נ ו י
121008	ק ר ב ת א ת ה פ ר ל פ נ י א ה ל מ ו ע ד ו ס מ כ א ה ר נ ו ב נ י ו א ת י ד י ה מ
121055	ר ו ש ח ט ת א ת ה פ ר ל פ נ י י ה ו ה פ ת ח א ה ל מ ו ע ד ו ל ק ח ת מ ד מ ה פ ר
121102	ק ר נ ת ה מ ז ב ח ב א צ ב ע כ ו א ת כ ל ה ד מ ת ש פ כ א ל י ס ו ד ה מ ז ב ח ו ל
121149	ה ח ל ב ה מ כ ס ה א ת ה ק ר ב ו א ת ה י ת ר ת ע ל ה כ ב ד ו א ת ש ת י ה כ ל י ת
121196	א ש ר ע ל י ה נ ו ה ק ט ר ת ה מ ז ב ח ה ו א ת ב ש ר ה פ ר ו א ת ע ר ו א ת פ ר
121243	א ש מ ח ו צ ל מ ח נ ה ח ט א ת ה ו א ו א ת ה א י ל א ח ד ת ק ח ו ס מ כ ו א ה ר
121290	ת י ד י ה מ ע ל ר א ש ה א י ל ו ש ח ט ת א ת ה א י ל ו ל ק ח ת א ת ד מ ו ו ז ר ק
121337	ח ס ב י ב ו א ת ה א י ל ת נ ת ח ל נ ת ח י ו ו ר ח צ ת ק ר ב ו ו כ ר ע י ו ו נ ת
121384	ו ו ע ל ר א ש ו ו ה ק ט ר ת א ת כ ל ה א י ל ה מ ז ב ח ה ע ל ה ה ו א ל י ה ו ה ר
121431	א ש ה ל י ה ו ה ה ו א ו ל ק ח ת א ת ה א י ל ה ש נ י ו ס מ כ א ה ר נ ו ב נ י ו א
121478	ל ר א ש ה א י ל ו ש ח ט ת א ת ה א י ל ו ל ק ח ת מ ד מ ו ו נ ת ת ה ע ל ת נ ו כ א
121525	ע ל ת נ ו כ א ז נ ב נ י ו ה י מ נ י ת ו ע ל ב ה נ י ד מ ה י מ נ י ת ו ע ל ב ה נ
121572	נ י ת ו ז ר ק ת א ת ה ד מ ע ל ה מ ז ב ח ס ב י ב ו ל ק ח ת מ נ ה ד מ א ש ר ע ל ה
121619	מ נ ה מ ש ח ה ו ה ז י ת ע ל א ה ר נ ו ע ל ב ג ד י ו ו ע ל ב נ י ו ו ע ל ב ג ד י
121666	ו ק ד ש ה ו א ו ב ג ד י ו ו ב נ י ו ו ב ג ד י ב נ י ו א ת ו ו ל ק ח ת מ נ ה א י
121713	א ל י ה ו א ת ה ח ל ב ה מ כ ס ה א ת ה ק ר ב ו א ת י ת ר ת ה כ ב ד ו א ת ש ת י ה
121760	ה ח ל ב א ש ר ע ל י ה נ ו א ת ש ו ק ה י מ י נ כ י א י ל מ ל א י מ ה ו א ו כ כ ר

Shape	Word	Translation	Verse	Position	Skip
א	אות	seal	Exodus 29:3	120693	335
ח	תשסח	2008	Exodus 29:3	120694	-1033
ת	תלאה	tribulation	Exodus 29:3	120710	276
א	אלוה	God	Exodus 29:3	120715	183
א	אמון	faithful	Exodus 29:4	120744	286
ת	תשסא	2001	Exodus 29:5	120794	332
ה	הצלה	salvation	Exodus 29:5	120821	52
כ	כוכב	star	Exodus 29:5	120835	-95
ת	תכלת	blue	Exodus 29:8	120928	188
ד	ד אדר	2/27	Exodus 29:9	120937	-240
א	אלטריכ	Al Tariq	Exodus 29:9	120976	-93
ק	קורן	Koran	Exodus 29:9	120982	90
ז	זיק	ray	Exodus 29:13	121212	91

60. Al Tariq/Blue: Al Tariq (of the) Koran (is the) Blue Star ray, Tribulation salvation seal (of) God (for the) faithful (on) 2/27/2001 (and in) 2008. (Two letters of "2008" are hidden beyond the slide border.)

Shape	Word	Translation	Verse	Position	Skip
ז	זהוב	golden	Exodus 27:7	117525	191
מ	מוות	death	Exodus 27:9	117628	-279
ע	עידן	age	Exodus 27:11	117706	473
נ	נאמן	faithful	Exodus 27:15	117899	-191
נ	נפש	soul	Exodus 27:15	117899	562
ל	לא עוד	nevermore	Exodus 28:2	118371	-93

61. Death/Nevermore: Death nevermore (for the) faithful soul(s) (of the) Golden Age.

It also confirms that, for those who remain faithful, there will be no physical death after the first resurrection. Those who do not remain faithful would logically join the remnant of the fourth root race. The remnant chose the mark of the beast and will be banished from earth for 1,000 years.

According to Revelation 20: 4, those faithful who died prior to the Tribulation period will be born into the Golden Age as members of the fifth root race. As long as they remain faithful, they will also live for 1,000 years, ascending at the end of that Age. According to the Bible Code, the Golden Age will repeat itself for 12 cycles of 1,000 years each in an effort to salvage the remnant souls of the fourth root race.

It would seem that, just as the test of Abraham and Isaac prophesied the coming of Jesus, the test of Israel during the Exodus prophesies the entrance of the new race of man into the Golden Age. We will be tested for 40 years in the wasteland of a destroyed world before we will be allowed to enter the Promised Land. As it is said in Zechariah 14:8-9: "And it shall come to pass, that in all the land, saith the Lord, two parts therein shall be cut off and die; but a third shall be left therein. And I will bring the third part through the fire and will refine them as silver is refined, and will try them as gold is tried; they shall call on my name and I will hear them: I will say, It is my people: they shall say, The Lord is my God."

We can graduate now, later, or never. The choice is ours alone.

THE TEN COMMANDMENTS
(Excerpts from Exodus 20)

1. I am the Lord thy God, Thou shalt have no other gods before me.
2. Thou shalt not make unto thee any graven image; thou shalt not bow down thyself to them nor serve them.
3. Remember the Sabbath day, to keep it holy.
4. Thou shalt not take the name of the Lord thy God in vain.
5. Honor thy father and thy mother.
6. Thou shalt not kill.
7. Thou shalt not commit adultery.
8. Thou shalt not steal.
9. Thou shalt not bear false witness against thy neighbor.
10. Thou shalt not covet anything that is thy neighbor's.

THE REVELATION TO SAINT JOHN THE DIVINE

1:1 The Revelation of Jesus Christ, which God gave unto him, to shew unto his
servants things which must shortly come to pass; and he sent and signified *it* by
his angel unto his servant John:
2 Who bare record of the word of God, and of the testimony of Jesus Christ, and
of all things that he saw.
3 Blessed is he that readeth, and they that hear the words of this prophecy, and
keep those things which are written therein: for the time is at hand.
4 John to the seven churches which are in Asia: Grace be unto you, and peace,
from him which is, and which was, and which is to come; and from the seven
Spirits which are before his throne;
5 And from Jesus Christ, who is the faithful witness, and the first begotten of the
dead, and the prince of the kings of the earth. Unto him that loved us, and
washed us from our sins in his own blood,
6 And hath made us kings and priests unto God and his Father; to him be glory
and dominion for ever and ever. Amen.
7 Behold, he cometh with clouds; and every eye shall see him, and they also
which pierced him: and all kindreds of the earth shall wail because of him. Even
so, Amen.
8 I am Alpha and Omega, the beginning and the ending, saith the Lord, which is,
and which was, and which is to come, the Almighty.

9 I John, who also am your brother, and companion in tribulation, and in the kingdom and patience of Jesus Christ, was in the isle that is called Patmos, for the word of God, and for the testimony of Jesus Christ.
10 I was in the Spirit on the Lord's day, and heard behind me a great voice, as of a trumpet,
11 Saying, I am Alpha and Omega, the first and the last: and, What thou seest, write in a book, and send it unto the seven churches which are in Asia; unto Ephesus, and unto Smyrna, and unto Pergamos, and unto Thyatira, and unto Sardis, and unto Philadelphia, and unto Laodicea.
12 And I turned to see the voice that spake with me. And being turned, I saw seven golden candlesticks;
13 And in the midst of the seven candlesticks *one* like unto the Son of Man, clothed with a garment down to the foot, and girt about the paps with a golden girdle.
14 His head and his hairs were white like wool, as white as snow; and his eyes were as a flame of fire;
15 And his feet like unto fine brass, as if they burned in a furnace; and his voice as the sound of many waters.
16 And he had in his right hand seven stars: and out of his mouth went a sharp twoedged sword: and his countenance was as the sun shineth in his strength.
17 And when I saw him, I felt at his feet as dead. And he laid his right hand upon me, saying unto me, Fear not; I am the first and the last:
18 I am he that liveth, and was dead; and, behold, I am alive for evermore, Amen; and have the keys of hell and of death.
19 Write the things which thou hast seen, and the things which are, and the things which shall be hereafter;
20 The mystery of the seven stars which thou sawest in my right hand, and the seven golden candlesticks. The seven stars are the angels of the seven churches: and the seven candlesticks which thou sawest are the seven churches.

2:1 Unto the angel of the church of Ephesus write; These things saith he that holdeth the seven stars in his right hand, who walketh in the midst of the seven golden candlesticks;
2 I know thy works, and thy labour, and thy patience, and how thou canst not bear them which are evil: and thou hast tried them which say they are apostles, and are not, and hast found them liars:
3 And hast borne, and hast patience, and for my name's sake hast laboured, and hast not fainted.
4 Nevertheless I have somewhat against thee, because thou hast left thy first love.
5 Remember therefore from whence thou art fallen, and repent, and do the first works; or else I will come unto thee quickly, and will remove thy candlestick out of his place, except thou repent.

6 But this thou hast, that thou hatest the deeds of the Nicolaitans, which I also
hate.
7 He that hath an ear, let him hear what the Spirit saith unto the churches; To
him that overcometh will I give to eat of the tree of life, which is in the midst of
the paradise of God.
8 And unto the angel of the church in Smyrna write; These things saith the first
and the last, which was dead, and is alive;
9 I know thy works, and tribulation, and poverty, (but thou art rich) and I
know the blasphemy of them which say they are Jews, and are not, but are the
synagogue of Satan.
10 Fear none of those things which thou shalt suffer: behold, the devil shall cast
some of you into prison, that ye may be tried; and you shall have tribulation ten
days: be thou faithful unto death, and I will give thee a crown of life.
11 He that hath an ear, let him hear what the Spirit saith unto the churches; He
that overcometh shall not be hurt of the second death.
12 And to the angel of the church in Pergamos write; These things saith he
which hath the sharp sword with two edges;
13 I know thy works, and where thou dwellest, even where Satan's seat is: and
thou holdest fast my name, and hast not denied my faith, even in those days
wherein Antipas was my faithful martyr, who was slain among you, where Satan
dwelleth.
14 But I have a few things against thee, because thou hast there them that hold
the doctrine of Balaam, who taught Balac to cast a stumblingblock before the
children of Israel, to eat things sacrificed unto idols, and to commit fornication.
15 So hast thou also them that hold the doctrine of the Nicolaitans, which thing
I hate.
16 Repent; or else I will come unto thee quickly, and will fight against them
with the sword of my mouth.
17 He that hath an ear, let him hear what the Spirit saith unto the churches; To
him that overcometh will I give to eat of the hidden manna, and will give him a
white stone, and in the stone a new name written, which no man knoweth saving
he that receiveth it.
18 And unto the angel of the church in Thyatira write; These things saith the
Son of God, who hath his eyes like unto a flame of fire, and his feet are like fine
brass;
19 I know thy works, and charity, and service, and faith, and thy patience, and
thy works; and the last to be more than the first.
20 Notwithstanding I have a few things against thee, because thou sufferest that
woman Jezebel, which calleth herself a prophetess, to teach and to seduce my
servants to commit fornication, and to eat things sacrificed unto idols.
21 And I gave her space to repent of her fornication; and she repented not.
22 Behold, I will cast her into a bed, and them that commit adultery with her
into great tribulation, except they repent of their deeds.

23 And 1 will kill her children with death; and all the churches shall know that
I am he which searcheth the reins and hearts: and I will give unto every one of
you according to your works.
24 But unto you I say, and unto the rest in Thyatira, as many as have not this
doctrine, and which have not known the depths of Satan, as they speak; 1 will
put upon you none other burden.
25 But that which ye have already hold fast till I come.
26 And he that overcometh, and keepeth my works unto the end, to him will I
give power over the nations:
27 And he shall rule them with a rod of iron; as the vessels of a potter shall they
be broken to shivers: even as I received of my Father.
28 And I will give him the morning star.
29 He that hath an ear, let him hear what the Spirit saith unto the churches.

3:1 And unto the angel of the church in Sardis write; These things saith he that
hath the seven Spirits of God, and the seven stars; I know thy works, that thou
hast a name that thou livest, and art dead.
2 Be watchful, and strengthen the things which remain, that are ready to die: for
I have not found thy works perfect before God.
3 Remember therefore how thou hast received and heard, and hold fast, and
repent. If therefore thou shalt not watch, I will come on thee as a thief, and thou
shalt not know what hour I will come upon thee.
4 Thou hast a few names even in Sardis which have not defiled their garments;
and they shall walk with me in white: for they are worthy.
5 He that overcometh, the same shall be clothed in white raiment; and I will not
blot out his name out of the book of life, but I will confess his name before my
Father, and before his angels.
6 He that hath an ear, let him hear what the Spirit saith unto the churches.
7 And to the angel of the church in Philadelphia write; These things saith he that
is holy, he that is true, he that hath the key of David, he that openeth, and no
man shutteth; and shutteth, and no man openeth;
8 I know thy works: behold, I have set before thee an open door, and no man
can shut it: for thou hast a little strength, and hast kept my word, and hast not
denied my name.
9 Behold, I will make them of the synagogue of Satan, which say they are Jews,
and are not, but do lie; behold, I will make them to come and worship before thy
feet, and to know that I have loved thee.
10 Because thou hast kept the word of my patience, I also will keep thee from
the hour of temptation, which shall come upon all the world, to try them that
dwell upon the earth.
11 Behold, I come quickly: hold that fast which thou hast, that no man take thy
crown.
12 Him that overcometh will I make a pillar in the temple of my God, and he

shall go no more out: and I will write upon him the name of my God, and the
name of the city of my God, *which* is new Jerusalem, which cometh down out of
heaven from my God: and *I will write upon him* my new name.
13 He that hath an ear, let him hear what the Spirit saith unto the churches.
14 And unto the angel of the church of the Laodiceans write; These things saith
the Amen, the faithful and true witness, the beginning of the creation of God;
15 I know thy works, that thou art neither cold nor hot: I would thou wert cold
or hot.
16 So then because thou art lukewarm, and neither cold nor hot, I will spue thee
out of my mouth.
17 Because thou sayest, I am rich, and increased with goods, and have need of
nothing; and knowest not that thou art wretched, and miserable, and poor, and
blind, and naked:
18 I counsel thee to buy of me gold tried in the fire, that thou mayest be rich;
and white raiment, that thou mayest be clothed, and that the shame of thy
nakedness do not appear; and anoint thine eyes with eyesalve, that thou mayest
see.
19 As many as I love, I rebuke and chasten: be zealous therefore, and repent.
20 Behold, I stand at the door, and knock: if any man hear my voice, and open
the door, I will come in to him, and will sup with him, and he with me.
21 To him that overcometh will I grant to sit with me in my throne, even as I
also overcame, and am set down with my Father in his throne.
22 He that hath an ear, let him hear what the Spirit saith unto the churches.

4:1 After this I looked, and, behold, a door was opened in heaven: and the first
voice which I heard was as it were of a trumpet talking with me; which said,
Come up hither, and I will shew thee things which must be hereafter.
2 And immediately I was in the spirit: and, behold, a throne was set in heaven,
and one sat on the throne.
3 And he that sat was to look upon like a jasper and a sardine stone: and there
was a rainbow round about the throne, in sight like unto an emerald.
4 And round about the throne were four and twenty seats, and upon the seats I
saw four and twenty elders sitting, clothed in white raiment; and they had on
their heads crowns of gold.
5 And out of the throne proceeded lightnings and thunderings and voices: and
there were seven lamps of fire burning before the throne, which are the seven
Spirits of God.
6 And before the throne there was a sea of glass like unto crystal: and in the
midst of the throne, and round about the throne, were four beasts full of eyes
before and behind.
7 And the first beast was like a lion, and the second beast like a calf, and the third
beast had a face as a man, and the fourth beast was like a flying eagle.
8 And the four beasts had each of them six wings about him; and they were full

of eyes within: and they rest not day and night, saying, Holy, holy, holy, Lord
God Almighty, which was, and is, and is to come.
9 And when those beasts give glory and honour and thanks to him that sat on
the throne, who liveth for ever and ever,
10 The four and twenty elders fall down before him that sat on the throne, and
worship him that liveth for ever and ever, and cast their crowns before the throne,
saying,
11 Thou art worthy, O Lord, to receive glory and honour and power: for thou
hast created all things, and for thy pleasure they are and were created.

5:1 And I saw in the right hand of him that sat on the throne a book written
within and on the backside, sealed with seven seals.
2 And I saw a strong angel proclaiming with a loud voice, Who is worthy to
open the book, and to loose the seals thereof?
3 And no man in heaven, nor in earth, neither under the earth, was able to open
the book, neither to look thereon.
4 And I wept much, because no man was found worthy to open and to read the
book, neither to look thereon.
5 And one of the elders saith unto me, Weep not: behold, the Lion of the tribe
of Juda, the Root of David, hath prevailed to open the book, and to loose the
seven seals thereof.
6 And I beheld, and, lo, in the midst of the throne and of the four beasts, and in
the midst of the elders, stood a Lamb as it had been slain, having seven horns and
seven eyes, which are the seven Spirits of God sent forth into all the earth.
7 And he came and took the book out of the right hand of him that sat upon the
throne.
8 And when he had taken the book, the four beasts and four and twenty elders
fell down before the Lamb, having every one of them harps, and golden vials full
of odours, which are the prayers of saints.
9 And they sung a new song, saying, Thou art worthy to take the book, and to
open the seals thereof: for thou wast slain, and hast redeemed us to God by thy
blood out of every kindred, and tongue, and people, and nation;
10 And hast made us unto our God kings and priests: and we shall reign on the
earth.
11 And I beheld, and I heard the voice of many angels round about the throne
and the beasts and the elders: and the number of them was ten thousand times
ten thousand, and thousands of thousands;
12 Saying with a loud voice, Worthy is the Lamb that was slain to receive power,
and riches, and wisdom, and strength, and honour, and glory, and blessing.
13 And every creature which is in heaven, and on the earth, and under the earth,
and such as are in the sea, and all that are in them, heard I saying, Blessing, and
honour, and glory, and power, be unto him that sitteth upon the throne, and
unto the Lamb for ever and ever.

14 And the four beasts said, Amen. And the four and twenty elders fell down
and worshipped him that liveth for ever and ever.

6:1 And I saw when the Lamb opened one of the seals, and I heard, as it were the
noise of thunder, one of the four beasts saying, Come and see.
2 And I saw, and behold a white horse: and he that sat on him had a bow; and a
crown was given unto him: and he went forth conquering, and to conquer.
3 And when he had opened the second seal, I heard the second beast say, Come
and see.
4 And there went out another horse that was red: and power was given to him
that sat thereon to take peace from the earth, and that they should kill one another:
and there was given unto him a great sword.
5 And when he had opened the third seal, I heard the third beast say, Come and
see. And I beheld, and lo a black horse; and he that sat on him had a pair of
balances in his hand.
6 And I heard a voice in the midst of the four beasts say, A measure of wheat for
a penny, and three measures of barley for a penny; and see thou hurt not the oil
and the wine.
7 And when he had opened the fourth seal, I heard the voice of the fourth beast
say, Come and see.
8 And I looked, and behold a pale horse: and his name that sat on him was
Death, and Hell followed with him. And power was given unto them over the
fourth part of the earth, to kill with sword, and with hunger, and with death,
and with the beasts of the earth.
9 And when he had opened the fifth seal, I saw under the altar the souls of them
that were slain for the word of God, and for the testimony which they held:
10 And they cried with a loud voice, saying, How long, O Lord, holy and true,
dost thou not judge and avenge our blood on them that dwell on the earth?
11 And white robes were given unto every one of them; and it was said unto
them, that they should rest yet for a little season, until their fellowservants also
and their brethren, that should be killed as they were, should be fulfilled.
12 And I beheld when he had opened the sixth seal, and, lo, there was a great
earthquake; and the sun became black as sackcloth of hair, and the moon became
as blood;
13 And the stars of heaven fell unto the earth, even as a fig tree casteth her
untimely figs, when she is shaken of a mighty wind.
14 And the heaven departed as a scroll when it is rolled together; and every
mountain and island were moved out of their places.
15 And the kings of the earth, and the great men, and the rich men, and the chief
captains, and the mighty men, and every bondman, and every free man, hid
themselves in the dens and in the rocks of the mountains;
16 And said to the mountains and rocks, Fall on us, and hide us from the face of
him that sitteth on the throne, and from the wrath of the Lamb:

17 For the great day of his wrath is come; and who shall be able to stand?

7:1 And after these things I saw four angels standing on the four corners of the
earth, holding the four winds of the earth, that the wind should not blow on the
earth, nor on the sea, nor on any tree.
2 And I saw another angel ascending from the east, having the seal of the living
God: and he cried with a loud voice to the four angels, to whom it was given to
hurt the earth and the sea,
3 Saying, Hurt not the earth, neither the sea, nor the trees, till we have sealed the
servants of our God in their foreheads.
4 And I heard the number of them which were sealed: and there were sealed an
hundred and forty and four thousand of all the tribes of the children of Israel.
5 Of the tribe of Juda were sealed twelve thousand. Of the tribe of Reuben were
sealed twelve thousand. Of the tribe of Gad were sealed twelve thousand.
6 Of the tribe of Aser were sealed twelve thousand. Of the tribe of Nephthalim
were sealed twelve thousand. Of the tribe of Manasses were sealed twelve
thousand.
7 Of the tribe of Simeon were sealed twelve thousand. Of the tribe of Levi were
sealed twelve thousand. Of the tribe of Issachar were sealed twelve thousand.
8 Of the tribe of Zabulon were sealed twelve thousand. Of the tribe of Joseph
were sealed twelve thousand. Of the tribe of Benjamin were sealed twelve
thousand.
9 After this I beheld, and, lo, a great multitude, which no man could number, of
all nations, and kindreds, and people, and tongues, stood before the throne, and
before the Lamb, clothed with white robes, and palms in their hands;
10 And cried with a loud voice, saying, Salvation to our God which sitteth upon
the throne, and unto the Lamb.
11 And all the angels stood round about the throne, and about the elders and
the four beasts, and fell before the throne on their faces, and worshipped God,
12 Saying, Amen: Blessing, and glory, and wisdom, and thanksgiving, and honour,
and power, and might, be unto our God for ever and ever. Amen.
13 And one of the elders answered, saying unto me, What are these which are
arrayed in white robes? and whence came they?
14 And I said unto him, Sir, thou knowest. And he said to me, These are they
which came out of great tribulation, and have washed their robes, and made
them white in the blood of the Lamb.
15 Therefore are they before the throne of God, and serve him day and night in
his temple: and he that sitteth on the throne shall dwell among them.
16 They shall hunger no more, neither thirst any more; neither shall the sun
light on them, nor any heat.
17 For the Lamb which is in the midst of the throne shall feed them, and shall
lead them unto living fountains of waters: and God shall wipe away all tears
from their eyes.

8:1 And when he had opened the seventh seal, there was silence in heaven about
the space of half an hour.
2 And I saw the seven angels which stood before God; and to them were given
seven trumpets.
3 And another angel came and stood at the altar, having a golden censer; and
there was given unto him much incense, that he should offer it with the prayers
of all saints upon the golden altar which was before the throne.
4 And the smoke of the incense, which came with the prayers of the saints,
ascended up before God out of the angel's hand.
5 And the angel took the censer, and filled it with fire of the altar, and cast it into
the earth: and there were voices, and thunderings, and lightnings, and an
earthquake.
6 And the seven angels which had the seven trumpets prepared themselves to
sound.
7 The first angel sounded, and there followed hail and fire mingled with blood,
and they were cast upon the earth: and the third part of trees was burnt up, and
all green grass was burnt up.
8 And the second angel sounded, and as it were a great mountain burning with
fire was cast into the sea: and the third part of the sea became blood;
9 And the third part of the creatures which were in the sea, and had life, died; and
the third part of the ships were destroyed.
10 And the third angel sounded, and there fell a great star from heaven, burning
as it were a lamp, and it fell upon the third part of the rivers, and upon the
fountains of waters;
11 And the name of the star is called Wormwood: and the third part of the
waters became wormwood; and many men died of the waters, because they were
made bitter.
12 And the fourth angel sounded, and the third part of the sun was smitten, and
the third part of the moon, and the third part of the stars; so as the third part of
them was darkened, and the day shone not for a third part of it, and the night
likewise.
13 And I beheld, and heard an angel flying through the midst of heaven, saying
with a loud voice, Woe, woe, woe, to the inhabiters of the earth by reason of the
other voices of the trumpet of the three angels, which are yet to sound!

9:1 And the fifth angel sounded, and I saw a star fall from heaven unto the earth:
and to him was given the key of the bottomless pit.
2 And he opened the bottomless pit; and there arose a smoke out of the pit, as
the smoke of a great furnace; and the sun and the air were darkened by reason of
the smoke of the pit.
3 And there came out of the smoke locusts upon the earth: and unto them was
given power, as the scorpions of the earth have power.

4 And it was commanded them that they should not hurt the grass of the earth,
neither any green thing, neither any tree; but only those men which have not the
seal of God in their foreheads.
5 And to them it was given that they should not kill them, but that they should
be tormented five months: and their torment was as the torment of a scorpion,
when he striketh a man.
6 And in those days shall men seek death, and shall not find it; and shall desire to
die, and death shall flee from them.
7 And the shapes of the locusts were like unto horses prepared unto battle; and
on their heads were as it were crowns like gold, and their faces were as the faces
of men.
8 And they had hair as the hair of women, and their teeth were as the teeth of
lions.
9 And they had breastplates, as it were breastplates of iron; and the sound of
their wings was as the sound of chariots of many horses running to battle.
10 And they had tails like unto scorpions, and there were stings in their tails: and
their power was to hurt men five months.
11 And they had a king over them, which is the angel of the bottomless pit,
whose name in the Hebrew tongue is Abaddon, but in the Greek tongue hath his
name Apollyon.
12 One woe is past; and, behold, there come two woes more hereafter.
13 And the sixth angel sounded, and I heard a voice from the four horns of the
golden altar which is before God,
14 Saying to the sixth angel which had the trumpet, Loose the four angels which
are bound in the great river Euphrates.
15 And the four angels were loosed, which were prepared for an hour, and a day,
and a month, and a year, for to slay the third part of men.
16 And the number of the army of the horsemen were two hundred thousand
thousand: and I heard the number of them.
17 And thus I saw the horses in the vision, and them that sat on them, having
breastplates of fire, and of jacinth, and brimstone: and the heads of the horses
were as the heads of lions; and out of their mouths issued fire and smoke and
brimstone.
18 By these three was the third part of men killed, by the fire, and by the smoke,
and by the brimstone, which issued out of their mouths.
19 For their power is in their mouth, and in their tails: for their tails were like
unto serpents, and had heads, and with them they do hurt.
20 And the rest of the men which were not killed by these plagues yet repented
not of the works of their hands, that they should not worship devils, and idols of
gold, and silver, and brass, and stone, and of wood: which neither can see, nor
hear, nor walk:
21 Neither repented they of their murders, nor of their sorceries, nor of their
fornication, nor of their thefts.

10:1 And I saw another mighty angel come down from heaven, clothed with a
cloud: and a rainbow was upon his head, and his face was as it were the sun, and
his feet as pillars of fire:
2 And he had in his hand a little book open: and he set his right foot upon the
sea, and his left foot on the earth,
3 And cried with a loud voice, as when a lion roareth: and when he had cried,
seven thunders uttered their voices.
4 And when the seven thunders had uttered their voices, I was about to write:
and I heard a voice from heaven saying unto me, Seal up those things which the
seven thunders uttered, and write them not.
5 And the angel which I saw stand upon the sea and upon the earth lifted up his
hand to heaven,
6 And sware by him that liveth for ever and ever, who created heaven, and the
things that therein are, and the earth, and the things that therein are, and the sea,
and the things which are therein, that there should be time no longer:
7 But in the days of the voice of the seventh angel, when he shall begin to sound,
the mystery of God should be finished, as he hath declared to his servants the
prophets.
8 And the voice which I heard from heaven spake unto me again, and said, Go
and take the little book which is open in the hand of the angel which standeth
upon the sea and upon the earth.
9 And I went unto the angel, and said unto him, Give me the little book. And he
said unto me, Take it, and eat it up; and it shall make thy belly bitter, but it shall
be in thy mouth sweet as honey.
10 And I took the little book out of the angel's hand, and ate it up; and it was in
my mouth sweet as honey: and as soon as I had eaten it, my belly was bitter.
11 And he said unto me, Thou must prophesy again before many peoples, and
nations, and tongues, and kings.

11:1 And there was given me a reed like unto a rod: and the angel stood, saying,
Rise, and measure the temple of God, and the altar, and them that worship therein.
2 But the court which is without the temple leave out, and measure it not; for it
is given unto the Gentiles: and the holy city shall they tread under foot forty and
two months.
3 And I will give power unto my two witnesses, and they shall prophesy a
thousand two hundred and threescore days, clothed in sackcloth.
4 These are the two olive trees, and the two candlesticks standing before the
God of the earth.
5 And if any man will hurt them, fire proceedeth out of their mouth, and
devoureth their enemies: and if any man will hurt them, he must in this manner
be killed.
6 These have power to shut heaven, that it rain not in the days of their prophecy:

and have power over waters to turn them to blood, and to smite the earth with
all plagues, as often as they will.
7 And when they shall have finished their testimony, the beast that ascendeth
out of the bottomless pit shall make war against them, and shall overcome them,
and kill them.
8 And their dead bodies shall lie in the street of the great city, which spiritually
is called Sodom and Egypt, where also our Lord was crucified.
9 And they of the people and kindreds and tongues and nations shall see their
dead bodies three days and an half, and shalt not suffer their dead bodies to be
put in graves.
10 And they that dwell upon the earth shall rejoice over them, and make merry,
and shall send gifts one to another; because these two prophets tormented them
that dwelt on the earth.
11 And after three days and an half the Spirit of life from God entered into
them, and they stood upon their feet; and great fear fell upon them which saw
them.
12 And they heard a great voice from heaven saying unto them, Come up hither.
And they ascended up to heaven in a cloud; and their enemies beheld them.
13 And the same hour was there a great earthquake, and the tenth part of the
city fell, and in the earthquake were slain of men seven thousand: and the remnant
were affrighted, and gave glory to the God of heaven.
14 The second woe is past; and, behold, the third woe cometh quickly.
15 And the seventh angel sounded; and there were great voices in heaven, saying,
The kingdoms of this world are become the kingdoms of our Lord, and of his
Christ; and he shall reign for ever and ever.
16 And the four and twenty elders, which sat before God on their seats, fell
upon their faces, and worshipped God,
17 Saying, We give thee thanks, O Lord God Almighty, which art, and wast,
and art to come; because thou hast taken to thee thy great power, and hast reigned.
18 And the nations were angry, and thy wrath is come, and the time of the dead,
that they should be judged, and that thou shouldest give reward unto thy servants
the prophets, and to the saints, and them that fear thy name, small and great; and
shouldest destroy them which destroy the earth.
19 And the temple of God was opened in heaven, and there was seen in his
temple the ark of his testament: and there were lightnings, and voices, and
thunderings, and an earthquake, and great hail.

12:1 And there appeared a great wonder in heaven; a woman clothed with the
sun, and the moon under her feet, and upon her head a crown of twelve stars:
2 And she being with child cried, travailing in birth, and pained to be delivered.
3 And there appeared another wonder in heaven; and behold a great red dragon,
having seven heads and ten horns, and seven crowns upon his heads.
4 And his tail drew the third part of the stars of heaven, and did cast them to the

earth: and the dragon stood before the woman which was ready to be delivered,
for to devour her child as soon as it was born.
5 And she brought forth a man child, who was to rule all nations with a rod of
iron: and her child was caught up unto God, and to his throne.
6 And the woman fled into the wilderness, where she hath a place prepared of
God, that they should feed her there a thousand two hundred and threescore
days.
7 And there was war in heaven: Michael and his angels fought against the dragon;
and the dragon fought and his angels,
8 And prevailed not; neither was their place found any more in heaven.
9 And the great dragon was cast out, that old serpent, called the Devil, and Satan,
which deceiveth the whole world: he was cast out into the earth, and his angels
were cast out with him.
10 And I heard a loud voice saying in heaven, Now is come salvation, and strength,
and the kingdom of our God, and the power of his Christ: for the accuser of our
brethren is cast down, which accused them before our God day and night.
11 And they overcame him by the blood of the Lamb, and by the word of their
testimony; and they loved not their lives unto the death.
12 Therefore rejoice, ye heavens, and ye that dwell in them. Woe to the inhabiters
of the earth and of the seal for the devil is come down unto you, having great
wrath, because he knoweth that he hath but a short time.
13 And when the dragon saw that he was cast unto the earth, he persecuted the
woman which brought forth the man child.
14 And to the woman were given two wings of a great eagle, that she might fly
into the wilderness, into her place, where she is nourished for a time, and times,
and half a time, from the face of the serpent.
15 And the serpent cast out of his mouth water as a flood after the woman, that
he might cause her to be carried away of the flood.
16 And the earth helped the woman, and the earth opened her mouth, and
swallowed up the flood which the dragon cast out of his mouth.
17 And the dragon was wroth with the woman, and went to make war with the
remnant of her seed, which keep the commandments of God, and have the
testimony of Jesus Christ.

13:1 And I stood upon the sand of the sea, and saw a beast rise up out of the sea,
having seven heads and ten horns, and upon his horns ten crowns, and upon his
heads the name of blasphemy.
2 And the beast which I saw was like unto a leopard, and his feet were as the feet
of a bear, and his mouth as the mouth of a lion: and the dragon gave him his
power, and his seat, and great authority.
3 And I saw one of his heads as it were wounded to death; and his deadly wound
was healed: and all the world wondered after the beast.
4 And they worshipped the dragon which gave power unto the beast: and they

worshipped the beast, saying, Who is like unto the beast? who is able to make
war with him?
5 And there was given unto him a mouth speaking great things and blasphemies;
and power was given unto him to continue forty and two months.
6 And he opened his mouth in blasphemy against God, to blaspheme his name,
and his tabernacle, and them that dwell in heaven,
7 And it was given unto him to make war with the saints, and to overcome
them: and power was given him over all kindreds, and tongues, and nations.
8 And all that dwell upon the earth shall worship him, whose names are not
written in the book of life of the Lamb slain from the foundation of the world.
9 If any man have an ear, let him hear.
10 He that leadeth into captivity shall go into captivity: he that killeth with the
sword must be killed with the sword. Here is the patience and the faith of the
saints.
11 And I beheld another beast coming up out of the earth; and he had two horns
like a lamb, and he spake as a dragon.
12 And he exerciseth all the power of the first beast before him, and causeth the
earth and them which dwell therein to worship the first beast, whose deadly
wound was healed.
13 And he doeth great wonders, so that he maketh fire come down from heaven
on the earth in the sight of men,
14 And deceiveth them that dwell on the earth by the means of those miracles
which he had power to do in the sight of the beast; saying to them that dwell on
the earth, that they should make an image to the beast, which had the wound by
a sword, and did live.
15 And he had power to give life unto the image of the beast, that the image of
the beast should both speak, and cause that as many as would not worship the
image of the beast should be killed.
16 And he causeth all, both small and great, rich and poor, free and bond, to
receive a mark in their right hand, or in their foreheads:
17 And that no man might buy or sell, save he that had the mark, or the name of
the beast, or the number of his name.
18 Here is wisdom. Let him that hath understanding count the number of the
beast: for it is the number of a man; and his number *is* Six hundred threescore
and six.

14:1 And I looked, and, lo, a Lamb stood on the mount Sion, and with him an
hundred forty and four thousand, having his Father's name written in their
foreheads.
2 And I heard a voice from heaven, as the voice of many waters, and as the voice
of a great thunder: and I heard the voice of harpers harping with their harps:
3 And they sung as it were a new song before the throne, and before the four
beasts, and the elders: and no man could learn that song but the hundred and

forty and four thousand, which were redeemed from the earth.
4 These are they which were not defiled with women; for they are virgins.
These are they which follow the Lamb whithersoever he goeth. These were
redeemed from among men, being the firstfruits unto God and to the Lamb.
5 And in their mouth was found no guile: for they are without fault before the
throne of God.
6 And I saw another angel fly in the midst of heaven, having the everlasting
gospel to preach unto them that dwell on the earth, and to every nation, and
kindred, and tongue, and people,
7 Saying with a loud voice, Fear God, and give glory to him; for the hour of his
judgment is come: and worship him that made heaven, and earth, and the sea,
and the fountains of waters.
8 And there followed another angel, saying, Babylon is fallen, is fallen, that great
city, because she made all nations drink of the wine of the wrath of her fornication.
9 And the third angel followed them, saying with a loud voice, If any man
worship the beast and his image, and receive his mark in his forehead, or in his
hand,
10 The same shall drink of the wine of the wrath of God, which is poured out
without mixture into the cup of his indignation; and he shall be tormented with
fire and brimstone in the presence of the holy angels, and in the presence of the
Lamb:
11 And the smoke of their torment ascendeth up for ever and ever: and they
have no rest day nor night, who worship the beast and his image, and whosoever
receiveth the mark of his name.
12 Here is the patience of the saints: here are they that keep the commandments
of God, and the faith of Jesus.
13 And I heard a voice from heaven saying unto me, Write, Blessed are the dead
which die in the Lord from henceforth: Yea, saith the Spirit, that they may rest
from their labours; and their works do follow them.
14 And I looked, and behold a white cloud, and upon the cloud one sat like unto
the Son of Man, having on his head a golden crown, and in his hand a sharp
sickle.
15 And another angel came out of the temple, crying with a loud voice to him
that sat on the cloud, Thrust in thy sickle, and reap: for the time is come for thee
to reap; for the harvest of the earth is ripe.
16 And he that sat on the cloud thrust in his sickle on the earth; and the earth
was reaped.
17 And another angel came out of the temple which is in heaven, he also having
a sharp sickle.
18 And another angel came out from the altar, which had power over fire; and
cried with a loud cry to him that had the sharp sickle, saying, Thrust in thy sharp
sickle, and gather the clusters of the vine of the earth; for her grapes are fully
ripe.

19 And the angel thrust in his sickle into the earth, and gathered the vine of the
earth, and cast it into the great winepress of the wrath of God.
20 *And the winepress was trodden without the city, and blood came out of the*
winepress, even unto the horse bridles, by the space of a thousand and six hundred
furlongs.

15:1 I saw another sign in heaven, great and marvellous, seven angels having the
seven last plagues, for in them is filled up the wrath of God.
2 And I saw as it were a sea of glass mingled with fire: and them that had gotten
the victory over the beast, and over his image, and over his mark, and over the
number of his name, stand on the sea of glass, having the harps of God.
3 And they sing the song of Moses the servant of God, and the song of the Lamb,
saying, Great and marvellous are thy works, Lord God Almighty; just and true
are thy ways, thou King of saints.
4 Who shall not fear thee, O Lord, and glorify thy name? for thou only art holy:
for all nations shall come and worship before thee; for thy judgments are made
manifest.
5 And after that I looked, and, behold, the temple of the tabernacle of the
testimony in heaven was opened:
6 And the seven angels came out of the temple, having the seven plagues, clothed
in pure and white linen, and having their breasts girded with golden girdles.
7 And one of the four beasts gave unto the seven angels seven golden vials full of
the wrath of God, who liveth for ever and ever.
8 And the temple was filled with smoke from the glory of God, and from his
power, and no man was able to enter into the temple, till the seven plagues of the
seven angels were fulfilled.

16:1 And I heard a great voice out of the temple saying to the seven angels, Go
your ways, and pour out the vials of the wrath of God upon the earth.
2 And the first went, and poured out his vial upon the earth; and there fell a
noisome and grievous sore upon the men which had the mark of the beast, and
upon them which worshipped his image.
3 And the second angel poured out his vial upon the sea; and it became as the
blood of a dead man: and every living soul died in the sea.
4 And the third angel poured out his vial upon the rivers and fountains of waters;
and they became blood.
5 And I heard the angel of the waters say, Thou art righteous, O Lord, which
art, and wast, and shalt be, because thou hast judged thus.
6 For they have shed the blood of saints and prophets, and thou hast given them
blood to drink; for they are worthy.
7 And I heard another out of the altar say, Even so, Lord God Almighty, true
and righteous are thy judgments.
8 And the fourth angel poured out his vial upon the sun; and power was given

unto him to scorch men with fire.
9 And men were scorched with great heat, and blasphemed the name of God,
which hath power over these plagues: and they repented not to give him glory.
10 And the fifth angel poured out his vial upon the seat of the beast; and his
kingdom was full of darkness; and they gnawed their tongues for pain,
11 And blasphemed the God of heaven because of their pains and their sores,
and repented not of their deeds.
12 And the sixth angel poured out his vial upon the great river Euphrates; and
the water thereof was dried up, that the way of the kings of the east might be
prepared.
13 And I saw three unclean spirits like frogs come out of the mouth of the
dragon, and out of the mouth of the beast, and out of the mouth of the false
prophet.
14 For they are the spirits of devils, working miracies, which go forth unto the
kings of the earth and of the whole world, to gather them to the battle of that
great day of God Almighty.
15 Behold, I come as a thief. Blessed is he that watcheth, and keepeth his garments,
lest he walk naked, and they see his shame.
16 And he gathered them together into a place called in the Hebrew tongue
Armageddon.
17 And the seventh angel poured out his vial into the air; and there came a great
voice out of the temple of heaven, from the throne, saying, it is done.
18 And there were voices, and thunders, and lightnings; and there was a great
earthquake, such as was not since men were upon the earth, so mighty an
earthquake, and so great.
19 And the great city was divided into three parts, and the cities of the nations
fell; and great Babylon came in remembrance before God, to give unto her the
cup of the wine of the fierceness of his wrath.
20 And every island fled away, and the mountains were not found.
21 And there fell upon men a great hail out of heaven, every stone about the
weight of a talent: and men blasphemed God because of the plague of the hail; for
the plague thereof was exceeding great.

17:1 And there came one of the seven angels which had the seven vials, and
talked with me, saying unto me, Come hither; I will shew unto thee the judgment
of the great whore that sitteth upon many waters:
2 With whom the kings of the earth have committed fornication, and the
inhabitants of the earth have been made drunk with the wine of her fornication.
3 So he carried me away in the spirit into the wilderness: and I saw a woman sit
upon a scarlet coloured beast, full of names of blasphemy, having seven heads
and ten horns.
4 And the woman was arrayed in purple and scarlet colour, and decked with
gold and precious stones and pearls, having a golden cup in her hand full of

abominations and filthiness of her fornication:
5 And upon her forehead was a name written, MYSTERY, BABYLON THE
GREAT, THE MOTHER OF HARLOTS AND ABOMINATIONS OF THE
EARTH.
6 And I saw the woman drunken with the blood of the saints, and with the
blood of the martyrs of Jesus: and when I saw her, I wondered with great
admiration.
7 And the angel said unto me, Wherefore didst thou marvel? I will tell thee the
mystery of the woman, and of the beast that carrieth her, which hath the seven
heads and ten horns.
8 The beast that thou sawest was, and is not; and shall ascend out of the bottomless
pit, and go into perdition: and they that dwell on the earth shall wonder, whose
names were not written in the book of life from the foundation of the world,
when they behold the beast that was, and is not, and yet is.
9 And here is the mind which hath wisdom. The seven heads are seven mountains,
on which the woman sitteth.
10 And there are seven kings: five are fallen, and one is, and the other is not yet
come; and when he cometh, he must continue a short space.
11 And the beast that was, and is not, even he is the eighth, and is of the seven,
and goeth into perdition.
12 And the ten horns which thou sawest are ten kings, which have received no
kingdom as yet; but receive power as kings one hour with the beast.
13 These have one mind, and shall give their power and strength unto the beast.
14 These shall make war with the Lamb, and the Lamb shall overcome them: for
he is Lord of lords, and King of kings: and they that are with him are called, and
chosen, and faithful.
15 And he saith unto me, The waters which thou sawest, where the whore
sitteth, are peoples, and multitudes, and nations, and tongues.
16 And the ten horns which thou sawest upon the beast, these shall hate the
whore, and shall make her desolate and naked, and shall eat her flesh, and burn
her with fire.
17 For God hath put in their hearts to fulfil his will, and to agree, and give their
kingdom unto the beast, until the words of God shall be fulfilled.
18 And the woman which thou sawest is that great city, which reigneth over the
kings of the earth.

18:1 And after these things I saw another angel come down from heaven, having
great power; and the earth was lightened with his glory.
2 And he cried mightily with a strong voice, saying, Babylon the great is fallen,
is fallen, and is become the habitation of devils, and the hold of every foul spirit,
and a cage of every unclean and hateful bird.
3 For all nations have drunk of the wine of the wrath of her fornication, and the
kings of the earth have committed fornication with her, and the merchants of

the earth are waxed rich through the abundance of her delicacies.
4 And I heard another voice from heaven, saying, Come out of her, my people,
that ye be not partakers of her sins, and that ye receive not of her plagues.
5 For her sins have reached unto heaven, and God hath remembered her iniquities.
6 Reward her even as she rewarded you, and double unto her double according
to her works: in the cup which she hath filled fill to her double.
7 How much she hath glorified herself, and lived deliciously, so much torment
and sorrow give her: for she saith in her heart, I sit a queen, and am no widow,
and shall see no sorrow.
8 Therefore shall her plagues come in one day, death, and mourning, and famine;
and she shall be utterly burned with fire: for strong is the Lord God who judgeth
her.
9 And the kings of the earth, who have committed fornication and lived
deliciously with her, shall bewail her, and lament for her, when they shall see the
smoke of her burning,
10 Standing afar off for the fear of her torment, saying, Alas, alas, that great city
Babylon, that mighty city! for in one hour is thy judgment come.
11 And the merchants of the earth shall weep and mourn over her; for no man
buyeth their merchandise any more:
12 The merchandise of gold, and silver, and precious stones, and of pearls, and
fine linen, and purple, and silk, and scarlet, and all thyine wood, and all manner
vessels of ivory, and all manner vessels of most precious wood, and of brass, and
iron, and marble,
13 And cinnamon, and odours, and ointments, and frankincense, and wine, and
oil, and fine flour, and wheat, and beasts, and sheep, and horses, and chariots,
and slaves, and souls of men.
14 And the fruits that thy soul lusted after are departed from thee, and all things
which were dainty and goodly are departed from thee, and thou shalt find them
no more at all.
15 The merchants of these things, which were made rich by her, shall stand afar
off for the fear of her torment, weeping and wailing,
16 And saying, Alas, alas, that great city, that was clothed in fine linen, and
purple, and scarlet, and decked with gold, and precious stones, and pearls!
17 For in one hour so great riches is come to nought. And every shipmaster, and
all the company in ships, and sailors, and as many as trade by sea, stood afar off.
18 And cried when they saw the smoke of her burning, saying, What city is like
unto this great city!
19 And they cast dust on their heads, and cried, weeping and wailing, saying,
Alas, alas, that great city, wherein were made rich all that had ships in the sea by
reason of her costliness! for in one hour is she made desolate.
20 Rejoice over her, thou heaven, and ye holy apostles and prophets; for God
hath avenged you on her.
21 And a mighty angel took up a stone like a great millstone, and cast it into the

sea, saying, Thus with violence shall that great city Babylon be thrown down,
and shall be found no more at all,
22 And the voice of harpers, and musicians, and of pipers, and trumpeters, shall
be heard no more at all in thee, and no craftsman, of whatsoever craft *he be*, shall
be found any more in thee; and the sound of a millstone shall be heard no more
at all in thee;
23 And the light of a candle shall shine no more at all in thee; and the voice of
the bridegroom and of the bride shall be heard no more at all in thee: for thy
merchants were the great men of the earth; for by thy sorceries were all nations
deceived.
24 And in her was found the blood of prophets, and of saints, and of all that
were slain upon the earth.

19:1 And after these things I heard a great voice of much people in heaven,
saying, Alleluia; Salvation, and glory, and honour, and power, unto the Lord our
God:
2 For true and righteous are his judgments: for he hath judged the great whore,
which did corrupt the earth with her fornication, and hath avenged the blood of
his servants at her hand.
3 And again they said, Alleluia. And her smoke rose up for ever and ever.
4 And the four and twenty elders and the four beasts fell down and worshipped
God that sat on the throne, saying, Amen; Alleluia.
5 And a voice came out of the throne, saying, Praise our God, all ye his servants,
and ye that fear him, both small and great.
6 And I heard as it were the voice of a great multitude, and as the voice of many
waters, and as the voice of mighty thunderings, saying, Alleluia: for the Lord
God omnipotent reigneth.
7 Let us be glad and rejoice, and give honour to him: for the marriage of the
Lamb is come, and his wife hath made herself ready.
8 And to her was granted that she should be arrayed in fine linen, clean and
white: for the fine linen is the righteousness of saints.
9 And he saith unto me, Write, Blessed are they which are called unto the marriage
supper of the Lamb. And he saith unto me, These are the true sayings of God.
10 And I fell at his feet to worship him. And he said unto me, See thou do it not:
I am thy fellowservant, and of thy brethren that have the testimony of Jesus:
worship God: for the testimony of Jesus is the spirit of prophecy.
11 And I saw heaven opened, and behold a white horse; and he that sat upon him
was called Faithful and True, and in righteousness he doth judge and make war.
12 His eyes were as a flame of fire, and on his head were many crowns; and he
had a name written, that no man knew, but he himself.
13 And he was clothed with a vesture dipped in blood: and his name is called
The Word of God.

14 And the armies which were in heaven followed him upon white horses,
clothed in fine linen, white and clean.
15 And out of his mouth goeth a sharp sword, that with it he should smite the
nations: and he shall rule them with a rod of iron: and he treadeth the winepress
of the fierceness and wrath of Almighty God.
16 And he hath on his vesture and on his thigh a name written, KING OF
KINGS, AND LORD OF LORDS.
17 And I saw an angel standing in the sun; and he cried with a loud voice, saying
to all the fowls that fly in the midst of heaven, Come and gather yourselves
together unto the supper of the great God;
18 That ye may eat the flesh of kings, and the flesh of captains, and the flesh of
mighty men, and the flesh of horses, and of them that sit on them, and the flesh
of all men, both free and bond, both small and great.
19 And I saw the beast, and the kings of the earth, and their armies, gathered
together to make war against him that sat on the horse, and against his army.
20 And the beast was taken, and with him the false prophet that wrought miracles
before him, with which he deceived them that had received the mark of the
beast, and them that worshipped his image. These both were cast alive into a
lake of fire burning with brimstone.
21 And the remnant were slain with the sword of him that sat upon the horse, which *sword*
proceeded out of his mouth: and all the fowls were filled with their flesh.

20:1 And I saw an angel come down from heaven, having the key of the
bottomless pit and a great chain in his hand.
2 And he laid hold on the dragon, that old serpent, which is the Devil, and Satan,
and bound him a thousand years,
3 And cast him into the bottomless pit, and shut him up, and set a seal upon
him, that he should deceive the nations no more, till the thousand years should
be fulfilled: and after that he must be loosed a little season.
4 And I saw thrones, and they sat upon them, and judgment was given unto
them: and I saw the souls of them that were beheaded for the witness of Jesus,
and for the word of God, and which had not worshipped the beast, neither his
image, neither had received his mark upon their foreheads, or in their hands; and
they lived and reigned with Christ a thousand years.
5 But the rest of the dead lived not again until the thousand years were finished.
This is the first resurrection.
6 Blessed and holy is he that hath part in the first resurrection: on such the
second death hath no power, but they shall be priests of God and of Christ, and
shall reign with him a thousand years.
7 And when the thousand years are expired, Satan shall be loosed out of his
prison,
8 And shall go out to deceive the nations which are in the four quarters of the
earth, Gog and Magog, to gather them together to battle: the number of whom is

as the sand of the sea.
9 And they went up on the breadth of the earth, and compassed the camp of the saints about, and the beloved city: and fire came down from God out of heaven, and devoured them.
10 And the devil that deceived them was cast into the lake of fire and brimstone, where the beast and the false prophet are, and shall be tormented day and night for ever and ever.
11 And I saw a great white throne, and him that sat on it, from whose face the earth and the heaven fled away; and there was found no place for them.
12 And I saw the dead, small and great, stand before God; and the books were opened: and another book was opened, which is *the* book of life: and the dead were judged out of those things which were written in the books, according to their works.
13 And the sea gave up the dead which were in it; and death and hell delivered up the dead which were in them: and they were judged every man according to their works.
14 And death and hell were cast into the lake of fire. This is the second death.
15 And whosoever was not found written in the book of life was cast into the lake of fire.

21:1 And I saw a new heaven and a new earth: for the first heaven and the first earth were passed away; and there was no more sea.
2 And I John saw the holy city, new Jerusalem, coming down from God out of heaven, prepared as a bride adorned for her husband.
3 And I heard a great voice out of heaven saying, Behold, the tabernacle of God is with men, and he will dwell with them, and they shall be his people, and God himself shall be with them, and be their God.
4 And God shall wipe away all tears from their eyes; and there shall be no more death, neither sorrow, nor crying, neither shall there be any more pain: for the former things are passed away.
5 And he that sat upon the throne said, Behold, I make all things new. And he said unto me, Write: for these words are true and faithful.
6 And he said unto me, it is done. I am Alpha and Omega, the beginning and the end. I will give unto him that is athirst of the fountain of the water of life freely.
7 He that overcometh shall inherit all things; and I will be his God, and he shall be my son.
8 But the fearful, and unbelieving, and the abominable, and murderers, and whoremongers, and sorcerers, and idolaters, and all liars, shall have their part in the lake which burneth with fire and brimstone: which is the second death.
9 And there came unto me one of the seven angels which had the seven vials full of the seven last plagues, and talked with me, saying, Come hither, I will shew thee the bride, the Lamb's wife.
10 And he carried me away in the spirit to a great and high mountain, and

shewed me that great city, the holy Jerusalem, descending out of heaven from
God,
11 Having the glory of God: and her light was like unto a stone most precious,
even like a jasper stone, clear as crystal;
12 And had a wall great and high, and had twelve gates, and at the gates twelve
angels, and names written thereon, which are the names of the twelve tribes of
the children of Israel:
13 On the east three gates; on the north three gates; on the south three gates; and
on the west three gates.
14 And the wall of the city had twelve foundations, and in them the names of
the twelve apostles of the Lamb.
15 And he that talked with me had a golden reed to measure the city, and the
gates thereof, and the wall thereof.
16 And the city lieth foursquare, and the length is as large as the breadth: and he
measured the city with the reed, twelve thousand furlongs. The length and the
breadth and the height of it are equal.
17 And he measured the wall thereof, an hundred and forty and four cubits,
according to the measure of a man, that is, of the angel.
18 And the building of the wall of it was of jasper: and the city was pure gold,
19 And the foundations of the wall of the city were garnished with all manner of
precious stones, The first foundation was jasper; the second, sapphire; the third,
a chalcedony; the fourth, an emerald;
20 The fifth, sardonyx; the sixth, sardius; the seventh, chrysolyte; the eighth,
beryl; the ninth, a topaz; the tenth, a chrysoprasus; the eleventh, a jacinth; the
twelfth, an amethyst.
21 And the twelve gates were twelve pearls; every several gate was of one pearl:
and the street of the city was pure gold, as it were transparent glass.
22 And I saw no temple therein: for the Lord God Almighty and the Lamb are
the temple of it.
23 And the city had no need of the sun, neither of the moon, to shine in it: for
the glory of God did lighten it, and the Lamb is the light thereof.
24 And the nations of them which are saved shall walk in the light of it: and the
kings of the earth do bring their glory and honour into it.
25 And the gates of it shall not be shut at all by day: for there shall be no night
there.
26 And they shall bring the glory and honour of the nations into it.
27 And there shall in no wise enter into it any thing that defileth, neither
whatsoever worketh abomination, or maketh a lie: but they which are written
in the Lamb's book of life.

22:1 And he shewed me a pure river of water of life, clear as crystal, proceeding
out of the throne of God and of the Lamb.
2 In the midst of the street of it, and on either side of the river, was there the tree

of life, which bare twelve manner of fruits, and yielded her fruit every month:
and the leaves of the tree were for the healing of the nations.
3 And there shall be no more curse: but the throne of God and of the Lamb shall
be in it; and his servants shall serve him:
4 And they shall see his face; and his name shall be in their foreheads.
5 And there shall be no night there; and they need no candle, neither light of the
sun; for the Lord God giveth them light: and they shall reign for ever and ever.
6 And he said unto me, These sayings are faithful and true: and the Lord God of
the holy prophets sent his angel to shew unto his servants the things which must
shortly be done.
7 Behold, I come quickly: blessed is he that keepeth the sayings of the prophecy
of this book.
8 And I John saw these things, and heard them. And when I had heard and seen,
I fell down to worship before the feet of the angel which shewed me these things.
9 Then saith he unto me, See thou do it not: for I am thy fellowservant, and of
thy brethren the prophets, and of them which keep the sayings of this book:
worship God.
10 And he saith unto me, Seal not the sayings of the prophecy of this book: for
the time is at hand.
11 He that is unjust, Let him be unjust still: and he which is filthy, Let him be
filthy still: and he that is righteous, Let him be righteous still: and he that is holy,
Let him be holy still.
12 And, behold, I come quickly; and my reward is with me, to give every man
according as his work shall be.
13 I am Alpha and Omega, the beginning and the end, the first and the last.
14 Blessed are they that do his commandments, that they may have right to the
tree of life, and may enter in through the gates into the city.
15 For without *are* dogs, and sorcerers, and whoremongers, and murderers, and
idolaters, and whosoever loveth and maketh a lie.
16 I Jesus have sent mine angel to testify unto you these things in the churches.
I am the root and the offspring of David, and the bright and morning star.
17 And the Spirit and the bride say, Come. And Let him that heareth say,
Come. And Let him that is athirst come. And whosoever will, Let him take the
water of life freely.
18 For I testify unto every man that heareth the words of the prophecy of this
book, if any man shall add unto these things, God shall add unto him the plagues
that are written in this book:
19 And if any man shall take away from the words of the book of this prophecy,
God shall take away his part out of the book of life, and out of the holy city, and
from the things which are written in this book.
20 He which testifieth these things saith, Surely I come quickly. Amen. Even
so, come, Lord Jesus.
21 The grave of our Lord Jesus Christ be with you all. Amen.

Joseph Noah

The Magic in a Circle

The magic in a circle,
Perhaps we'll never comprehend,
Existing in eternity
No beginning and no end.

The atoms we're composed of
Seem to form a common bond,
With the movement of the planets
And the galaxies beyond.

Within this sphere of motion
We all fulfill a role,
Free agents on the course of life,
Though components of the whole.

Concentric motion trapped in time
Perpetuates a plan,
A plan of such great magnitude
It confounds the mind of man.

The spiral ever lifting
As from life to life we grasp,
That our destiny is godliness
And we're approaching it at last.

The mystery soon to be unveiled
As history turns a page,
When the faithful find the courage
To declare the Golden Age.

Till then have faith
And live the Master's plan,
No doubt the universe contains
A special time for man.

__Joseph Noah__ was born in Pennsylvania and raised on a small country farm near the coal regions. Trained in engineering, he has practiced that profession for extended periods of time in the United States, the Caribbean, Europe and the Middle and Far East. He is currently retired, and divides his time between Texas and Montana.

Works Cited and Related Reading

Ali, Abdullah Yusuf. *The Meaning of the Holy Quran.* Brentwood, MD: Amana, 1993.

Bennett, William J. *The De-Valuing of America: The Fight for Our Culture and Our Children.* New York: Summit, 1996.

-----. *The Index of Leading Cultural Indicators.* New York: Broadway Books, 1999.

Bunson, Matthew. *Angels A to Z.* New York: Three Rivers Press, 1996.

Cambridge Factfinder, The. Cambridge, U.K.: University of Cambridge Press, 1998.

Chatterji, J. C. *The Wisdom of the Vedas.* Wheaton, IL: Theosophical Publishing House, 1992.

Complete Poetry and Selected Prose of John Donne & The Complete Poetry of William Blake. New York: Modern Library, 1941. pp. 331-332.

Davis, Lee. *Encyclopedia of Natural Disasters.* London, U.K.: Headline, 1992.

Drosnin, Michael. *The Bible Code.* New York: Simon & Schuster, 1997.

Frejer, B. Ernest. *Edgar Cayce Companion.* Virginia Beach, VA: A.R.E., 1995.

Gibran, Kahlil. *The Prophet.* New York: Alfred Knopf, 1998.

Halevi, Zev ben Shimon. *Kabbalah, The Divine Plan.* New York: Harper Collins, 1996.

Hansen, Ph.D., Kenneth. *Dead Sea Scrolls: The Untold Story.* Tulsa, OK: Council Oaks Books, 1997.

Hitchcock, Mark. *The Complete Book of Bible Prophecy.* Wheaton, IL: Dyndale House, 1996.

Jaspers, Karl.*Socrates, Buddha, Confucius, Jesus.* New York: Harvest Book,1990.

Lost Books of the Bible, the Forgotten Books of Eden. New York: World Bible, 1926.

Marrs, Jim. *Rule by Secrecy.* New York: Harper Collins, 2000.

Puryear, Herbert B., Ph.D. *The Edgar Cayce Primer.* New York: Bantam, 1982.

-----. *Why Jesus Taught Reincarnation.* Scottsdale, AZ: New Paradigm Press, 1995.

Scallion, Gordon Michael. *Notes from the Cosmos.* Chesterfield, NH: Matrix Institute, 1997.

Schlessinger, Dr. Laura. *The Ten Commandments.* New York: Harper Collins, 1998.

Stearn, Jess. *Edgar Cayce, The Sleeping Prophet.* New York: Bantam Books, 1989.

White, John. *Pole Shift.* Virginia Beach, VA: A.R.E., 1991.

Timms, Moira. *Beyond Prophecies and Predictions.* New York: Ballantine, 1996.

World Almanac and Book of Facts, 2001. Mahwah, N.J.: World Almanac, 2001.

Yenne, Bill. *The Atlas of the Solar System.* New York: Exeter Books, 1987.

Index

S

T

U

V

W

Z